Whitman Peck

First Lessons in Latin

Salzwasser

Whitman Peck

First Lessons in Latin

1. Auflage | ISBN: 978-3-84605-456-7

Erscheinungsort: Frankfurt, Deutschland

Erscheinungsjahr: 2020

Salzwasser Verlag GmbH

Reprint of the original, first published in 1869.

REVISED AND ENLARGED EDITION.

FIRST

LESSONS IN LATIN;

OR,

AN INTRODUCTION

TO

ANDREWS AND STODDARD'S

LATIN GRAMMAR.

BY E. A. ANDREWS, LL. D.

WITH NEW EXERCISES,

SELECTED AND ARRANGED BY

WHITMAN PECK, A. M.

FORTY-SECOND EDITION.

BOSTON:
PUBLISHED BY CROCKER & BREWSTER,
51 WASHINGTON STREET.
1869.

PREFACE.

THIS revision of the "First Lessons in Latin," like the former editions, contains an Abstract of "Andrews and Stoddard's Latin Grammar," Rules for Translating certain Latin Forms and Idioms, Exercises in Latin Syntax, and a Vocabulary. The Reading Lessons are omitted, their place being supplied by the greater number of Exercises.

The abstract of the Grammar comprises, as before, the most important principles of that work, together with its paradigms; but with a different arrangement of the Parts of Speech and Rules of Syntax, so as to meet the changes introduced in the plan of the Exercises.

In this edition, also, " to prevent the erroneous habits of pronunciation which students often acquire in the commencement of their Latin course, the inflected words are divided into syllables, and the place of the accent carefully marked."

In the preparation of the Vocabulary, pains have been taken to exhibit the derivation of words, and the proper succession of their meanings.

The principal difference between this and the previous editions of the "First Lessons" is in the Exercises. As now presented, they are believed to be better designed to render pupils familiar, *first*, with the rudiments of Latin Grammar, including the inflections of the different Parts of Speech, with the corresponding variations in the meaning of words; and, *secondly*, with the application of the principal Rules of Syntax. To this end they have been so prepared as to accompany the study of the book from the commencement, though, for the sake of greater convenience in referring to what has been studied, the different Parts of Speech, the Rules of Syntax, and the Exercises, instead of being mingled, have been, as before,

III

separately arranged, since it is desirable that while the pupil is learning the different declensions and conjugations, they should be presented to his view in the same connection, and thus associated in his memory.

An important part of the plan has been, to annex to the Exercises on each new lesson, Promiscuous Exercises, requiring the repeated application of what the pupil has previously studied; so that while he advances step by step, he shall not forget what he has once learned. Instead also of many examples of the same kind being arranged together, so that after one is understood no effort is required to learn the rest, they have been carefully intermingled, so that the pupil will need to exercise his own judgment in applying what he has learned, particularly the Rules of Syntax.

These modifications of the original plan of the Exercises are introduced after a thorough practical test of their value made by Whitman Peck, A. M., of Fishkill, N.Y., an experienced and skilful instructor, who is entitled to the credit of such changes, and also of the selection of the Examples not found in the former editions of this work. The Exercises, with few exceptions, are taken from good Latin writers, many of them from Nepos and Cæsar, in order that pupils may become accustomed to a classical style.

In the arrangement of the Parts of Speech, the Verb was first introduced, as being indispensable to the formation of a complete sentence, and then the other parts, in such order that sentences could be conveniently selected for each without introducing those not yet learned.

Frequent reviews of what the pupil has learned will be found of great benefit; and the teacher will exercise his discretion in leaving to a second or third reading certain portions of the book, such as the Rules for the Gender and of the oblique cases of the third declension, the Remarks under the Rules of Syntax, &c.

It is believed that the student who masters the contents of this book will be qualified to enter upon the study of the Latin Reader, Cæsar, or Nepos, with pleasure and profit.

HORACE ANDREWS.

NEW YORK, June 2, 1864.

CONTENTS.

LATIN LESSONS.

THE Latin language is the language spoken by the ancient Romans.

Latin Grammar teaches the principles of the Latin language.

It is divided into Orthography, Orthoëpy, Etymology, Syntax, and Prosody.

ORTHOGRAPHY.

Orthography treats of the letters and other characters of written language, and the proper mode of spelling words.

The letters of the Latin language are twenty-five.

They have the same names as the corresponding characters in English.

They are A, a; B, b; C, c; D, d; E, e; F, f; G, g; H, h; I, i; J, j; K, k; L, l; M, m; N, n; O, o; P, p; Q, q; R, r; S, s; T, t; U, u; V, v; X, x; Y, y; Z, z.

W is not found in Latin words, and K is seldom used.

Letters are divided into *vowels* and *consonants*.

The vowels are *a, e, i, o, u,* and *y.*

Of the consonants, *l, m, n,* and *r,* are called *liquids.*

X and *z* are called double letters. *X* stands for *cs* or *gs ;* and *z* for *ts* or *ds*.

The other consonants, except *h* and *s*, are called *mutes*.

Two vowels in immediate succession, in the same syllable, are called a *diphthong ;* as, *ae* in *mu'-sae*, or *eu* in *heu*.

A *short* vowel is marked by a curved line over it; as, *i* in *dom'-ĭ-nus*.

A *long* vowel is marked by a horizontal line over it; as, *o* in *ser-mō'-nis*.

A *common* or *doubtful* vowel is marked by both a curved and a horizontal line; as, *u* in *vol'-ŭ-cris*.

The *acute* accent (') marks the emphatic syllable of a word; as, *reg'-num*, a kingdom.

The *grave* accent (`) is sometimes written over particles to distinguish them from other words spelled in the same manner; as, *quòd*, because; *quod*, which.

The *circumflex* accent (ˆ) denotes a contraction ; as, *num-mûm* for *num-mō'rum*.

The *diœrĕsis* (¨) denotes that the vowel over which it stands does not form a diphthong with the preceding vowel.; as, *aër*, the air.

(*Here learn Exercise I.*)

ORTHOËPY.

Orthoëpy treats of the right pronunciation of words.

NOTE.—The ancient pronunciation of the Latin language is in a great measure lost. In Europe, two systems of pronouncing this language are in use,—the *English* and the *Continental.* The former is exhibited in this work. In both methods the consonants are pronounced in nearly the same manner. According to the *Continental* system, each of the vowels, when standing at the end of a syllable, is considered as having but one sound, which, however, may be either short or long. Thus, —

Short ă, as in hat.	Long ŏ, as in no.
Long ā, as in father.	Short ŭ, as in tub.
Short ĕ, as in met.	Long ū, as in full.
Long ē, as in there.	Æ or œ, as *e* in there.
Short ĭ, as in sit.	Au, as *ou* in our.
Long ī, as in machine.	Eu, as in feudal.
Short ŏ, as in not.	Ei, as *i* in ice.

These sounds are sometimes slightly modified when followed by a consonant in the same syllable.

OF THE VOWELS.

A vowel, when ending an accented syllable, has always its *long* English sound; as, *pa'-ter, de'dit, vi'- vus, to'-tus, tu'-ba, Ty'-rus;* in which the accented vowels are pronounced as in *fatal, metre, vital, total, tutor, tyrant.*

A, at the end of an unaccented syllable, has nearly the sound of *a* in *father*, or in *ah*, but shorter and less distinct; as, *mu'-sa*, pronounced *mu'-zah*.

E, o, and *u*, at the end of an unaccented syllable, have nearly the same sound as when accented, but shorter and less distinct; as, *re'-te, vo'-lo, u'-su-i.*

I final, except in *tibi* and *sibi*, has its long sound; as, *qui, au'-di.*

I, at the end of an unaccented syllable not final, has usually an indistinct sound like short *e;* as, *Fa'-bi-us*, pronounced *fa'-be-us.*

Y is pronounced like *i* in the same situation.

A vowel has its *short* English sound when followed by a consonant in the same syllable; as, *mag'-nus, reg'- num, fin'go, hoc, fus'-tis, cyg'-nus*, in which the vowels are pronounced as in *magnet, seldom, finish, copy, lustre, symbol.*

Es, at the end of a word, is pronounced like the English word *ease;* as, *ig'-nes.*

Os, at the end of plural cases, is pronounced like *ose* in *dose;* as, *nos, il'-los.*

Post is pronounced like the same word in English; so also its compounds.

OF THE DIPHTHONGS.

Ae and *oe*, when diphthongs, are pronounced as *e* would be in the same situation; as, *œ'-tas*, *œs'-tas*, *pœ'-na*, *œs'-trum*.

Ei, when a diphthong, and not followed by another vowel, is pronounced like *i ;* as in *hei*.

Au, when a diphthong, is pronounced like *aw ;* as, *laus*, pronounced *laws*.

Eu, when a diphthong, is pronounced like long *u ;* as, *heu*.

OF THE CONSONANTS.

The consonants have, in general, the same power in Latin as in English words.

C and *g* have their soft sound, like *s* and *j*, before *e*, *i*, and *y*, and the diphthongs *œ* and *œ*.

Ch has always the sound of *k ;* as, *char'-ta*, pronounced *kar'-tah*.

(Here learn Exercise II.)

OF QUANTITY.

The *penult* of a word is the last syllable but one.

The *antepenult* is the last syllable but two.

The *quantity* of a syllable is the relative time occupied in pronouncing it.

A *short* syllable requires, in pronunciation, half the time of a *long* one.

The following are the general rules for the quantity of syllables.

1. A vowel before another vowel or *h* is short.
2. Diphthongs not beginning with *u* are long.
3. A vowel before *x, z, j*, or any two consonants, except a mute followed by a liquid, is long *by position*, as it is called.
4. A vowel before a mute, followed by a liquid, is *common*, i. e. either long or short; as *a* in *pa'-tris*.

OF ACCENT.

Accent is a particular stress of voice upon certain syllables of words.

In words of two syllables, the penult is always accented; as, *pă'-ter, mā'-ter, pen'-na.*

In words of more than two syllables, if the *penult* is *long*, it is accented; but if it is *short*, the accent is on the *antepenult;* as, *ă-mī'-cus, dom'-i-nus.*

If the penult is *common*, the accent, in prose, is upon the *antepenult;* as, *phar'-ĕ-tra;* but genitives in *ius,* in which *i* is common, accent their *penult* in prose; as, *u-nī'-us.*

In every Latin word there are as many syllables as there are separate vowels and diphthongs.

(Here learn Exercise III.)

ETYMOLOGY.

Etymology treats of the different classes of words, their derivation, and various inflections.

The parts of speech in Latin are eight, — *Verb, Substantive* or *Noun, Adjective, Adverb, Preposition, Conjunction, Interjection,* and *Pronoun.*

To verbs belong *Participles, Gerunds,* and *Supines.*

Inflection, in Latin grammar, signifies a change in the termination of a word.

It is of three kinds, — *declension, conjugation,* and *comparison.*

Nouns, pronouns, adjectives, participles, gerunds, and supines, are *declined.*

Verbs are *conjugated.*

Adjectives and adverbs are *compared.*

2

VERBS.

A verb is a word by which something is affirmed of a person or thing.

That of which anything is affirmed is called the subject of the verb; as, *puer legit*, the boy reads; *virtus laudātur*, virtue is praised. In these propositions, *puer*, the boy, and *virtus*, virtue, are the subjects of the verbs.

Verbs are either *active* or *neuter*, sometimes called *transitive* and *intransitive*.

I. An *active* or *transitive verb* expresses such an action as requires the addition of an object to complete the sense; as, *amo tc*, I love thee.

Most active verbs have two forms, which are called the *active* and the *passive voices*.

A verb in the *active voice* represents the agent as *acting upon* some person or thing, called the *object ;* as, *puer* legit *librum*, the boy *is reading* a book.

A verb in the *passive voice* represents the object as *acted upon* by the agent; as, *liber* legĭtur *a puĕro*, a book *is read* by the boy.

II. A *neuter* or *intransitive verb* expresses such an action or state as does not require the addition of an object to complete the sense; as, *equus currit*, the horse runs; *ego sedeo*, I sit.

Neuter verbs have in general the form of the active voice only.

REMARK. — The neuter verbs *audeo*, I dare; *fido*, I trust; *gaudeo*, I rejoice; and *soleo*, I am wont, have the passive form in the perfect and its cognate tenses; as, *ausus sum*, I dared. Hence they are called *neuter passives*.

A *deponent verb* is an active or neuter verb, having the form of the passive voice only; as *sequor*, I follow; *morior*, I die.

REMARK. — They are called *deponent* verbs, from *depŏno*, to lay aside, as having laid aside their active form and their passive signification.

Changes are made in the terminations of verbs to denote their different *voices*, *moods*, *tenses*, *numbers*, and *persons*.

(Here learn Exercise IV.)

MOODS.

Moods are forms of the verb denoting the *manner* of the action or state expressed by the verb.

There are in Latin four moods, — the *indicative*, the *subjunctive*, the *imperative*, and the *infinitive*.

The *indicative* mood is used in independent and absolute *assertions* and *inquiries ;* as, *amo*, I love ; *audisne ?* dost thou hear ?

The *subjunctive* mood is used to express an action or state simply as conceived by the mind; as, *si me* obsĕcret, *redibo ;* if he *entreat* me, I will return.

The *imperative* mood is used in commanding, exhorting, or entreating; as, *ama*, love thou.

The *infinitive* mood is used to denote an action or state indefinitely, without limiting it to any person or thing as its subject; as, *amāre*, to love.

(Here learn Exercise V.)

TENSES.

Tenses are forms of the verb denoting the *time* of the action or state expressed by the verb.

Latin verbs have six tenses, — the *present, imperfect, future, perfect, pluperfect,* and *future perfect.*

The *present tense* represents an action as now going on, and not completed; as, *amo*, I love, *or* am loving.

The *imperfect tense* represents an action as going on at some past time, but not then completed; as, *amā-bam*, I was loving. Sometimes it denotes customary past action; as, *legēbam*, I used to read; or attempting to act; as, *pelliciēbat*, he tried to entice.

The *future tense* denotes that an action will be going

on hereafter, without reference to its completion; as, *amābo*, I shall love, *or* shall be loving.

The *perfect tense* represents an action either as just completed, or as completed in some indefinite past time; as, *amāvi*, I have loved, *or* I loved.

In the former sense, it is called the *perfect definite;* in the latter, which is more common, it is called the *perfect indefinite, historical perfect,* or *aorist.*

The *pluperfect tense* represents a past action as completed, at or before the time of some other past action or event; as, *littĕras* scripsĕram, *quum nuncius venit; I had written* the letter when the messenger arrived.

The *future perfect tense* denotes that an action will be completed, at or before the time of some other future action or event; as, *quum* cœnavĕro, *proficiscar;* when *I shall have supped,* I will go.

(*Here learn Exercise VI.)*

NUMBERS.

Number, in verbs, is the form by which they denote whether their subject is one person or thing, or more than one.

Verbs have two numbers, — the singular and the plural. The singular is used when the subject is only one person or thing; the plural when it is more than one.

PERSONS.

Person, in verbs, is the form by which they denote the person of their subject. In each number there are three persons, — the *first, second,* and *third.*

The speaker is of the *first* person, the person spoken to is of the *second* person, and the person or thing spoken of is of the *third* person.

PARTICIPLES, GERUNDS, AND SUPINES.

A *participle* is a word derived from a verb, and partaking of its meaning, but having the form of an adjective.

Gerunds are verbal nouns, used only in the genitive, dative, accusative, and ablative singular.

Supines also are verbal nouns of the fourth declension, in the accusative and ablative singular; as, *amātum*, to love; *amātu*, to be loved. The supine in *um* is called the *former* supine; that in *u*, the *latter*.

CONJUGATION.

The conjugation of a verb is the regular formation and arrangement of its several parts, according to their voices, moods, tenses, numbers, and persons.

There are four conjugations, which are characterized by the vowel before *re* in the present of the infinitive active.

> In the first conjugation it is *ā* long.
> In the second, ... *ē* long.
> In the third, ... *ĕ* short.
> In the fourth, ... *ī* long.

A verb consists of two parts, — the *root* and the *termination.* The root is the part which is not changed by inflection. The termination is the part annexed to the root.

The *first* or *general* root of a verb consists of those letters that are found in every part; as, *am* in amo, am*ābam*, am*avĕrim*, am*ātus*. This root is found by removing the termination of the present infinitive.

NOTE. — The termination of the present infinitive,
In the first conjugation, active voice, is *āre*; passive, *āri*;
In the second " " " " *ēre*; " *ēri*;
In the third " " " " *ĕre*; " *i*;
In the fourth " " " " *īre*; " *īri*.

A verb has also two special roots; the first of which is found in the *perfect*, and is called the *second* root; the other is found in the *supine* or *perfect participle*, and is called the *third* root.

In regular verbs of the first, second, and fourth conjugations, the *second* root is formed by adding, respec-

2*

tively, *āv, u,* and *īv* to the *general* root; and the *third* root by a similar addition of *āt, ĭt,* and *īt.*

REMARK.—The tenses formed from the second root are sometimes contracted; as, *amâstis* for *amavistis.*

In the third conjugation, the second root either is the same as the first, or is formed from it by adding *s* (usually when the first root ends with a consonant); the third root is formed by adding *t.*

REMARK 1. — *C, g, h,* and *qu,* at the end of the first root, form with *s* the double letter *x* in the second root; in the third root *c* remains, and the others are changed into *c* before *t;* as, *dico, dicĕre,* (*dicsi,* i. e.), *dixi, dictum; rego, regĕre,* (*regsi,* i. e.), *rexi, rectum; veho, vehĕre, vexi, vectum; coquo, coquĕre, coxi, coctum.*

REMARK 2. — *B* is changed into *p* before *s* and *t;* as, *scribo, scribĕre, scripsi, scriptum.*

REMARK 3. — *D* and *t* before *s* are either dropped or changed into *s;* as, *claudo, claudĕre, clausi; cedo, cedĕre, cessi; mitto, mittĕre, misi.*

REMARK 4. — In verbs whose first root ends in *d* or *t,* the third root is formed by adding *s* (instead of *t*), dropping the *d* and *t,* or changing them into *s;* as, *claudo, clausum; cedo, cessum.*

The present and perfect indicative, the supine in *um,* and the present infinitive, are called the *principal parts* of the verb.

In the passive voice, the principal parts are the present indicative and infinitive, and the perfect participle.

(*Here learn Exercise VII.*)

SUM. *I am.*

The *substantive* or *auxiliary* verb *sum* is very irregular in those parts which, in other verbs, are formed from the first root. It is called an *auxiliary* verb because it is used in conjunction with participles to supply the want of simple forms in other verbs. From its denoting existence, it is called the *substantive* verb. When used to connect an attribute to a subject, it is called the *copula;* as, *terra est rotunda,* the earth is round.

NOTE. — Auxiliary verbs and the word with which they are connected constitute but one verb; as, The times *are changed,* The times *will be changed,* The times *will have been changed.*

Sum is thus conjugated: —

PRINCIPAL PARTS.

Pres. Indic.	Pres. Infin.	Perf. Indic.	Fut. Part.
Sum,	es'se,	fu'i,	fu-tū'-rus.

INDICATIVE MOOD.

Present Tense.

Singular. | **Plural.**

Person.
1. sum, *I am,** | su'-mus, *we are,*
2. es, *thou † art,* | es'-tis, *ye ‡ are,*
3. est, *he is ;* | sunt, *they are.*

Imperfect.

1. e'-ram, *I was,* | e-rā'-mus, *we were,*
2. e'-ras, *thou wast,* | e-rā tis, *ye were,*
3. e'-rat, *he was;* | e'-rant, *they were.*

Future. *shall* or *will.*

1. e'-ro, *I shall be,* | er'-ĭ-mus, *we shall be,*
2. e'-ris, *thou wilt be,* | er'-ĭ-tis, *ye will be,*
3. e'-rit, *he will be;* | e'-runt, *they will be.*

Perfect. *have been* or *was.*

1. fu'-i, *I have been,* | fu'ĭ-mus, *we have been,*
2. fu-is'-ti, *thou hast been,* | fu-is'-tis, *ye have been,*
3. fu'-it, *he has been;* | fu-ē -runt *or* -re, *they have been.*

Pluperfect.

1. fu'-ĕ-ram, *I had been,* | fu-e-rā'-mus, *we had been,*
2. fu'-ĕ-ras, *thou hadst been,* | fu-e-rā'-tis, *ye had been,*
3. fu'-ĕ-rat, *he had been;* | fu'-ĕ-rant, *they had been.*

* In the singular number the subject of the first person is *ego*, I; of the second, *tu*, thou; of the third, *ille*, he, or some other pronoun or noun in the singular: in the plural, the subject of the first person is *nos*, we; of the second, *vos*, ye or you; of the third, *illi*, they, or some other pronoun or noun in the plural.

In writing Latin, the subjects of verbs in the first and second persons are commonly omitted, unless they are emphatic.

In the paradigms in this book, the subject is omitted before the verb in Latin.

† In the second person singular in English, the plural form *you* is commonly used, except in solemn discourse; as, *tu es*, you are.

‡ The plural pronoun of the second person is either *ye* or *you*.

Future Perfect. *shall or will have.*

1. fu'-ĕ-ro, *I shall have been,*   fu-er'-ĭ-mus, *we shall have been,*
2. fu'-ĕ-ris, *thou wilt have been,*   fu-er'-ĭ-tis, *ye will have been,*
3. fu'-ĕ-rit, *he will have been ;*   fu'-ĕ-rint, *they will have been.*

SUBJUNCTIVE MOOD.

Present. *may or can.*

1. sim, *I may be,*   si'-mus, *we may be,*
2. sis, *thou mayst be,*   si'-tis, *ye may be,*
3. sit, *he may be ;*   sint, *they may be.*

Imperfect. *might, could, would, or should.*

1. es'-sem, *I would be,*   es-sē'-mus, *we would be,*
2. es'-ses, *thou wouldst be,*   es-sē'-tis, *ye would be,*
3. es'-set, *he would be ;*   es'-sent, *they would be.*

Perfect.

1. fu'-ĕ-rim, *I may have been,*   fu-er'-ĭ-mus, *we may have been,*
2. fu'-ĕ-ris, *thou mayst have been,*   fu-er'-ĭ-tis, *ye may have been,*
3. fu'-ĕ-rit, *he may have been ;*   fu'-ĕ-rint, *they may have been.*

Pluperfect. *might, could, would, or should have.*

1. fu-is'-sem, *I would have been,*   fu-is-sē'-mus, *we would have been,*
2. fu-is'-ses, *thou wouldst have been,*   fu-is-sē'-tis, *ye would have been,*
3. fu-is'-set, *he would have been ;*   fu-is'-sent, *they would have been.*

IMPERATIVE MOOD.

Pres.   2. es, *be thou,*   es'-te, *be ye,*
Fut.   2. es'-to, *thou shalt be,*   es-tō'-te, *ye shall be,*
    3. es'-to, *let him be ;*   sun'-to, *let them be.*

INFINITIVE MOOD.

Present. es'-se, *to be,*
Perfect. fu-is'-se, *to have been,*
Future. fu-tū'-rus (a, um,) es'-se, *or* fo'-re, *to be about to be.*

PARTICIPLE.

Future. fu-tū'-rus, *about to be.*

(*Here learn Exercise VIII.*)

FIRST CONJUGATION.

ACTIVE VOICE.

PRINCIPAL PARTS.

Pres. Indic.	Pres. Infin.	Perf. Indic.	Supine.
A'-mo,	a-mā'-re,	a-mā'-vi,	a-mā'-tum.

INDICATIVE MOOD.

Present. *love, do love, am loving.*

Sing.	a'-mo	I love,
	a'-mas,	thou lovest,
	a'-mat,	he loves ;
Plur.	a-mā'mus,	we love,
	a-mā'-tis,	ye love,
	a'-mant,	they love.

Imperfect. *was loving, loved, did love.*

Sing.	a-mā'-bam,	I was loving,
	a-mā'-bas,	thou wast loving,
	a-mā'-bat,	he was loving ;
Plur.	am-a-bā'-mus,	we were loving,
	am-a-bā'-tis,	ye were loving,
	a-mā'-bant,	they were loving.

Future. *shall or will.*

Sing.	a-mā'-bo,	I shall love,
	a-mā'-bis,	thou wilt love,
	a-mā'-bit,	he will love ;
Plur.	a-mab'-ĭ-mus,	we shall love,
	a-mab'-ĭ-tis,	ye will love,
	a-mā'-bunt,	they will love.

Perfect. *loved,* or *have loved.*

Sing.	a-mā'-vi,	I have loved,
	am-a-vis'-ti,	thou hast loved,
	a-mā'-vit,	he has loved ;
Plur.	a-mav'-ĭ-mus,	we have loved,
	am-a-vis'-tis,	ye have loved,
	am-a-vĕ'-runt *or* re,	they have loved.

Pluperfect. *had.*

Sing.	a-mav´-ĕ-ram,	*I had loved,*
	a-mav´-ĕ-ras,	*thou hadst loved,*
	a-mav´-ĕ-rat,	*he had loved ;*
Plur.	am-a-ve-rā´-mus,	*we had loved,*
	am-a-ve-rā´-tis,	*ye had loved,*
	a-mav´-ĕ-rant,	*they had loved.*

Future Perfect. *shall* or *will have.*

Sing.	a-mav´-ĕ-ro,	*I shall have loved,*
	a-mav´-ĕ-ris,	*thou wilt have loved,*
	a-mav´-ĕ-rit,	*he will have loved ;*
Plur.	am-a-ver´i-mus,	*we shall have loved,*
	am-a-ver´-į-tis,	*ye will have loved,*
	a-mav´-ĕ-rint,	*they will have loved.*

SUBJUNCTIVE MOOD.

Present. *may* or *can.*

Sing.	a´-mem,	*I may love,*
	a´-mes,	*thou mayst love,*
	a´-met,	*he may love ;*
Plur.	a-mē´-mus,	*we may love,*
	a-mē´-tis,	*ye may love,*
	a´-ment,	*they may love.*

Imperfect. *might, could, would,* or *should.*

Sing.	a-mā´-rem,	*I would love,*
	a-mā´-res,	*thou wouldst love,*
	a-mā´-ret,	*he would love ;*
Plur.	am-a-rē´-mus,	*we would love,*
	am-a-rē´-tis,	*ye would love,*
	a-mā´-rent,	*they would love.*

Perfect. *may,* or *can have.*

Sing.	a-mav´-ĕ-rim,	*I may have loved,*
	a-mav´-ĕ-ris,	*thou mayst have loved,*
	a-mav´-ĕ-rit,	*he may have loved ;*
Plur.	am-a-ver´-i-mus,	*we may have loved,*
	am-a-ver´-i-tis,	*ye may have loved,*
	a-mav´-ĕ-rint,	*they may have loved.*

Pluperfect. *might, could, would,* or *should have.*

Sing.	am-a-vis'-sem,	*I would have loved,*
	am-a-vis'-ses,	*thou wouldst have loved,*
	am-a-vis'-set,	*he would have loved;*
Plur.	am-a-vis-sē'-mus,	*we would have loved,*
	am-a-vis-sē'-tis,	*ye would have loved,*
	am-a-vis'-sent,	*they would have loved.*

IMPERATIVE MOOD.

Pres. Sing.	a'-ma,	*love thou,*
Plur.	a-mā'-te,	*love ye,*
Fut. Sing.	a-mā'to,	*thou shalt love,*
	a-mā'-to,	*he shall love;*
Plur.	am-a-tō'-te,	*ye shall love,*
	a-man'-to,	*they shall love.*

INFINITIVE MOOD.

Present.	a-mā'-re,	*to love,*
Perfect.	am-a-vis'-se,	*to have loved,*
Future.	am-a-tū'-rus (a, um,) es'-se.	*to be about to love.*

PARTICIPLES.

Present.	a'-mans,	*loving,*
Future.	am-a-tū'-rus, (a, um,)	*about to love.*

GERUND.

G.	a-man'-di,	*of loving,*
D.	a-man'-do,	*for loving,*
Ac.	a-man'-dum,	*loving,*
Ab.	a-man'-do,	*by loving.*

SUPINE.

Former.	a-mā'-tum,	*to love.*

(Here learn Exercise IX.)

PASSIVE VOICE.
PRINCIPAL PARTS.

Pres. Indic.	Pres. Infin.	Perf. Part.
A'mor,	a-mā'-ri,	a-mā'-tus.

INDICATIVE MOOD.

Present. *am.*

Sing.	a-mor	*I am loved,*
	a-mā'-ris *or* -re,	*thou art loved,*
	a-mā'-tur,	*he is loved;*
Plur.	a-mā'-mur,	*we are loved,*
	a-mam'-ı-ni,	*ye are loved,*
	a-man'-tur,	*they are loved.*

Imperfect. *was.*

Sing.	a-mā'-bar,	*I was loved,*
	am-a-bā'-ris *or* -re,	*thou wast loved,*
	am-a-bā'-tur,	*he was loved;*
Plur.	am-a-bā'-mur,	*we were loved,*
	am-a-bam'-ı-ni,	*ye were loved,*
	am-a-ban'-tur,	*they were loved.*

Future. *shall* or *will be.*

Sing.	a-mā'-bor,	*I shall be loved,*
	a-mab'-ĕ-ris *or* re,	*thou wilt be loved,*
	a-mab'-ı-tur,	*he will be loved;*
Plur.	a-mab'-ı-mur,	*we shall be loved,*
	am-a-bim'-ı-ni,	*ye will be loved,*
	am-a-bun'-tur,	*they will be loved.*

Perfect. *have been,* or *was.*

S.	a-mā'-tus sum *or* fu'-i,	*I have been loved,*
	a-mā'-tus es *or* fu-is'-ti,	*thou hast been loved,*
	a-mā'-tus est *or* fu'-it,	*he has been loved;*
P.	a-mā'-ti su'-mus *or* fu'-ı-mus,	*we have been loved,*
	a-mā'-ti es'-tis *or* fu-is'-tis,	*ye have been loved,*
	a-mā'-ti sunt, fu-ē'-runt *or* -re,	*they have been loved.*

Pluperfect. *had been.*

S.	a-mā'-tus e'-ram *or* fu'-ĕ-ram	*I had been loved,*
	a-mā'-tus e'-ras *or* fu'-ĕ-ras,	*thou hadst been loved,*
	a-mā'-tus e'-rat *or* fu'-ĕ-rat,	*he had been loved;*
P.	a-mā'-ti e-rā'-mus *or* fu-e-rā'-mus,	*we had been loved,*
	a-mā'-ti e-rā'-tis *or* fu-e-rā'-tis,	*ye had been loved,*
	a-mā'-ti e'-rant *or* fu'-ĕ-rant,	*they had been loved.*

Future Perfect. *shall have been.*

S. a-mā´-tus e´-ro *or* fu´-ĕ-ro,   *I shall have been loved,*
a-mā´-tus e´-ris *or* fu´-ĕ-ris,   *thou wilt have been loved,*
a-mā´-tus e´-rit *or* fu´-ĕ-rit,   *he will have been loved;*
P. a-mā´-ti er´-ĭ-mus *or* fu-er´-ĭ-mus, *we shall have been loved,*
a-mā´-ti er´-ĭ-tis *or* fu-er´-ĭ-tis, *ye will have been loved,*
a-mā´-ti e´-runt *or* fu´-ĕ-rint,   *they will have been loved.*

SUBJUNCTIVE MOOD.

Present. *may* or *can be.*

Sing. a´-mer,   *I may be loved,*
a-mē´-ris *or* -re,   *thou mayst be loved,*
a-mē´-tur,   *he may be loved;*
Plur. a-mē´-mur,   *we may be loved,*
a-mem´-ĭn-ĭ,   *ye may be loved,*
a-men´-tur,   *they may be loved.*

Imperfect. *might, could, would,* or *should be.*

Sing. a-mā´-rer,   *I would be loved,*
am-a-rĕ´-ris *or* -re,   *thou wouldst be loved,*
ám-a-rē´-tur,   *he would be loved;*
Plur. am-a-rē´-mur,   *we would be loved,*
am-a-rem´-ĭn-ĭ,   *ye would be loved,*
am-a-ren´-tur,   *they would be loved.*

Perfect. *may have been.*

S. a-mā´-tus sim *or* fu´-ĕ-rim,   *I may have been loved,*
a-mā´-tus sis *or* fu´-ĕ-ris,   *thou mayst have been loved,*
a-mā´-tus sit *or* fu´-ĕ-rit,   *he may have been loved;*
P. a-mā´-ti si´-mus *or* fu-er´-ĭ-mus, *we may have been loved,*
a-mā´-ti si´-tis *or* fu-er´-ĭ-tis, *ye may have been loved,*
a-mā´-ti sint *or* fu´-ĕ-rint,   *they may have been loved.*

Pluperfect. *might, could, would,* or *should have been.*

S. a-mā´-tus es´-sem *or* fu-is´-sem, *I would have been loved,*
a-mā´-tus es´-ses *or* fu-is´-ses, *thou wouldst have been loved,*
a-mā´-tus es´-set *or* fu-is´-set, *he would have been loved;*
P. a-mā´-ti es-sē´mus *or* fu-is-sē´-mus, *we would have been loved,*
a-mā´-ti es-sē´-tis *or* fu-is-sē´-tis, *ye would have been loved,*
a-mā´-ti es´-sent *or* fu-is´-sent, *they would have been loved.*

IMPERATIVE MOOD.

Pres. Sing	a-mā′-re,		be thou loved,
Plur.	a-mam′-ɪ-ni,		be ye loved ;
Fut. Sing.	a-mā′-tor,		thou shalt be loved,
	a-mā′tor,		he shall be loved ;
Plur.	(* am-a-bim′-ɪ-ni,		ye shall be loved,)
	a-man′-tor,		they shall be loved.

INFINITIVE MOOD.

Present.	a-mā′-ri,	to be loved.
Perfect.	a-mā′-tus es′-se or fu-is′-se,	to have been loved.
Future.	a-mā′-tum i′-ri,	to be about to be loved.

PARTICIPLES.

Perfect.	a-mā′-tus,	loved, or having been loved.
Future.	a-man′-dus,	to be loved.

SUPINE.

Latter.	a-mā′-tu,	to be loved.

FORMATION OF THE TENSES.

The first root of *amo* is *am*, the second *amāv*, and the third *amāt*.

From the first root, *am*, are derived in the

Active.	*Passive.*
amo,	amor,
amābam,	amābar,
amābo,	amābor,
amem,	amer,
amārem,	amārer,
ama,	-amāre,
amāto,	amātor,
amāre,	amāri,
amans,	amandus.
amandi,	

From the second root, *amāv*, are derived in the
Active.

amāvi,	amavĕrim,
amavĕram	amavissem,
amāvĕro,	amavisse.

From the third root, *amāt*, are derived in the

Active.	Passive.
amatūrus esse,	amātus sum,
amatūrus,	amātus eram,
amātum.	amātus ero,
	amātus sim,
	amātus essem
	amātus esse,
	amātum iri,
	amātus
	amātu.

(Here learn Exercise X.)

SECOND CONJUGATION.

ACTIVE VOICE.   **PASSIVE VOICE.**

PRINCIPAL PARTS.

Pres. Indic.	mo'-ne-o,		Pres. Indic.	mo'-ne-or,
Pres. Infin.	mo-nĕ'-re,		Pres. Infin.	mo-nĕ'-ri,
Perf. Indic.	mon'-u-i,		Perf. Part.	mon'-ı-tus.
Supine.	mon'-ı-tum.			

INDICATIVE MOOD.
Present.

I advise.   *I am advised.*

Sing	mo'-ne-o,		Sing.	mo'-ne-or,
	mo'-nes,			mo-nĕ'-ris or -re,
	mo'-net;			mo-nĕ'-tur;
Plur.	mo-nĕ'-mus,		Plur.	mo-nĕ'-mur,
	mo-nĕ'-tis,			mo-nem'-ı-ni,
	mo'-nent.			mo-nen'-tur.

Imperfect.

I was advising.	*I was advised.*
S. mo-nē´-bam, mo-nē´-bas, mo-nē´-bat ; mon-e-bā´-mus, mon-e-bā´-tis, mo-nē´-bant.	S. mo-nē´-bar, mon-e-bā´-ris *or* -re, mon-e-bā´-tur ; P. mon-e-bā´-mur, mon-e-bam´-ɪ-ni, mon-e-ban´-tur.

Future.

I shall or *will advise.*	*I shall* or *will be advised.*
S. mo-nē´-bo, • mo-nē´-bis, mo-nē´-bit ; P. mo-neb´-ɪ-mus, mo-neb´-ɪ-tis, mo-nē-bunt.	S. mo-nē´-bor, mo-neb´-ĕ-ris *or* -re, mo-neb´-ɪ-tur ; P. mo-neb´-ɪ-mur, mon-e-bim´-ɪ-ni, mon-e-bun´-tur.

Perfect.

I advised or *have advised.*'	*I was* or *have been advised.*
S. mon´-u-i, mon-u-is´-ti, mon´-u-it ; P. mo-nu´-ɪ-mus, mon-u-is´-tis, mon-u-ē´-runt *or* -re.	S. mon´-ɪ-tus sum *or* fu´-i, mon´-ɪ-tus es *or* fu-is´-ti, mon´-ɪ-tus est *or* fu´-it ; P. mon´-ɪ-ti su´-mus *or* fu´-ɪ-mus, mon´-ɪ-ti es´-tis *or* fu-is´-tis, mon´-ɪ-ti sunt, fu-ē´-runt *or* -re.

Pluperfect.

I had advised.	*I had been advised.*
S. mo-nu´-ĕ-ram, mo-nu´-ĕ-ras, mo-nu´-ĕ-rat ; P. mon-u-e-rā´-mus, mon-u-e-rā´-tis, mo-nu´-ĕ-rant.	S. mon´-ɪ-tus e´-ram *or* fu´-ĕ-ram, mon´-ɪ-tus e´-ras *or* fu´-ĕ-ras, mon´-ɪ-tus e´-rat *or* fu´-ĕ-rat ; P. mon´-ɪ-ti e-rā´-mus *or* fu-e-rā´-mus, mon´-ɪ-ti e-rā´-tis *or* fu-e-rā´-tis, mon´-ɪ ti e´-rant *or* fu´-ĕ-rant.

Future Perfect.

I shall have advised.	*I shall have been advised.*
S. mo-nu'-ĕ-ro, mo-nu'-ĕ-ris, mo-nu'-ĕ-rit; P. mon-u-er'-ĭ-mus, mon-u-er'-ĭ-tis, mo-nu'-ĕ-rint.	S. mon'-ĭ-tus e'-ro *or* fu'-ĕ-ro, mon'-ĭ-tus e'-ris *or* fu'-ĕ-ris, mon'-ĭ-tus e'-rit *or* fu'-ĕ-rit; P. mon'-ĭ-ti er'-ĭ-mus *or* fu-er'-ĭ-mus, mon'-ĭ-ti er'-ĭ-tis *or* fu-er'-ĭ-tis, mon'-ĭ-ti e'-runt *or* fu'-ĕ-rint.

SUBJUNCTIVE MOOD.

Present.

I may or *can advise.*	*I may* or *can be advised.*
S. mo'-ne-am, mo'-ne-as, mo'-ne-at; P. mo-ne-ā'-mus, mo-ne-ā'-tis, mo'-ne-ant.	S. mo'-ne-ar, mo-ne-ā'-ris *or* -re, mo-ne-ā'-tur; P. mo-ne-ā'-mur, mo-ne-am'-ĭ-ni, mo-ne-an'-tur.

Imperfect.

I might, could, would, or *should advise.*	*I might, could, would,* or *should be advised.*
S. mo-nē'-rem, mo-nē'-res, mo-nē'-ret; P. mon-e-rē'mus, mon-e-rē'-tis, mo-nē'-rent.	S. mo-nē'-rer, mon-e-rē'-ris *or* -re, mon-e-rē'-tur; P. mon-e-rē'-mur, mon-e-rem'-ĭ-ni, mon-e-ren'-tur.

Perfect.

I may have advised.	*I may have been advised.*
S. mo-nu'-ĕ-rim, mo-nu'-ĕ-ris, mo-nu'-ĕ-rit; P. mon-u-er'-ĭ-mus, mon-u-er'-ĭ-tis, mo-nu'-ĕ-rint.	S. mon'-ĭ-tus sim *or* fu'-ĕ-rim, mon'-ĭ-tus sis *or* fu'-ĕ-ris, mon'-ĭ-tus sit *or* fu'-ĕ-rit; P. mon'-ĭ-ti si'-mus *or* fu-er'-ĭ-mus, mon'-ĭ-ti si'-tis *or* fu-er'-ĭ-tis, mon'-ĭ-ti sint *or* fu'-ĕ-rint.

Pluperfect.

I might, could, would or should have advised.	*I might, could, would, or should have been advised.*

S.   mon-u-is'-sem,
      mon-u-is'-ses,
      mon-u-is'-set ;
 P.   mon-u-is-sē'-mus,
      mon-u-is-sē'-tis,
      mon-u-is'-sent.
	S. mon'-I-tus es'-sem *or* fu-is'-sem,
	      mon'-I-tus es'-ses *or* fu-is'-ses,
	      mon'-I-tus es'-set *or* fu-is'-set ;
	 P. mon'-I-ti es-sē'-mus *or* fu-is-sē-'mus,
	      mon'-I-ti es-sē'-tis, *or* fu-is-sē'-tis,
	      mon'-I-ti es'-sent *or* fu-is'-sent.

IMPERATIVE MOOD.

| P. S.   mo'-ne, *advise thou ;*
   P.   mo-nē'-te, *advise ye.*
 F. S.   mo-nē'-to, *thou shalt advise,*

       mo-nē'-to, *he shall advise ;*

   P.   mon-e-tō'te, *ye shall advise,*

       mo-nen'-to, *they shall advise.* | P. S.   mo-nē'-re, *be thou advised ;*
   P.   mo-nem'-I-ni, *be ye advised.*
 F. S.   mo-nē'-tor, *thou shalt be advised,*
       mo-nē'-tor, *he shall be advised ;*
   P.   (mon-e-bim'-I-ni,   *ye shall be advised,*)
       mo-nen-tor, *they shall be advised.* |

INFINITIVE MOOD.

| *Pres.*   mo-nē'-re, *to advise.*
 Perf.   mon-u-is'-se, *to have advised.*

 Fut.   mon-i-tū'-rus es'-se, *to be about to advise.* | *Pres.*   mo-nē'-ri, *to be advised.*
 Perf.   mon'-I-tus es'-se *or* fu-is'-se, *to have been advised.*
 Fut.   mon'-I-tum i'-ri, *to be about to be advised.* |

PARTICIPLES.

| *Pres.*   mo-nens, *advising.*
 Fut.   mon-i-tū'-rus, *about to advise.* | *Perf.*   mon'-I-tus, *advised.*
 Fut.   mo-nen'-dus, *to be advised.* |

GERUND.

| G.   mo-nen'-di, *of advising,*
 D.   mo-nen'-do,
 Ac.   mo-nen'-dum,
 Ab.   mo-nen'-do. | |

SUPINES.

Former.	*Latter.*
mon'-I-tum, *to advise.*	mon'-I-tu, *to be advised.*

FORMATION OF THE TENSES.

The first root of *moneo* is *mon*, the second *monu*, and the third *monĭt*.

From the first root, *mon*, are derived in the

Active.	*Passive.*
moneo,	moneor,
monēbam,	monēbar,
monēbo,	monēbor,
moneam,	monear,
monērem,	monērer,
mone,	monēre,
monēto,	monētor,
monēre,	monēri,
monens,	monendus.
monendi,	

From the second root, *monu*, are derived in the

Active.

monui,	69	monuĕrim,
monuĕram,		monuissem,
monuĕro,	96	monuisse.

From the third root, *monĭt*, are derived in the

Active.	*Passive.*
monitūrus esse,	monĭtus sum,
monitūrus,	monĭtus eram,
monĭtum.	monĭtus ero,
	monĭtus sim,
	monĭtus essem,
	monĭtus esse,
	monĭtum iri,
	monĭtus,
	monĭtu.

(Here learn Exercise XI.)

THIRD CONJUGATION.

ÁCTIVE.   **PASSIVÉ.**

PRINCIPAL PARTS.

Pres. Indic.	Ré′go,		*Pres. Indic.*	re′-gor,
Pres. Infin.	reg′-ĕ-re,		*Pres. Infin.*	re′-gi,
Perf. Indic.	rex′-i,		*Perf. Part.*	rec′-tus.
Supine.	rec′-tum.			

INDÍCATIVE MOOD.

Present.

I rule.   *I am ruled.*

Sing.	re′-go,		*Sing.*	re′-gor,
	re′-gis,			reg′-ĕ-ris *or* -re,
	re′-git ;			reg′-I-tur ;
Plur.	reg′-I-mus,		*Plur.*	reg′-I-mur,
	reg′-I-tis,			re-gim′-I-ni,
	re′-gunt.			re-gun′-tur.

Imperfect.

I was ruling.   *I was ruled.*

S.	re-gē′-bam,		*S.*	re-gē′-bar,
	re-gē′-bas,			reg-e-bā′-ris *or* -re,
	re-gē′-bat ;			reg-e-bā′-tur ;
P.	reg-e-bā′-mus,		*P.*	reg-e-bā′-mur,
	reg-e-bā′-tis,			reg-e-bam′-I-ni,
	re-gē′-bant.			reg-e-ban′-tur.

Future.

I shall or *will rule.*   *I shall* or *will be ruled.*

S.	re′-gam,		*S.*	re′-gar,
	re′-ges,			re-gē′-ris *or* -re,
	re′-get ;			re-gē′-tur ;
P.	re-gē′-mus,		*P.*	re-gē′-mur,
	re-gē′-tis,			re-gem′-I-ni
	re′-gent.			re-gen′-tur.

ACTIVE.   PASSIVE.

Perfect.

I ruled or *have ruled.* | *I was* or *have been ruled*

S. rex'-i,
    rex-is'-ti,
    rex'-it ;
P   rex'-ĭ-mus,
    rex-is'-tis,
    rex-ē'-runt *or* -re.

S. rec'-tus sum *or* fu'-i,
    rec'-tus es *or* fu-is'-ti,
    rec'-tus est *or* fu'-it ;
P. rec'-ti su'-mus *or* fu'-ĭ-mus,
    rec'-ti es'-tis *or* fu-is'-tis,
    rec'-ti sunt, fu-ē'-runt, *or* -re.

Pluperfect.

I had ruled. | *I had been ruled.*

S. rex'-ĕ-ram,
    rex'-ĕ-ras,
    rex'-ĕ-rat ;
P. rex-e-rā'-mus,
    rex-e-rā'-tis,
    rex'-ĕ-rant.

S. rec'-tus e'-ram *or* fu'-ĕ-ram,
    rec'-tus e'-ras *or* fu'-ĕ-ras,
    rec'-tus e'-rat *or* fu'-ĕ-rat ;
P. rec'-ti e-rā'-mus *or* fu-e-rā'-mus,
    rec'-ti e-rā'-tis *or* fu-e-rā'-tis,
    rec'-ti e'-rant *or* fu'-ĕ-rant.

Future Perfect.

I shall have ruled. | *I shall have been ruled.*

S. rex'-ĕ-ro,
    rex'-ĕ-ris,
    rex'-ĕ-rit ;
P. rex-er'-ĭ-mus,
    rex-er'-ĭ-tis,
    rex'-ĕ-rint.

S. rec'-tus e'-ro *or* fu'-ĕ-ro,
    rec'-tus e'-ris *or* fu'-ĕ-ris,
    rec'-tus e'-rit *or* fu'-ĕ-rit ;
P. rec'-ti er'-ĭ-mus *or* fu-er'-ĭ-mus,
    rec'-ti er'-ĭ-tis *or* fu-er'-ĭ-tis,
    rec'-ti e'-runt *or* fu'-ĕ-rint.

SUBJUNCTIVE MOOD.
Present.

I may or *can rule.* | *I may* or *can be ruled.*

S. re'-gam,
    re'-gas,
    re'-gat ;
P. re-gā'-mus,
    re-gā'-tis,
    re'-gant.

S. re'-gar,
    re-gā'-ris *or* -re,
    re-gā'-tur ;
P. re-gā'-mur,
    re-gam'-ĭ-ni,
    re-gan'-tur.

ACTIVE. **PASSIVE.**

Imperfect.

I might, could, would or should rule. | *I might, could, would or should be ruled.*

S. reg'-ĕ-rem,
reg'-ĕ-res,
reg'-ĕ-ret ;
P. reg-e-rē'-mus,
reg-e-rē'-tis,
reg'-ĕ-rent.

S. reg'-ĕ-rer,
reg-e-rē'-ris or -re,
reg-e-rē'-tur ;
P. reg-e-rē'-mur,
reg-e-rem'-ĭ-ni,
reg-e-ren'-tur.

Perfect.

I may have ruled. | *I may have been ruled.*

S. rex'-ĕ-rim,
rex'-ĕ-ris,
rex'-ĕ-rit ;
P. rex-er'-ĭ-mus,
rex-er'-ĭ-tis;
rex'-ĕ-rint.

S. rec'-tus sim or fu'-ĕ-rim,
rec'-tus sis or fu'-ĕ-ris,
rec'-tus sit or fu'-ĕ-rit ;
P. rec'-ti si'-mus or fu-er'-ĭ-mus,
rec'-ti si'-tis or fu-er'-ĭ-tis,
rec'-ti sint or fu'-ĕ-rint.

Pluperfect.

I might, could, would or should have ruled. | *I might, could, would, or should have been ruled.*

S. rex-is'-sem,
rex-is'-ses,
rex-is'-set ;
P. rex-is-sē'-mus,
rex-is-sē'-tis,
rex-is'-sent.

S. rec'-tus es'-sem or fu-is'-sem,
rec'-tus es'-ses or fu-is'-ses,
rec'-tus es'-set or fu-is'-set;
P. rec'-ti es-sē'mus or fu-is-sē'-mus,
rec'-ti es-sē'-tis or fu-is-sē'-tis,
rec'-ti es'-sent or fu-is'-sent.

IMPERATIVE MOOD.

Pres. S. re'-ge, *rule thou ;*
P. reg'-ĭ-te, *rule ye.*
Fut. S. reg'-ĭ-to, *thou shalt rule,*
reg'-ĭ-to, *he shall rule ;*
P. reg-i-tō'-te, *ye shall rule,*
re-gun'-to, *they shall rule.*

Pres. S. reg'-ĕ-re, *be thou ruled ;*
P. re-gim'-ĭ-ni, *be ye ruled.*
Fut. S. reg'-ĭ-tor, *thou shalt be ruled,*
reg'-ĭ-tor, *he shall be ruled ;*
P. (re-gim'-ĭ-ni, *ye shall be ruled.*)
re-gun'-tor, *they shall be ruled.*

ACTIVE.   PASSIVE.

INFINITIVE MOOD.

Pres. reg'-ĕ-re, *to rule.*   *Pres.* re'-gi, *to be ruled.*
Perf. rex-is'-se. *to have ruled.*   *Perf.* rec'-tus es'-se, *or* fu-is'-se, *to*
Fut. rec-tū'-rus es'-se, *to be about*   *have been ruled.*
      to rule.   *Fut.* rec'-tum i'-ri, *to be about to*
                           be ruled.

PARTICIPLES.

Pres. re'-gens, *ruling.*   *Perf.* rec'-tus, *ruled.*
Fut. rec-tū'-rus, *about to rule.*   *Fut.* re-gen'-dus, *to be ruled.*

GERUND.

G.   re-gen'-di, *of ruling,*
D.   re-gen'-do,
Ac.   re-gen'-dum,
Ab.   re-gen'-do.

SUPINES.

Former.   *Latter.*

rec'-tum, *to rule.*   rec'-tu, *to be ruled.*

FORMATION OF THE TENSES.

The first root of *rego* is *reg*, the second *rex*, and the third *rect*.

From the first root, *reg*, are derived in the

Active.	Passive.
rego,	regor,
regēbam,	regēbar,
regam,	regar,
regam,	regar,
regĕrem,	regĕrer,
rege,	regĕre,
regito,	regitor,
regĕre,	regi,
regens,	regendus.
regendi.	

ACTIVE.   PASSIVE.

INFINITIVE MOOD.

	Active		Passive
Pres.	cap'-ĕ-re.	*Pres.*	ca'-pi.
Perf.	ce-pis'-se.	*Perf.*	cap'-tus es'-se *or* fu-is'-se.
Fut.	cap-tū'-rus es'-se.	*Fut.*	cap'-tum i'-ri.

PARTICIPLES.

	Active		Passive
Pres.	ca'-pi-ens.	*Perf.*	cap'-tus.
Fut.	cap-tū'-rus.	*Fut.*	ca-pi-en'-dus.

GERUND.

G.   ca-pi-en'-dĭ, &c.

SUPINES.

Former.   cap'-tum.   *Latter.*   cap'-tu.

FORMATION OF THE TENSES.

The first root of *capio* is *cap*, the second *cep*, and the third *capt*.

From the first root, *cap*, are derived in the

Active.	*Passive.*
capio,	capior,
capiēbam,	capiēbar,
capiam,	capiar,
capiam,	capiar,
capĕrem,	capĕrer,
cape,	capĕre,
capito,	capitor,
capĕre,	capi,
capiens,	capiendus.
capiendi.	

From the second root, *cep*, are derived in the

Active.

cepi,	cepĕrim,
cepĕram,	cepissem,
cepĕro,	cepisse.

From the third root, *capt*, are derived in the

Active.	Passive.
captūrus esse,	captus sum,
captūrus,	captus eram,
captum.	captus ero,
	captus sim,
	captus essem,
	captus esse,
	captum iri,
	captus,
	captu.

(*Here learn Exercise XII.*)

FOURTH CONJUGATION.

ACTIVE.   **PASSIVE.**

PRINCIPAL PARTS.

Pres. Indic.	Au'-di-o,	*Pres. Indic.*	au'-di-or,
Pres. Infin.	au-dī'-re,	*Pres. Infin.*	au-dī'-ri,
Perf. Indic.	au-dī'-vi,	*Perf. Part.*	au-dī'-tus.
Supine.	au-dī'-tum.		

INDICATIVE MOOD.
Present.

I hear.	*I am heard.*
S. au'-di-o,	S. au'-di-or,
au'-dis,	au-dī'-ris *or* -re,
au'-dit;	au-dī'-tur;
P. au-dī'-mus,	P. au-dī'-mur,
au-dī'-tis,	au-dim'-i-ni,
au'-di-unt.	au-di-un'-tur.

Imperfect.

I was hearing.	*I was heard.*
S. au-di-ē'-bam,	S. au-di-ē'-bar,
au-di-ē'-bas,	au-di-e-bā'-ris *or* -re,
au-di-ē'-bat;	au-di-e-bā'-tur;
P. au-di-e-bā'-mus,	P. au-di-e-bā'-mur,
au-di-e-bā'-tis,	au-di-e-bam'-i-ni,
au-di-ē'-bant.	au-di-e-ban'-tur.

<table>
<tr><td>A C T I V E.</td><td>P A S S I V E.</td></tr>
</table>

Future.

I shall or *will hear.*	*I shall* or *will be heard.*
S. au′-di-am, au′-di-es, au′-di-et; *P.* au-di-ē′-mus, au-di-ē′-tis, au′-di-ent.	*S.* au′-di-ar, au-di-ē′-ris *or* -re, au-di-ē′-tur; *P.* au-di-ē′-mur, au-di-em′-ĭ-ni, au-di-en′-tur.

Perfect.

I heard or *have heard.*	*I have been* or *was heard.*
S. au-dī-vi, au-di-vis′-ti, au-dī′-vit; *P.* au-div′-ĭ-mus, au-di-vis′-tis, au-di-vē′-runt *or* -re.	*S.* au-dī′-tus sum *or* fu′-i, au-dī′-tus es *or* fu-is′-ti, au-dī′-tus est *or* fu′-it; *P.* au-dī′-ti su′-mus *or* fu′-ĭ-mus. au-dī′-ti es′-tis *or* fu-is′-tis, au-dī′-ti sunt, fu-ē′-runt *or* -re.

Pluperfect.

I had heard.	*I had been heard.*
S. au-div′-ĕ-ram, au-div′-ĕ-ras, au-div′-ĕ-rat; *P.* au-di-ve-rā′mus, au-di-ve-rā′-tis, au-div′-ĕ-rant.	*S.* au-dī′-tus e′-ram *or* fu′-ĕ-ram, au-dī′-tus e′-ras *or* fu′-ĕ-ras, au-dī′-tus e′-rat *or* fu′-ĕ-rat; *P.* au-dī′-ti e-rā′-mus *or* fu-e-rā′-mus, au-dī′-ti e-rā′-tis *or* fu-e-rā′-tis, au-dī′-ti e′-rant *or* fu′-ĕ-rant.

Future Perfect.

I shall have heard.	*I shall have been heard.*
S. au-div′-ĕ-ro, au-div′-ĕ-ris, au-div′-ĕ-rit; *P.* au-dī′-ver′-ĭ-mus, au-di-ver′-ĭ-tis, au-div′-ĕ-rint.	*S.* au-dī′-tus e′-ro *or* fu′-ĕ-ro, au-dī′-tus e′-ris *or* fu′-ĕ-ris, au-dī′-tus e′-rit *or* fu′-ĕ-rit; au-dī′-ti er′-ĭ-mus *or* fu-er′-ĭ-mus, au-dī′-ti er′-ĭ-tis *or* fu-er′-ĭ-tis, au-dī′-ti e′-runt *or* fu′-ĕ-rint.

ACTIVE.   PASSIVE.

SUBJUNCTIVE MOOD.

Present.

I may or *can hear.*   *I may* or *can be heard.*

S.	au'-di-am,	S. au'-di-ar,
	au'-di-as,	au-di-ā'-ris *or* -re,
	au'-di-at;	au-di-ā'-tur;
P.	au-di-ā'-mus,	P. au-di-ā'-mur,
	au-di-ā'-tis,	au-di-am'-ĭ-ni,
	au'-di-ant.	au-di-an'-tur.

Imperfect.

I might, could, would, or   *I might, could, would,* or
should hear.   *should be heard.*

S.	au-dī'-rem,	S. au-dī'rer,
	au-dī'-res,	au-di-rē'-ris *or* -re,
	au-dī'-ret;	au-di-rē'-tur;
P.	au-di-rē'-mus,	P. au-di-rē'-mur,
	au-di-rē'-tis,	au-di-rem'-ĭ-ni,
	au-dī'-rent.	au-di-ren'-tur.

Perfect.

I may have heard.   *I may have been heard.*

S.	au-div'-ĕ-rim,	S. au-dī'-tus sim *or* fu'-ĕ-rim,
	au-div'-ĕ-ris,	au-dī'-tus sis *or* fu'-ĕ-ris,
	au-div'-ĕ-rit;	au-dī'-tus sit *or* fu'-ĕ-rit;
P.	au-di-ver'-ĭ-mus,	P. au-dī'-ti si'-mus *or* fu-er'-ĭ-mus,
	au-di-ver'-ĭ-tis,	au-dī'-ti si'-tis *or* fu-er'-ĭ-tis,
	au-div'-ĕ-rint.	au-dī'-ti sint *or* fu'-ĕ-rint.

Pluperfect.

I might, could, would,   *I might, could, would,* or *should*
or *should have heard.*   *have been heard.*

S.	au-di-vis'-sem,	S. au-dī'-tus es'-sem *or* fu-is'-sem,
	au-di-vis'-ses,	au-dī'-tus es'-ses *or* fu-is'-ses,
	au-di-vis'-set;	au-dī'-tus es'-set *or* fu-is'-set;
P.	au-di-vis-sē'-mus,	P. au-dī'-ti es-sē'-mus *or* fu-is-sē'-mus,
	au-di-vis-sē'-tis,	au-dī'-ti es-sē'-tis *or* fu-is-sē'-tis,
	au-di-vis'-sent.	au-dī'-ti es'-sent *or* fu-is'-sent.

ACTIVE.   PASSIVE.

IMPERATIVE MOOD.

Pres. S. au'-di, *hear thou;*
     P. au-dĭ'-te, *hear ye.*
Fut. S. au-dĭ'-to, *thou shalt hear,*
     au-dĭ'-to, *he shall hear;*
     P. au-di-tō'-te, *ye shall hear,*
     au-di-un'-to, *they shall hear.*

Pres. S. au-dĭ'-re, *be thou heard;*
     P. au-dim'-ĭ-ni,   *be ye heard.*
Fut. S. au-dĭ'-tor, *thou shalt be heard,*
     au-dĭ'-tor, *he shall be heard;*
     P. (au-di-em'-ĭ-ni, *ye shall be heard,)*
     au-di-un'-tor, *they shall be heard.*

INFINITIVE MOOD.

Pres. au-dĭ'-re, *to hear.*
Perf. au-di-vis'-se, *to have heard.*
Fut. au-di-tū'-rus es'-se, *to be about to hear.*

Pres. au-dĭ'-ri, *to be heard.*
Perf. au-dĭ'-tus es'-se *or* fu-is'-se, *to have been heard.*
Fut. au-dĭ'-tum i'-ri, *to be about to be heard.*

PARTICIPLES.

Pres. au'-di-ens, *hearing.*
Fut. au-di-tū'-rus, *about to hear.*

Perf. au-dĭ'-tus, *heard.*
Fut. au-di-en'-dus, *to be heard.*

GERUND.

G. au-di-en'-di, *of hearing.*
D. au-di-en'-do,
Ac. au-di-en'-dum,
Ab. au-di-en'-do.

SUPINES.

Former. au-dĭ'-tum, *to hear.* | *Latter.* au-dĭ'-tu, *to be heard.*

FORMATION OF THE TENSES.

The first root of *audio* is *aud,* the second *audīv,* and the third *audīt.*

From the first root, *aud*, are derived in the

Active.	*Passive.*
audio,	audior,
audiēbam,	audiēbar,
audiam,	audiar,
audiam,	audiar,
audīrem,	audirer,
audi,	audire,
audīto,	auditor,
audire,	audiri,
audiens,	audiendus.
audiendi.	

From the second root, *audiv*, are derived in the

Active.

audīvi,	audivĕrim,
audivĕram,	audivissem,
audivĕro,	audivisse,

From the third root, *audīt*, are derived in the

Active.	*Passive.*
auditūrus esse,	audītus sum,
auditūrus,	audītus eram,
audītum.	audītus ero,
	audītus sim,
	aūdītus essem,
	audītus esse,
	audītum iri,
	audītus,
	audītu.

(*Here learn Exercises XIII., XIV., XV.*)

The following table exhibits a connected view of the verbal terminations in all the conjugations. By annexing these to the several roots, all the parts of a verb may be formed.

Terminations added to the First Root.

ACTIVE VOICE.

INDICATIVE MOOD.

PRESENT TENSE.

Conjugation.	SINGULAR. Persons.			PLURAL. Persons.		
	1.	2.	3.	1.	2.	3.
1.	-o,	-as,	-at;	-āmus,	-ātis,	-ant.
2.	-eo,	-es,	-et;	-ēmus,	-ētis,	-ent.
3.	-o,	-is,	-it;	-imus,	-itis,	-unt.
4.	-io,	-is,	-it;	-imus,	-itis,	-iunt.

IMPERFECT.

	1.	2.	3.	1.	2.	3.
1.	-ābam,	-ābas,	-ābat;	-ābāmus,	-ābātis,	-ābant.
2.	-ēbam,	-ēbas,	-ēbat;	-ēbāmus,	-ēbātis,	-ēbant.
3.	-ēbam,	-ēbas,	-ēbat;	-ēbāmus,	-ēbātis,	-ēbant.
4.	-iēbam,	-iēbas,	-iēbat;	-iēbāmus,	-iēbātis,	-iēbant.

FUTURE.

	1.	2.	3.	1.	2.	3.
1.	-ābo,	-ābis,	-ābit;	-ābimus,	-ābitis,	-ābunt.
2.	-ēbo,	-ēbis,	-ēbit;	-ēbimus,	-ēbitis,	-ēbunt.
3.	-am,	-es,	-et;	-ēmus,	-ētis,	-ent.
4.	-iam,	-ies,	-iet;	-iēmus,	-iētis,	-ient.

SUBJUNCTIVE MOOD.

PRESENT TENSE.

	1.	2.	3.	1.	2.	3.
1.	-em,	-es,	-et;	-ēmus,	-ētis,	-ent.
2.	-eam,	-eas,	-eat;	-eāmus,	-eātis,	-eant.
3.	-am,	-as,	-at;	-āmus,	-ātis,	-ant.
4.	-iam,	-ias,	-iat;	-iāmus,	-iātis,	-iant.

PASSIVE VOICE.

INDICATIVE MOOD.

PRESENT TENSE.

	SINGULAR. Persons.			PLURAL. Persons.		
	1.	2.	3.	1.	2.	3.
1.	-or,	-āris *or* -āre,	-ātur;	-āmur,	-amīni,	-antur.
2.	-eor,	-ēris *or* -ēre,	-ētur;	-ēmur,	-emīni,	-entur.
3.	-or,	-eris *or* -ēre,	-itur;	-imur,	-imīni,	-untur.
4.	-ior,	-iris *or* -īre,	-itur;	-imur,	-imīni,	-iuntur.

IMPERFECT.

	1.	2.	3.	1.	2.	3.
1.	-ābar,	-abāris *or* -abāre,	-abātur;	-abāmur,	-abamīni,	-abantur.
2.	-ēbar,	-ebāris *or* -ebāre,	-ebātur;	-ebāmur,	-ebamīni,	-ebantur.
3.	-ēbar,	-ebāris *or* -ebāre,	-ebātur;	-ebāmur,	-ebamīni,	-ebantur.
4.	-iēbar,	-iebāris *or* -iebāre,	-iebātur;	-iebāmur,	-iebamīni,	-iebantur.

FUTURE.

	1.	2.	3.	1.	2.	3.
1.	-ābor,	-abēris *or* -abēre,	-abitur;	-abimur,	-abimīni,	-abuntur.
2.	-ēbor,	-ebēris *or* -ebēre,	-ebitur;	-ebimur,	-ebimīni,	-ebuntur.
3.	-ar,	-ēris *or* -ēre,	-ētur;	-ēmur,	-emīni,	-entur.
4.	-iar,	-iēris *or* -iēre,	-iētur;	-iēmur,	-iemīni,	-ientur.

SUBJUNCTIVE MOOD.

PRESENT TENSE.

	1.	2.	3.	1.	2.	3.
1.	-er,	-ēris *or* -ēre,	-ētur;	-ēmur,	-emīni,	-entur.
2.	-ear,	-eāris *or* -eāre,	-eātur;	-eāmur,	-eamīni,	-eantur.
3.	-ar,	-āris *or* -āre,	-ātur;	-āmur,	-amīni,	-antur.
4.	-iar,	-iāris *or* -iāre,	-iātur;	-iāmur,	-iamīni,	-iantur.

IMPERFECT.

Present.
1. -a;
2. -e;
3. -e;
4. -i;

1. -ārem,	-ārēs,	-āret;	-ārēmus,	-ārētis,	-ārent.
2. -ērem,	-ērēs,	-ēret;	-ērēmus,	-ērētis,	-ērent.
3. -ĕrem,	-ĕrēs,	-ĕret;	-ĕrēmus,	-ĕrētis,	-ĕrent.
4. -īrem,	-īrēs,	-īret;	-īrēmus,	-īrētis,	-īrent.

1. -ārer, or	-ārēre,	-ārēris;	-arēmur,	-aremini,	-arentur.
2. -ērer, or	-ērēre,	-ērēris;	-erēmur,	-eremini,	-erentur.
3. -ĕrer, or	-ĕrēre,	-ĕrēris;	-erēmur,	-eremini,	-erentur.
4. -īrer, or	-īrēre,	-īrēris;	-irēmur,	-iremini,	-irentur.

IMPERATIVE MOOD.

Present.
1. -ā; -āte, -anto.
2. -ē; -ēte, -ento.
3. -ĕ; -ĭte, -unto.
4. -ī; -īte, -iunto.

Future.
1. -āto, -āto; -ātōte, -anto.
2. -ēto, -ēto; -etōte, -ento.
3. -ĭto, -ĭto; -itōte, -unto.
4. -ĭto, -ĭto; -itōte, -iunto.

Present.
1. -āre, -emini.
2. -ēre, -emini.
3. -ĕre, -imini.
4. -īre, -imini.

Future.
1. -ātor, -ātor; -antor.
2. -ētor, -ētor; -entor.
3. -ĭtor, -ĭtor; -untor.
4. -ĭtor, -ĭtor; -iuntor.

INFIN. Pres.
1. -āre,   (-ābamĭni,)
2. -ēre,   (-ēbimĭni,)
3. -ĕre,   (-imĭni,)
4. -īre,   (-iemĭni,)

INFIN. Pres.
1. -ārī,
2. -ērī,
3. -ī,
4. -īrī.

PART. Pres.
1. -ans,
2. -ens,
3. -ens,
4. -iens.

GER.
1. -andi,
2. -endi,
3. -endi,
4. -iendi.

PART. Fut.
1. -andus,
2. -endus,
3. -endus,
4. -iendus.

Note.— Verbs in *io* of the third conjugation have two connecting vowels in all the parts in which they occur in verbs of the fourth conjugation, and these vowels are the same in both.

Terminations added to the Second and Third Roots.

The terminations of the tenses which are formed from the second and third roots are the same in all the conjugations. Thus:—

ACTIVE VOICE.—SECOND ROOT.

INDICATIVE MOOD.

	Singular.			*Plural.*		
Perf.	-ī,	-istī,	-it;	-ĭmus,	-istĭs,	-ērunt or -ēre.
Plup.	-ĕram,	-ĕrās,	-ĕrat;	-ĕrāmus,	-ĕrātis,	-ĕrant.
Fut. Perf.	-ĕro,	-ĕris,	-ĕrit;	-ĕrimus,	-ĕritis,	-ĕrint.

SUBJUNCTIVE MOOD.

Perf.	-ĕrim,	-ĕris,	-ĕrit;	-ĕrimus,	-ĕritis,	-ĕrint.
Plup.	-issem,	-isses,	-isset;	-issēmus,	-issētis,	-issent.

INFIN. Perf. -isse.

THIRD ROOT. INF. Fut. -ūrus esse. PART. Fut. -ūrus. F.SUP. -um. PART. Perf. -us. INF. Fut. -um iri. L.SUP. -u.

PASSIVE VOICE.—THIRD ROOT.

INDICATIVE MOOD.

Singular.

Perf.	-us sum or ful,	-us es,	or fulsti, etc.
Plup.	-us eram or fuĕram,	-us eras,	or fuĕras, etc.
Fut. Perf.	-us ero or fuĕro,	-us eris,	or fuĕris, etc.

SUBJUNCTIVE MOOD.

Perf.	-us sim	or fuĕrim,	-us sis or fuĕris, etc.
Plup.	-us essem	or fuissem,	-us esses,or fuissem, etc.

INFIN. Perf. -us esse or fuisse.

DEPONENT VERBS.

Deponent verbs are conjugated like the passive voice, and have also the participles, gerunds, supines, and participial formations of the active voice.

The following is an example of an active deponent verb of the first conjugation : —

PRINCIPAL PARTS.

Mǐ'-ror, mi-rā'-ri, mi-rā'-tus, *to admire.*

INDICATIVE MOOD.

Pres.	mǐ'-ror, mi-rā'-ris, &c.	*I admire, &c.*
Imperf.	mi-rā'-bar, &c.	*I was admiring.*
Fut.	mi-rā'-bor,	*I shall admire.*
Perf.	mi-rā'-tus sum *or* fu'-i,	*I have admired.*
Plup.	mi-rā'-tus e'-ram *or* fu'-ĕ-ram,	*I had admired.*
Fut. Perf.	mi-rā'-tus e'-ro *or* fu'-ĕ-ro	*I shall have admired.*

SUBJUNCTIVE MOOD.

Pres.	mǐ'-rer, mi-rē'-ris, &c.	*I may admire, &c.*
Imperf.	mi-rā'-rer,	*I would admire.*
Perf.	mi-rā'-tus sim *or* fu'-ĕ-rim,	*I may have admired.*
Plup.	mi-rā'-tus es'-sem *or* fu-is'-sem,	*I would have admired.*

IMPERATIVE MOOD.

Pres. S.	mi·rā'-re,	*admire thou ;*
P.	mi-ram'-ĭ-ni,	*admire ye.*
Fut. S.	mi-rā'-tor,	*thou shalt admire,*
	mi-rā'-tor,	*he shall admire ;*
P.	(mir-a-bim'-ĭ-ni,	*ye shall admire,)*
	mi-ran'-tor,	*they shall admire.*

INFINITIVE MOOD.

Pres.	mi-rā'-ri,	*to admire.*
Perf.	mi-rā'-tus es'-se *or* fu-is'-se,	*to have admired.*
Fut. Act.	mir-a-tū'-rus es'-se,	*to be about to admire.*
Fut. Pas.	mi-rā'-tum i'-ri, ·	*to be about to be admired.*

PARTICIPLES.

Pres.	mǐ'-rans,	*admiring.*
Perf.	mi-rā'-tus,	*having admired.*
Fut. Act.	mir-a-tū'-rus,	*about to admire.*
Fut. Pass.	mi-ran'-dus,	*to be admired.*

GERUND.

G. mi-ran'-di, *of admiring, &c.*

SUPINES.

Former. mi-rā'-tum, *to admire.*
Latter. mi-rā'-tu, *to be admired.*

IMPERSONAL VERBS.

Impersonal verbs are those which are used only in the third person singular, and do not admit of a *personal* subject. Their English is generally preceded by the pronoun *it*, especially in the active voice ; as, *delectat,* it delights.

They are thus conjugated :—

	1st *Conj.*	2d *Conj.*	3d *Conj.*	4th *Conj.*
Ind. Pres.	delectat,	decet,	contingit,	evĕnit.
Imp.	delectābat,	decēbat,	contingēbat,	eveniēbat.
	&c.,	&c.,	&c.	

REMARK 1.—Most neuter and many active verbs may be used impersonally in the passive voice ; as, *currĭtur*, it is run, *pugnātur*, it is fought.

REMARK 2.—The parts of the verb used impersonally are, in each voice, the several tenses of the indicative, subjunctive, and infinitive moods, except the future infinitive active.

NEUTER PASSIVE VERBS.

(*See Remark on page 14.*)

Of these verbs, *audeo, gaudeo,* and *soleo,* are of the second conjugation ; the other of the third.

Audeo is thus conjugated :—

PRINCIPAL PARTS.

Pres. Indic. Audeo.   *Pres. Infin.* audēre.   *Perf. Part.* ausus.

INDICATIVE MOOD.

Pres.	audeo, &c.,	*I dare, &c.*
Imp.	audēbam,	*I was daring.*
Fut.	audēbo,	*I shall dare.*
Perf.	ausus sum *or* fui,	*I dared.*
Plup.	ausus eram *or* fuĕram,	*I had dared.*
Fut. Perf.	ausus ero *or* fuĕro,	*I shall have dared.*

SUBJUNCTIVE MOOD.

Pres.	audeam, &c.,	*I may dare, &c.*
Imp.	audērem,	*I would dare.*
Perf.	ausus sim,	*I may have dared.*
Plup.	ausus essem,	*I would have dared.*

IMPERATIVE MOOD.

Pres.	aude, &c.,	*dare thou, &c.*
Fut.	audēto, &c.,	*thou shalt dare, &c.*

INFINITIVE MOOD.

Pres.	audēre,	*to dare.*
Perf.	ausus esse,	*to have dared.*
Fut.	ausūrus esse,	*to be about to dare.*

PARTICIPLES.

Pres.	audens, *daring.*	*Fut. Act.*	ausūrus, *about to dare.*
Perf.	ausus, *having dared.*	*Fut. Pass.*	audendus, *to be dared.*

GERUND.

Gen.   audendi, *of daring, &c.*

SUPINES.

Former.   ausum, *to dare.*
Latter.   ausu, *to be dared.*

(Here learn Exercise XVIII.)

IRREGULAR VERBS.

NOTE. — These may be omitted by the pupil until they are introduced in the Exercises ; also, the Defective Verbs.

Irregular verbs are such as deviate from the common forms in some of the parts derived from the first root.

They are *sum, volo, fero, edo, fio, eo,* and their compounds.

NOTE. — In general, only the irregular parts of the following verbs are fully exhibited. The other parts may be supplied by a comparison with the regular verbs already conjugated. The regular parts of *volo, fero,* and their compounds, follow the analogy of the third conjugation; *fio, eo,* and their compounds, that of the fourth.

Sum has been already conjugated, (see page 19). In the same manner are conjugated its compounds, *absum, adsum, desum, insum, intersum, obsum, præsum, subsum,* and *supersum.*

Prosum, to do good, to benefit, has *d* after *pro* when the simple verb begins with *e;* as,

Ind. pres. pro′-sum, prod′-es, prod′-est, &c.
— *imperf.* prod′-ĕ-ram, prod′-ĕ-ras, &c.

Possum, I can, is compounded of *potis,* able, and *sum.*

PRINCIPAL PARTS.

Pres. Ind.	*Pres. Infin.*	*Perf. Ind.*
pos′-sum,	pos′-se,	pot′-u-i, *I can* or *I am able.*

INDICATIVE MOOD.

Present. *I am able.*

Sing.	pos′-sum,	po′-tes,	po′-test;
Plur.	pos′-sŭ-mus,	po′-tes-tis,	pos′-sunt.

Imperfect. *I was able.*

Sing.	pot′-ĕ-ram,	pot′-ĕ-ras,	pot′-ĕ-rat;
Plur.	pot-e-rā′-mus,	pot-e-rā′-tis,	pot′-ĕ-rant.

Future. *I shall* or *will be able.*

Sing.	pot′-ĕ-ro,	pot′-ĕ-ris,	pot′-ĕ-rit;
Plur.	po-ter′-ĭ-mus,	po-ter′-ĭ-tis,	pot′-ĕ-runt.

Perfect. *I have been able.*

Sing.	pot'-u-i,	pot-u-is'-ti,	pot'-u-it ;
Plur.	po-tu'-i-mus,	pot-u-is'-tis,	pot-u-ē'-runt *or* -re

Pluperfect. *I had been able.*

Sing.	po-tu'-ĕ-ram,	po-tu'-ĕ-ras,	po-tu'-ĕ-rat ;
Plur.	pot-u-e-rā'-mus	pot-u-e-rā'-tis,	po-tu'-ĕ-rant.

Future Perfect. *I shall or will have been able.*

Sing.	po-tu'-ĕ-ro,	po-tu'-ĕ-ris,	po-tu'-ĕ-rit ;
Plur.	pot-u-er'i-mus,	pot-u-er'-i-tis,	po-tu'-ĕ-rint.

SUBJUNCTIVE MOOD.

Present. *I may or can be able.*

Sing.	pos'-sim,	pós'-sis,	pos'-sit ;
Plur.	pos-sī'-mus,	pos-sī'-tis,	pos'-sint.

Imperfect. *I might be able.*

Sing.	pos'-sem,	pos'-ses,	pos'-set ;
Plur.	pos-sē-mus,	pos-sē'-tis,	pos'-sent.

Perfect. *I may have been able.*

Sing.	po-tu'-ĕ-rim,	po-tu'-ĕ-ris,	po-tu'-ĕ-rit ;
Plur.	pot-u-er'-i-mus,	pot-u-er'-i-tis,	po-tu'-ĕ-rint.

Pluperfect. *I might have been able.*

Sing.	pot-u-ís'-sem,	pot-u-is'-ses,	pot-u-is'-set ;
Plur.	pot-u-is-sē'-mus,	pot-u-is-sē'-tis,	pot-u-is'-sent.

(No imperative.)

INFINITIVE MOOD.
Present. pos'-se. *Perfect.* pot-u-is'-se.

PARTICIPIAL ADJECTIVE.
po'-tens, *able.*

NOLO is compounded of the obsolete *ne* (for *non*, not) and *volo ;* MALO of *magis*, more, and *volo*. They are thus conjugated : —

PRINCIPAL PARTS.

Pres. Indic.	Pres. Infin.	Perf. Indic.	
Vo'-lo,	vel'-le,	vol'-u-i,	*to be willing,* or *to wish.*
No'-lo,	nol'-le,	nol'-u-i,	*to be unwilling.*
Ma'-lo,	mal'-le,	mal'-u-i,	*to be more willing.*

INDICATIVE.

Present.

S. Vo'-lo, vis, vult ;　　　P. vol'-ŭ-mus, vul'-tis, vo'-lunt.
　No'-lo, non'-vis, non'-vult ;　　nol'-ŭ-mus, non-vul'-tis, no'-lunt.
　Ma'-lo, ma'-vis, ma'-vult ;　　mal'-ŭ-mus, ma-vul'-tis, ma'-lunt.

Imp.	vo-lē'-bam.	no-lē'-bam.	ma-lē'-bam.
Fut.	vo'-lam.	no'-lam.	ma'-lam.
Perf.	vol'-u-i.	nol'-u-i.	mal'-u-i.
Plup.	vo-lu'-ĕ-ram.	no-lu'-ĕ-ram.	ma-lu'-ĕ-ram.
Fut. Perf.	vo-lu'-ĕ-ro.	no-lu'-ĕ-ro.	ma-lu'-ĕ-ro.

SUBJUNCTIVE.

Present.

S. ve'-lim, ve'-lis, ve'-lit ;　　P. ve-lī'-mus, ve-lī'-tis, ve'-lint.
　no'-lim, no'-lis, no'-lit ;　　no-lī'-mus, no-lī'-tis, no'-lint.
　ma'-lim, ma'-lis, ma'-lit ;　　ma-lī'-mus, ma-lī'-tis, ma'-lint.

Imperfect.

S. vel'-lem, vel'-les, vel'-let ;　P. vel-lē'-mus, vel-lē'-tis, vel'-lent.
　nol'-lem, nol'-les, nol'-let ;　　nol-lē'-mus, nol-lē'-tis, nol'-lent.
　mal'-lem, mal'-les, mal'-let ;　　mal-lē'-mus, mal-lē'-tis, mal'-lent.

Perf.	vo-lu'-ĕ-rim.	no-lu'-ĕ-rim.	ma-lu'-ĕ-rim.
Plup.	vol-u-is'-sem.	nol-u-is'-sem.	mal-u-is'-sem.

Pres. Sing. 2. no'-li ;		Fut. Sing. 2. no-lī'-to.	
		3. no-lī'-to.	
Plur. 2. no-lī'-te.		Plur. 2. nol-i-tō'-te.	
		3. no-lun'-to.	

INFINITIVE.

Pres. vel'-le.	nol'-le.	mal'-le.
Perf. vol-u-is'-se.	nol-u-is'-se.	mal-u-is'-se.

PARTICIPLE.

Pres. vo'-lens.   no'-lens.

Fero, to bear, is thus conjugated : —

ACTIVE.   **PASSIVE.**

PRINCIPAL PARTS.

Pres. Indic. Fe'-ro,		*Pres. Indic.* Fe'-ror,
Pres. Infin. fer'-re,		*Pres. Infin.* fer'-ri,
Perf. Indic. tu'-li,		*Perf. Part.* la'-tus.
Supine. la'-tum.		

INDICATIVE.

Present.

S. fe'-ro, fers, fert ;	*S.* fe'-ror, fer'-ris *or* -re, fer'-tur ;
P. fer-i-mus, fer'-tis, fe'-runt.	*P.* fer-i-mur, fe-rim'-i-ni, fe-run'-tur.

Imp.	fe-re'-bam.	*Imp.*	fe-re'-bar.
Fut.	fe'-ram.	*Fut.*	fe'-rar.
Perf.	tu'-li.	*Perf.*	la'-tus sum *or* fu'-i.
Plup.	tu'-le-ram.	*Plup.*	la'-tus e'-ram *or* fu'-e-ram.
Fut. Perf.	tu'-le-ro.	*F. P.*	la'-tus e'-ro *or* fu'-e-ro.

SUBJUNCTIVE.

Pres.	fe'-ram.	*Pres.*	fe'-rar.
Imp. S.	fer'-rem, fer'-res, fer'-ret ;	*Imp. S.*	fer'-rer, fer-re'-ris *or* -re,
P.	fer-re'-mus, fer-re'-tis,		fer-re'-tur ;
	fer'-rent.	*P.*	fer-re'-mur, fe-ren'-i-ni, fer-ren'-tur.
Perf.	tu'-le-rim.	*Perf.*	la'-tus sim *or* fu'-e-rim.
Plup.	tu-lis'-sem.	*Plup.*	la'-tus es'-sem *or* fu-is'-sem.

IMPERATIVE.

Pres. S.	fer.	*Pres. S.*	fer'-re.
P.	fer'-te.	*P.*	fe-rim'-i-ni.
Fut. S. 2.	fer'-to.	*Fut. S.* 2.	fer'-tor.
3.	fer'-to.	3.	fer'-tor.
P. 2.	fer-to'-te.	*P.* 2.	(fe-rim'-i-ni,)
3.	fe-run'-to.	3.	fe-run'-tor.

ACTIVE.	PASSIVE.

INFINITIVE.

Pres.	fer'-re.	*Pres.*	fer'-ri.
Perf.	tu-lis'-se.	*Perf.*	la'-tus es'-se *or* fu-is'-se.
Fut.	la-tū'-rus es'-se.	*Fut.*	la'-tum i'-ri.

PARTICIPLES.

Pres.	fe'-rens.	*Perf.*	la'-tus.
Fut.	la-tū'-rus.	*Fut.*	fe-ren'-dus.

GERUND.

fe-ren'-di, &c.

SUPINES.

Former.	lā'-tum.	*Latter.*	la'-tu.

Fio, to be made, *or* to become, is used as the passive voice of *facio*, which has no regular passive.

Pres. Indic.	*Pres. Infin.*	*Perf. Part.*
Fi'-o,	fi'-ĕ-ri,	fac'-tus.

INDICATIVE.

Pres. S.	fi'-o, fis, fit;	*Plup.*	fac'-tus e'-ram *or* fu'-ĕ-
P.	fi'-mus, fi'-tis, fi'-unt.		ram.
Imp.	fi-ē'-bam.	*Fut. Perf.*	fac'-tus e'-ro *or* fu'-ĕ-ro.
Fut.	fi'-am.		
Perf.	fac'-tus sum *or* fu'-i.		

4# SUBJUNCTIVE.

Pres.	fi'-am.	*Plup.*	fac'-tus es'-sem *or* fu-is'-
Imp.	fi'-ĕ-rem.		sem.
Perf.	fac'-tus sim *or* fu'-ĕ-rim.		

IMPERATIVE.	INFINITIVE.

Sing.	fi;	*Pres.*	fi'-ĕ-ri.
Plur.	fi'-te.	*Perf.*	fac'-tus es'-se *or* fu-is'-se.
		Fut.	fac'-tum i'-ri.

PARTICIPLES.	SUPINE.

Perf.	fac'-tus.	*Latter.*	fac'-tu.
Fut.	fa-ci-en'-dus.		

5*

Edo, to eat, is conjugated regularly as a verb of the third conjugation; but in the present of the indicative, imperative, and infinitive moods, and in the imperfect of the subjunctive, it has also forms similar to those of the corresponding tenses of *sum*. Thus:

INDICATIVE.

Present.

Sing. e´-do, e´-dis, e´-dit,
    (*or* es, est ;)
	Plur. ed´-ĭ-mus, ed´-ĭ-tis e´-dunt,
	    (*or* es´-tis.)

SUBJUNCTIVE.

Imperfect.

S. ed´-ĕ-rom, ed´-ĕ-res, ed´-ĕ-ret,
   (*or* es´-sem, es´-ses, es´-set ;)
	P. ed-e-rē´-mus, ed-e-rē´-tis, ed´-ĕ-rent,
	   (*or* es-sē´-mus, es-sē´-tis, es´-sent.)

IMPERATIVE.

Pres. S. e´-de,
    (*or* es.)
 Fut. S. ed´-ĭ-to,
    (*or* es-to.)
	Plur. ed´-ĭ-te,
	    (*or* es-te.)
	 Plur. ed-i-tō´-te, e-dun´-to,
	    (*or* es-tō´-te.)

INFINITIVE.

Pres. ed ĕ-re, (*or* es-se.)

PASSIVE.

Pres. ed ĭ-tur, (*or* es-tur.)
Fut. ed-e-tur, (*or* es-sē-tur.)

Eo, to go, is thus conjugated :—

Pres. Indic.	Pres. Inf.	Perf. Indic.	Perf. Part.
E´-o,	i´-re.	i´-vi.	i´-tum.

INDICATIVE.

SUBJUNCTIVE.

Pres. *S.* e′-am, e′-as, e′-at; *P.* e-ā′-mus, e-ā′-tis, e′-ant.
Imp. *S.* i′-rem, i′-res, i′-ret; *P.* i-rē′-mus, i-rē′-tis, i′-rent.
Perf. iv′-ĕ-rim.
Plup. i-vis′-sem.

IMPERATIVE.

Pres. *S.* i,
    P. ĭ-te.
Fut. *S.* 2 í -to,
      3 í -to ;
    P. 2 i-to′-te,
      3 e-un′-to.

INFINITIVE.

Pres. i′-re.
Perf. i-vis′-se.
Fut. i-tū′-rus es′-se.

PARTICIPLES.

Pres. i′-ens, (*gen.* e-un′-tis.)
Fut. i-tū′-rus.

GERUND.

e-un′-di, &c.

The compounds of *eo* are conjugated like the simple verb, but most of them have *ii* in the perfect rather than *ivi.*

DEFECTIVE VERBS.

Defective verbs are those which are not used in certain tenses, numbers, or persons.

The following list contains such verbs as are remarkable for wanting many of their parts : —

1. Odi, *I hate.*
2. Cœpi, *I have begun.*
3. Memĭni, *I remember.*
4. Aio, } *I say.*
5. Inqnam, }
6. Fari, *to speak.*
7. Quæso, *I pray.*
8. Ave, } *hail.*
9. Salve, }

Odi, cœpi, and *memĭni,* are used chiefly in the perfect and in the other parts formed from the second root, and are thence called *preteritive* verbs. Thus : —

1. IND. *perf.* o′-di *or* o′-sus sum; *plup.* od′-ĕ-ram; *f. perf.* od′-ĕ-ro.
    SUBJ. *perf.* od′ĕ-rim; *plup.* o-dis′-sem.

INF. *perf.* o-dis'-se ; *fut.* o-sŭ'-rum esse.
PART. *fut.* o-sŭ'-rus ; *perf.* o'-sus.

Exōsus and *perōsus*, like *osus*, are used actively.

2. IND. *perf.* cœ'-pi ; *plup.* cœp'-ĕ-ram ; *f. perf.* cœp'-ĕ-ro.
SUBJ. *perf.* cœp'-ĕ-rim ; *plup.* cœ-pis'-sem.
INF. *perf.* cœ-pis'-se ; *fut.* cœp-tū'-rum esse.
PART. *fut.* cœp-tū'-rus ; *perf.* cœp'-tus.

3. IND. *perf.* mem'-ĭ-ni ; *plup.* me-min'-ĕ-ram ; *f. perf.* me-min'-ĕ-ro.
SUBJ. *perf.* me-min'-ĕ-rim ; *plup.* mem-i-nis'-sem.
INF. *perf.* mem-i-nis'-se.
IMPERAT. 2 *pers.* S. me-men'-to ; P. mem-en-tō'-te.

Odi and *memĭni* have, in the perfect, the sense of
the present, and, in the pluperfect and future perfect,
the sense of the imperfect and future.

4. IND. *pres.* S. ai'-o,* a'-is, a'-it ; P. ——, ——, ai'-unt.*
—— *imp.* S. ai-ē'-bam, ai-ē'-bas, ai-ē'-bat ;
P. ai-e-bā'-mus, ai-e-bā'-tis, ai-ē'-bant.
SUBJ. *pres.* ——, ai'-as, ai'-at ; ——, ——, ai'-ant.
IMPERAT. a'-i.   PART. *pres.* ai'-ens.

5. IND. *pres.* S. in'-quam, in'-quis, in'-quit ;
P. in'-quĭ-mus, in'-quĭ-tis, in'-qui-unt.
—— *imp.* ——, ——, in-qui-ē'-bat *and* in-quī'-bat ; ——, ——,.
in-qui-ē'-bant.
—— *fut.* ——, in'-qui-es, in'-qui-et ; ——, ——, ——.
—— *perf.* ——, in-quis'-ti, in'-quit ; ——, ——, ——.
SUBJ. *pres.* ——, in'-qui-as, in'-qui-at ; ——, in-qui-ā'-tis, in'-qui-
ant.
IMPERAT. in'-que, in'-quĭ-to.

6. IND. *pres.* ——, ——, fa'-tur. *fut.* fa'-bor, ——, fab'-ĭ-tur.
—— *perf.* fa'-tus est ; *plup.* fa'-tus eram.
IMPERAT. fa'-re.
INFIN. *pres.* fa'-ri *or* fa'-ri-er.
PART. *pres.* fans ; *perf.* fa'-tus ; *fut.* fan'-dus.
GERUND, *gen.* fan'-di ; *abl.* fan'-do.
SUPINE, fa'-tu.

7. IND. *pres.* S. quæ'-so, ——, quæ'-sit ; P. quæs'-ŭ-mus, ——, ——.
INF. *pres.* quæs'-ĕ-re.

8. IMPERAT. S. a'-ve, a-vē'-te ; a-vē'-to. INF. a-vē'-re.

Pronounced *a'-yo, a'-yunt,* &c.

9. IND. *pres.* sal'-ve-o ; *fut.* sal-vĕ'-bis.
   INF. *pres.* sal-vĕ'-re.
   IMPERAT. *S.* sal'-ve, sal-vĕ'-te ; sal-vĕ'-to..

Among defective verbs is sometimes included *fore*,
which is thus conjugated : —

Subj. imperf. *S.* fo'-rem, fo'-res, fo'-ret; *P.* ——, ——, fo'-rent.
Inf. pres. fo'-re.

Forem has the same meaning as *essem*, and *fore* the
same as *futūrus esse*.

NOUNS.

A substantive or noun is the *name* of an object.

A *proper* noun is the name of *an individual* object;
as, *Cæsar ; Roma*, Rome.

A *common* noun is the name of a *class of objects*, to
each of which it is applicable; as, *homo*, man, *or* a
man ; *avis*, a bird.

A *collective* noun is one which, in the singular number, denotes *a collection of individuals ;* as, *popŭlus*,
a people.

An *abstract* noun is the name of a *quality, action*,
or other *attribute ;* as, *bonĭtas*, goodness; *gaudium*,
joy.

A *material* noun is the name of a *substance considered in the gross ;* as, *lignum*, wood ; *ferrum*, iron.

GENDER.

Nouns have three genders, — *masculine, feminine*,
and *neuter*.

The gender of Latin nouns depends either on their
signification, or on their declension and termination.

Names, proper and appellative, of all male beings,
and names of rivers, winds, and months, are *masculine ;* as, *Homērus*, Homer ; *pater*, a father ; *equus*, a
horse ; *Aprīlis*, April.

Names, proper and appellative, of all female beings, and names of countries, towns, trees, plants, ships, islands, poems, and gems, are *feminine;* as, *Helĕna,* Helen; *mater,* a mother; *juvenca,* a heifer; *piru*, a pear-tree.

Some words are either masculine or feminine. These, if they denote things having life, are said to be of the *common* gender; if things without life, of the *doubtful* gender; as *parens,* a parent; *finis,* an end.

Nouns which are neither masculine nor feminine, are said to be of the *neuter* gender.

NUMBER.

Latin nouns have two numbers, the *Singular* and the *Plural,* which are distinguished by their terminations.

The singular number denotes one object; the plural, more than one.

PERSON.

The person of a noun or pronoun is the character sustained by the object which it represents, as being the speaker, the person spoken to, or the person or thing spoken of.

Hence, as in verbs, there are three persons.

CASES.

Cases are those terminations of nouns which denote their relations to other words.

Latin nouns have six cases, viz.: *Nominative, Genitive, Dative, Accusative, Vocative,* and *Ablative.*

The nominative denotes the relation of a *subject* to a finite verb; as, *ego scribo, I* write.

The genitive denotes *origin, possession,* and many other relations, which, in English, are expressed by the preposition *of,* or by the *possessive* case; as, vita *Cæsaris,* the life of *Cæsar,* or *Cæsar's* life.

The dative denotes that *to* or *for* which anything is, or is done; as, *Ille* mihi *librum dedit*, He gave the book *to me.*

The accusative is either the *object* of an active verb, or of certain prepositions, or the *subject* of an infinitive.

The vocative is the form appropriated to the name of any object which is addressed.

The ablative denotes *privation*, and many other relations, especially those expressed in English by the prepositions *with, from, in,* or *by.*

REMARK. — The inflected cases, *i. e.,* all except the nominative and vocative, are sometimes called the *oblique* cases.

DECLENSIONS.

There are in Latin five different modes of declining nouns, called the *first, second, third, fourth,* and *fifth* declensions.

These may be distinguished by the termination of the genitive singular, which, in the first declension, ends in *æ,* in the second in *i,* in the third in *is,* in the fourth in *ûs,* and in the fifth in *eï.*

Every inflected word consists of two parts, — a *root* and a *termination.*

The *root* is the part which is not changed by inflection.

The *termination* is the part annexed to the root.

REMARK. — The root of a *declined* word may be found by removing the termination of any of its oblique cases. The case commonly selected for this purpose is the genitive singular.

The following table exhibits a comparative view of the terminations of the five declensions : —

Singular.

	I.	II. M.	N.	III. M. & F.	N.	IV. M.	N.	V.
Nom.	a,	us, er,	um,	or &c., &c., e, &c.	is,	us,	u,	es,
Gen.	æ,	i,			i,	ûs,		ei,
Dat.	æ,	o,			i,	ui,	u,	ei,
Acc.	am,	um,		em, (im,)	e, &c.	um,	u,	em,
Voc.	a,	e, er,	um,	or &c. &c. e, &c.	e,	us,	u,	es,
Abl.	a,	o,			(i,)		u.	e.

Plural.

	I.	II.			III.		IV.		V.
Nom.	æ,	i,		a,	es,	a, (ia,)	us,	ua,	es,
Gen.	ārum,	ōrum,			um,	(ium,)	uum,		ērum,
Dat.	is,	is,				ĭbus,	ĭbus, (ŭbus,)		ēbus,
Acc.	as,	os,		a,	es,	a, (ia,)	us,	ua,	es,
Voc.	æ,	i,		a,	es,	a, (ia,)	us,	ua,	es,
Abl.	is.	is.				ĭbus.	ĭbus, (ŭbus.)		ēbus.

Remarks.

1. The accusative singular of masculines and feminines always ends in *m*.

2. The vocative singular is like the nominative, except in nouns in *us* of the second declension.

3. The nominative and vocative plural are alike.

4. The genitive plural always ends in *um*.

5. The dative and ablative plural end alike; — in the 1st and 2d declensions, in *is;* in the 3d, 4th, and 5th, in *bus*.

6. The accusative plural of masculines and feminines always ends in *s*.

7. Nouns of the neuter gender have the accusative and vocative like the nominative, in both numbers; and these cases, in the plural, end in *a*.

FIRST DECLENSION.

Nouns of the first declension end in *a, e, as, es.*

Those in *a* and *e* are feminine; those in *as* and *es* are masculine.

Latin nouns of this declension end only in *a.*
They are thus declined : —

	Singular.	
Nom.	Mu´-sa,	*a muse ;*
Gen.	mu´-sæ,	*of a muse ;*
Dat.	mu´-sæ,	*to a muse ;*
Acc.	mu´-sam,	*a muse ;*
Voc.	mu´-sa,	*O muse ;*
Abl.	mu´-sa,	*with a muse ;*

	Plural.	
Nom.	mu´-sæ,	*muses ;*
Gen.	mu-sä´-rum,	*of muses ;*
Dat.	mu´-sis,	*to muses ;*
Acc.	mu´-sas,	*muses ;*
Voc.	mu´-sæ,	*O muses ;*
Abl.	mu´-sis,	*with muses.*

In like manner decline

Au´-la, *a hall.*
Cu´-ra, *care.*
Ga´-le-a, *a helmet.*

Mach´-i-na, *a machine.*
Pen´-na, *a quill, a wing.*
Sa-git´-ta, *an arrow.*

Dea, a goddess, and *filia,* a daughter, have generally *ābus* in the dative and ablative plural.

GREEK NOUNS.

Nouns of the first declension in *e, as,* and *es,* and some also in *a,* are Greek.

Greek nouns in *e, as,* and *es,* are thus declined in the singular number : —

N.	Pe-nel´-ŏ-pe,	*N.*	Æ-nē´-as,	*N.*	An-chī´-ses,
G.	Pe-nel´-ŏ-pes,	*G.*	Æ-nē´-æ,	*G.*	An-chī´-sæ,
D.	Pe-nel´-ŏ-pæ,	*D.*	Æ-nē´-æ,	*D.*	An-chī´-sæ,
Ac.	Pe-nel´-ŏ-pen,	*Ac.*	Æ-nē´-am *or* -an,	*Ac.*	An-chī´-sen,
V.	Pe-nel´-ŏ-pe,	*V.*	Æ-nē´-a,	*V.*	An-chī´-se *or* a,
Ab.	Pe-nel´-ŏ-pe.	*Ab.*	Æ-nē´-a.	*Ab.*	An-chī´-sa *or* e.

In like manner decline

E-pit´-ŏ-me, *an abridgment.*
This´-be.
Bo´-re-as, *the north wind.*
Mi´-das.

Ti-ā´-ras, *a turban.*
Co-mē´-tes, *a comet.*
Dy-nas´-tes, *a sovereign.*
Pri-am´-I-des, *a son of Priam.*

Greek nouns which admit of a plural are declined in that number like the plural of *musa*.

(*Here learn Exercises XIX., XX.*)

SECOND DECLENSION.

Nouns of the second declension end in *er*, *ir*, *us*, *um*,

Those ending in *um* and *on* are neuter; the rest are masculine.

Nouns in *er*, *us*, and *um*, are thus declined : —

Singular.

	A lord.	A son-in-law.	A field.	A kingdom.
N.	Dom'-ĭ-nus,	Ge'-ner,	A'-ger,	Reg'-num,
G.	dom'-ĭ-ni,	gen'-ĕ-ri,	a'-gri,	reg'-ni,
D.	dom'-ĭ-no,	gen'-ĕ-ro,	a'-gro,	reg'-no,
Ac.	dom'-ĭ-num,	gen'-ĕ-rum,	a'-grum,	reg'-num,
V.	dom'-ĭ-ne,	ge'-ner,	a'-ger,	reg'-num,
Ab.	dom'-ĭ-no,	gen'-ĕ-ro,	a'-gro,	reg'-no,

Plural.

N.	dom'-ĭ-ni,	gen'-ĕ-ri,	a'-gri,	reg'-na,
G.	dom-i-nō'-rum,	gen-e-rō'-rum,	a-grō'-rum,	reg-nō'-rum,
D.	dom'-ĭ-nis,	gen'-ĕ-ris,	a'-gris,	reg'-nis,
Ac.	dom'-ĭ-nos,	gen'-ĕ-ros,	a'-gros,	reg'-na,
V.	dom'-ĭ-ni,	gen'-ĕ-ri,	a'-gri,	reg'-na,
Ab.	dom'-ĭ-nis.	gen'-ĕ-ris.	a'-gris.	reg'-nis.

Like *domĭnus* decline

An'-ĭ-mus, *the mind.*
Clip'-e-us, *a shield.*
Cor'-vus, *a raven.*
Fo'-cus, *a hearth.*

Gla'-di-us, *a sword.*
Lu'-cus, *a grove.*
Nu'-mĕ-rus, *a number.*
O-ce'-ă-nus, *the ocean.*

Like *gener* decline.

A-dul'-ter, ĕri, *an adulterer.*
Ar'-mĭ-ger, ĕri, *an armor-bearer.*

Cel'-tĭ-ber, ĕri, *a Celtiberian.*
I'-ber, ĕri, *a Spaniard.*

Li'-ber, ĕri, *Bacchus.*

Pu'-er, ĕri, *a boy.*

So'-cer, ĕri, *a father-in-law.*

Ves'-per, ĕri, *the evening.*

Like *ager* decline

A'-per, *a wild boar.*

Aus'-ter, *the south wind.*

Fa'-ber, *a workman.*

Li'-ber, *a book.*

Ma-gis'-ter, *a master.*

On'-ă-ger, *a wild ass.*

Al-ex-an'-der.

Teu'-cer.

Like *regnum* decline

An'-trum, *a cave.*

A'-tri-um, *a hall.*

Bel'-lum, *war.*

Ex-em'-plum, *an example.*

Ne-go'-ti-um,* *a business.*

Ni'-trum, *natron.*

Præ-sid'-i-um, *a defence.*

Sax'-um, *a rock.*

Scep'-trum, *a sceptre.*

Tem'-plum, *a temple.*

Vir, a man, with its compounds, and *Trevir*, (the only nouns in *ir*,) are declined like *gener.*

Proper names in *ius* omit *e* in the vocative; as, *Horatius, Horāti.* So also *filius*, a son, has *fili.*

Deus, a god, has *deus* in the vocative, and in the plural it has commonly *dii* and *diis*, instead of *dei* and *deis.*

Greek Nouns.

Nouns of the second declension ending in *os* and *on* are Greek. They are thus declined : —

Barbĭton, *a lyre.*

Singular.	*Singular.*	*Singular.*
N. De'-los,	An-dro'-ge-os,	*N.* bar'-bĭ-ton,
G. De'-li,	An-dro'-ge-o, *or* i,	*G.* bar'-bĭ-ti,
D. De'-lo,	An-dro'-ge-o,	*D.* bar'-bĭ-to,
Ac. De'-lon, *or* um,	An-dro'-ge-o, *or* on,	*Ac.* bar'-bĭ-ton,
V. De'-le,	An-dro'-ge-os,	*V.* bar'-bĭ-ton,
Ab. De'-lo.	An-dro'-ge-o.	*Ab.* bar'-bĭ-to.

REMARK. — The plurals of Greek nouns in *os* and *on* are declined like those of *domĭnus* and *regnum.*

(Here learn Exercises XXI., XXII., XXIII.)

* Pronounced *ne go'-she-um.*

THIRD DECLENSION.

The number of final letters in the third declension is twelve. Five are vowels, — *a, e, i, o, y ;* and seven are consonants, — *c, l, n, r, s, t, x.* The number of its final syllables exceeds fifty.

The following are examples of the most common forms of nouns of this declension, declined through all their cases : —

Honor, *honor ;* masc.

	Singular.	Plural.
N.	ho′-nor,	ho-nō′-res,
G.	ho-nō′-ris,	ho-nō′-rum,
D.	ho-nō′-ri,	ho-nor′-ĭ-bus,
Ac.	ho-nō′-rem,	ho-nō′-res,
V.	ho′-nor,	ho-nŏ′-res,
Ab.	ho-nō′-re,	ho-nor′-ĭ-bus.

Sermo, *speech ;* masc.

	Singular.	Plural.
N.	ser′-mo,	ser-mō′-nes, —
G.	ser-mō′-nis,	ser-mō′-num,
D.	ser-mō′-ni,	ser-mon′-ĭ-bus,
Ac.	ser-mō′-nem,	ser-mō′-nes,
V.	ser′-mo,	ser-mō′-nes,
Ab.	ser-mō′-ne,	ser-mon′-ĭ-bus.

Rupes, *a rock ;* fem.

	Singular.	Plural.
N.	ru′-pes,	ru′-pes,
G.	ru′-pis,	ru′-pi-um,
D.	ru′-pi,	ru′-pĭ-bus,
Ac.	ru′-pem,	ru′-pes,
V.	ru′-pes,	ru′-pes,
Ab.	ru′-pe,	ru′-pĭ-bus.

Turris, *a tower ;* fem.

	Singular.	Plural.
N.	tur′-ris,	tur′-res,
G.	tur′-ris,	tur′-ri-um,
D.	tur′-ri, (rem,)	tur′-rĭ-bus,
Ac.	tur′-rim *or*	tur′-res,
V.	tur′-ris,	tur′-res,
Ab.	tur′-ri *or* -re,	tur′-rĭ-bus.

Ars, *art ;* fem.

	Singular.	Plural.
N.	ars,	ar′-tes,
G.	ar′-tis,	ar′-ti-um,*
D.	ar′-ti,	ar′-tĭ-bus,
Ac.	ar′-tem,	ar′-tes,
V.	ars,	ar′-tes,
Ab.	ar′-te,	ar′-tĭ-bus.

Nox, *night ;* fem.

	Singular.	Plural.
N.	nox,	noc′-tes,
G.	noc′-tis,	noc′-ti-um,†
D.	noc′-ti,	noc′-tĭ-bus,
Ac.	noc′-tem,	noc′-tes,
V.	nox,	noc′-tes,
Ab.	noc′-te,	noc′-tĭ-bus.

* Pronounced *ar′-she-um.*   † *noc′-she-um.*

Miles, *a soldier ;* com. gen.

Singular.	Plural.
N. mi'-les,	mil'-ĭ-tes,
G. mil'-ĭ-tis,	mil'-ĭ-tum,
D. mil'-ĭ-ti,	mi-lit'-ĭ-bus,
Ac. mil'-ĭ-tem,	mil'-ĭ-tes,
V. mi'-les,	mil'-ĭ-tes,
Ab. mĭl'-ĭ-te,	mi-lit'-ĭ-bus.

Iter, *a journey ;* neut.

Singular.	Plural.
N. i'-ter,	i-tin'-ĕ ra,
G. i-tin'-ĕ-ris,	i-tin'-ĕ-rum,
D. i-tin'-ĕ-ri,	it-i-ner'-ĭ-bus,
Ac. i'-ter,	i-tin'-ĕ-ra,
V. ĭ'-ter,	i-tin'-ĕ-ra,
Ab. i-tin'-ĕ-re,	it-i-ner'-ĭ-bus.

Pater, *a father ;* masc.

Singular.	Plural.
N. pa'-ter,	pa'-tres,
G. pa'-tris,	pa'-trum,
D. pa'-tri,	pat'-rĭ-bus,
Ac. pa'-trem,	pa'-tres,
V. pa'-ter,	pa'-tres,
Ab. pa'-tre,	pat'-rĭ-bus.

Lapis, *a stone ;* masc.

Singular.	Plural.
N. la'-pis,	lap'-ĭ-des,
G. lap'-ĭ-dis,	lap'-ĭ-dum,
D. lap'-ĭ-di,	la-pid'-ĭ-bus,
Ac. lap'-ĭ-dem,	lap'-ĭ-des,
V. la'-pis,	lap'-ĭ-des,
Ab. lap'-ĭ-de,	la-pid'-ĭ-bus.

Sedile, *a seat ;* neut.

Singular.	Plural.
N. se-dī'-le,	se-dil'-i-a,
G. se-dī'-lis,	se-dil'-i-um,
D. se-dī'-li,	se-dil'-ĭ-bus,
Ac. se-dī'-le,	se-dil'-i-a,
V. se-dī'-le,	se-dil'-i-a,
Ab. se-dī'-li,	se-dil'-ĭ-bus.

Virgo, *a virgin ;* fem.

Singular.	Plural.
N. vir'-go,	vir'-gĭ-nes,
G. vir'-gĭ-nis,	vir'-gĭ-num,
D. vir'-gĭ-ni,	vir-gin'-ĭ-bus,
Ac. vir'-gĭ-nem,	vir'-gĭ-nes,
V. vir'-go,	vir'-gĭ-nes,
Ab. vir'-gĭ-ne,	vir-gin'-ĭ-bus.

Carmen, *a verse ;* neut.

Singular.	Plural.
N. car'-men,	car'-mĭ-na,
G. car'-mĭ-nis,	car'-mĭ-num,
D. car'-mĭ-ni,	car-min'-ĭ-bus,
Ac. car'-men,	car'-mĭ-na,
V. car'-men,	car'-mĭ-na,
Ab. car'-mĭ-ne,	car-min'-ĭ-bus.

Animal, *an animal ;* neut.

Singular.	Plural.
N. an'-ĭ-mal,	an-i-ma'-li-a,
G. an-i-mā'-lis,	an-i-ma'-li-um,
D. an-i-mā'-li,	an-i-mal'-ĭ-bus,
Ac. an'-ĭ-mal,	an-i-ma'-li-a,
V. an'-ĭ-mal,	an-i-ma'-li-a,
Ab. an-i-mā'-li,	an-i-mal'-ĭ-bus.

Opus, *a work ;* neut. | **Caput,** *a head ;* neut.

Singular.	Plural.	Singular.	Plural.
N. o′-pus,	op′-ĕ-ra,	N. ca′-put,	cap′-ĭ-ta,
G. op′-ĕ-ris,	op′-ĕ-rum,	G. cap′-ĭ-tis,	cap′-ĭ-tum,
D. op′-ĕ-ri,	o-per′-ĭ-bus,	D. cap′-ĭ-ti,	ca-pit′-ĭ-bus,
Ac. o′-pus,	op′-ĕ-ra,	Ac. ca′-put,	cap′-ĭ-ta,
V. o′-pus,	op′-ĕ-ra,	V. ca′-put,	cap′-ĭ-ta,
Ab. op′-ĕ-re,	o-per′-ĭ-bus.	Ab. cap′-ĭ-te,	ca-pit′-ĭ-bus.

Poëma, *a poem ;* neut.

Singular.	Plural.
N. po-ē′-ma,	po-em′-ă-ta,
G. po-em′-ă-tis,	po-em′-ă-tum,
D. po-em′-ă-ti,	po-e-mat′-ĭ-bus *or* po-em′-ă-tis,
Ac. po-ē′-ma,	po-em′-ă-ta,
V. po-ē′-ma,	po-em′-ă-ta,
Ab. po-em′-ă-te,	po-e-mat′-ĭ-bus *or* po-em′-ă-tis.

RULES FOR THE GENDER OF NOUNS OF THE THIRD DECLENSION.

MASCULINES.

Nouns ending in *o, er, or, es* increasing in the genitive, *os* and *n,* are masculine.

EXCEPTION 1. — Most nouns in *io* are feminine, when they signify things incorporeal; as, *ratio,* reason.

Exc. 2. — Most nouns in *do* and *go,* of more than two syllables, are feminine; as, *arundo,* a reed ; *imāgo,* an image.

FEMININES.

Nouns ending in *as, es* not increasing in the genitive, *is, ys, aus, s* preceded by a consonant, and *x,* are feminine.

Exc. 1. — Latin nouns in *nis* are masculine or doubtful; as, *ignis,* fire, mas.; *amnis,* a river, mas. or fem.

Exc. 2. — *Dens,* a tooth, *fons,* a fountain, *mons,* a mountain, and *pons,* a bridge, are masculine.

Exc. 3. — Most nouns in *ex* are masculine.

NEUTERS.

Nouns ending in *a, e, i, y, c, l, t, ar, ur, us,* and *men,* are neuter.

Exc. — Nouns in *us,* having *ūtis* or *ūdis* in the genitive, are feminine; as, *juventus,* youth; *incus,* an anvil.

Note. — There are many other exceptions to these general rules for the gender, which will be found in the larger Grammars.

RULES FOR THE OBLIQUE CASES OF NOUNS OF THE THIRD DECLENSION.

Note. — There are many other exceptions to the following rules for the oblique cases besides those here given.

GENITIVE SINGULAR.

The genitive singular of Latin nouns of the third declension always ends in *is;* in Greek nouns sometimes in *os* and *us.*

Nouns in *a* form their genitive in *ātis;* as, *di-a-dē'-ma, di-a-dem'-ă-tis,* a crown.

Nouns in *e* change *e* into *is;* as, *re'-te, re'-tis,* a net.

Nouns in *o* form their genitive in *ōnis;* as, *ser'-mo, ser-mō'-nis,* speech.

Exc. — Nouns in *do* and *go* form their genitive in *ĭnis;* as, *a-run'-do, a-run'-dĭ-nis,* a reed; *i-mā'-go, i-mag'-ĭ-nis,* an image.

Nouns in *l, n,* and *r,* form their genitive by adding *is;* as, *con'-sul, con'-sŭ-lis,* a consul; *ca'-non, can'-ŏ-nis,* a rule; *ho'-nor, ho-nō'-ris,* honor.

Exc. 1. — Neuters in *en* form their genitive in *ĭnis;* as, *flu'-men, flu'-mĭ-nis,* a river,

Exc. 2. — Nouns in *ter* drop *e* in the genitive; as *pa'-ter, pa'-tris,* a father. So also *imber,* a shower, and names of months in *ber;* as, *Oc-tō'-ber, Oc-tō'-bris.*

Nouns in *as* form their genitive in *ātis;* as, *œ'-tas, œ-tā'-tis,* age.

Nouns in *es* form their genitive by changing *es* into *is*, *ĭtis*, *ĕtis*, or *ētis*; as, *ru'-pes*, *ru'-pis*, a rock; *mī-les*, *mil'-i-tis*, a soldier; *se'-ges*, *seg'-ĕ-tis*, growing corn.; *quies*, *quiētis*, rest.

Nouns in *is* have their genitive the same as the nominative; as, *au'-ris*, *au'-ris*, the ear.

Nouns in *os* form their genitive in *ōris* or *ōtis*; as, *flos*, *flo'-ris*, a flower; *ne'-pos*, *ne-pō'-tis*, a grandchild.

Nouns in *us* form their genitive in *ĕris* or *ōris*; as, *ge'-nus*, *gen'-ĕ-ris*, a kind; *tem'-pus*, *tem'-pŏ-ris*, time. Some in *uris*, *ūtis*, *udis*.

Nouns in *s*, with a consonant before it, form their genitive by changing *s* into *is* or *tis*; as, *trabs*, *tra'-bis*, a beam; *pars*, *par'-tis*, a part.

Nouns in *x* form their genitive by changing *x* into *cs* or *gs*, and inserting *i* before *s*; as *vox*, *vo'-cis*, the voice; *lex*, *legis*, a law.

Exc. — Nouns in *ex* form their genitive in *ĭcis*; as, *pol'-lex*, *pol'-li-cis*, the thumb.

DATIVE SINGULAR.

The dative singular ends in *i*.

ACCUSATIVE SINGULAR.

The accusative singular of neuter nouns is like the nominative. The accusative singular of masculines and feminines ends in *em*; but some Latin nouns in *is*, which do not increase in the genitive, have *im*; and some Greek nouns have *im*, *in*, or *a*.

VOCATIVE SINGULAR.

The vocative is like the nominative.

ABLATIVE SINGULAR.

The ablative singular commonly ends in *e*.

Exc. 1. — Neuters in *e*, *al*, and *ar*, have the ablative in *i*; as, *sedile*, *sedili*; *animal*, *animāli*; *calcar*, *cal-cāri*.

Exc. 2. — Nouns which have *im* alone, or both *im* and *in* in the accusative, and names of months in *er* or *is*, have *i* in the ablative; as, *vis, vim, vi; December, Decembri; Aprilis, Aprili.*

Exc. 3. — Nouns which have *em* or *im* in the accusative, have their ablative in *e* or *i*; as, *turris, turre*, or *turri.*

NOMINATIVE PLURAL.

— The nominative plural of masculines and feminines ends in *es;* but neuters have *a*, and those whose ablative singular ends in *i* only, or in *e* and *i*, have *ia.*

GENITIVE PLURAL.

The genitive plural commonly ends in *um*, sometimes in *ium.*

Nouns which, in the ablative singular, have *i* only, or *e* and *i*, make the genitive plural in *ium;* as, *sedile, sedili, sedilium; turris, turre* or *turri, turrium.*

Nouns in *es* and *is*, which do not increase in the genitive singular, have *ium;* as, *nubes, nubium; hostis, hostium.*

Monosyllables ending in two consonants have *ium* in the genitive plural; as, *urbs, urbium; gens, gentium.*

Nouns of two or more syllables, in *ns* or *rs*, and names of nations in *as*, have commonly *ium;* as, *cliens, clientium; Arpinas, Arpinatium.*

DATIVE AND ABLATIVE PLURAL.

— The dative and ablative plural end in *ibus.*

ACCUSATIVE PLURAL

The accusative plural ends, like the nominative, in *es, a, ia.*

The following nouns are irregular : —

Jupiter.

Singular.
N. Ju´-pĭ-ter,
G. Jo´-vis,
D. Jo´-vi,
Ac. Jo´-vem,
V. Ju´-pĭ-ter,
Ab. Jo´-ve.

Vis, *strength.*

Singular.	*Plural.*
N. vis,	vi´-res,
G. vis,	vir´-i-um,
D. —,	vir´-ĭ-bus,
Ac. vim,	vi´-res,
V. vis,	vi´-res,
Ab. vi,	vir´-ĭ-bus.

Bos, *an ox or cow.*

Singular.	*Plural.*
N. bos,	bo´-ves,
G. bo´-vis,	bo´-um,
D. bo´-vi,	bo´-bus *or* bu´-bus,
Ac. bo´-vem,	bo´-ves,
V. bos,	bo´-ves,
Ab. bo´-ve,	bo´-bus *or* bu´-bus.

(Here learn Exercises XXIV., XXV., XXVI.)

FOURTH DECLENSION.

Nouns of the fourth declension end in *us* and *u.* Those in *us* are masculine ; those in *u* are neuter.

They are thus declined : —

Fructus, *fruit.*

Singular.	*Plural.*
N. fruc´-tus,	fruc´-tus,
G. fruc´-tûs,	fruc´-tu-um,
D. fruc´-tu-i,*	fruc´-tĭ-bus,
Ac. fruc´-tum,	fruc´-tus,
V. fruc´-tus,	fruc´-tus,
Ab. fruc´-tu,	fruc´-tĭ-bus.

Cornu, *a horn.*

Singular.	*Plural.*
N. cor´-nu,	cor´-nu-a,
G. cor´-nûs,	cor´-nu-um,
D. cor´-nu,	cor´-nĭ-bus,
Ac. cor´-nu,	cor´-nu-a,
V. cor´-nu,	cor´-nu-a,
Ab. cor´-nu,	cor´-nĭ-bus.

In like manner decline

Can´-tus, *a song.*
Cur´-rus, *a chariot.*
Ex-er´-cĭ-tus, *an army.*
Fluc´-tus, *a wave.*

Mo´-tus, *motion.*
Se-nā´-tus, *the senate.*
Ge´-lu, *ice.*
Ve´-ru, *a spit.*

* Pronounced *fruct´-yu-i* or *fruc´-tshu-i,* etc.

EXCEPTIONS IN GENDER.

The following are feminine : —

Acus, *a needle,*
Domus, *a house.*
Ficus, *a fig.*

Manus, *a hand.*
Portĭcus, *a gallery.*
Tribus, *a tribe.*

EXCEPTIONS IN DECLENSION.

Domus, a house, is partly of the fourth declension and partly of the second. It is thus declined : —

Singular.	*Plural.*
N. do′-mus,	do′-mus,
G. do′-mûs *or* do′-mi,	dom′-u-um *or* do-mō′-rum,
D. dom′-u-i *or* do′-mo,	dom′-ĭ-bus,
Ac. do′-mum,	do′-mus *or* do′-mos,
V. do′-mus,	do′-mus,
Ab. do′-mo,	dom′-ĭ-bus.

The following nouns have *ŭbus* in the dative and ablative plural : —

Acus, *a needle.*
Arcus, *a bow.*
Artus, *a joint.*

Lacus, *a lake.*
Partus, *a birth.*
Pecu, *a flock.*

Specus, *a den.*
Tribus, *a tribe.*

Genu, a knee, *portus*, a harbor, *tonĭtrus*, thunder, and *veru*, a spit, have *ĭbus* or *ŭbus*.

FIFTH DECLENSION.

Nouns of the fifth declension end in *es*, and are of the feminine gender.

They are thus declined : —

Res, *a thing.*		**Dies**, *a day.*	
Singular.	*Plural.*	*Singular.*	*Plural.*
N. res,	res,	N. di′-es,	di′-es,
G. re′-i,	re′-rum,	G. di-ē′-i,	di-ē′-rum,
D. re′-i,	re′-bus,	D. di-ē′-i,	di-ē′-bus,
Ac. rem,	res,	Ac. di′-em,	di′-es,
V. res,	res,	V. di′-es,	di′-es,
Ab. re,	re′-bus.	Ab. di′-e,	di-ē′-bus.

Dies, a day, is masculine or feminine in the singular, and always masculine in the plural; *meridies,* mid-day, is masculine only.

(*Here learn Exercises XXVII., XXVIII., XXIX., XXX., XXXI., XXXII., XXXIII.*)

———

ADJECTIVES.

An adjective is a word which qualifies or limits the meaning of a substantive.

Adjectives are declined like substantives, and are either of the first and second declensions, or of the third only.

ADJECTIVES OF THE FIRST AND SECOND DECLENSION.

The masculine of adjectives belonging to the first and second declensions ends either in *us* or *er.*

Adjectives of the first and second declension form their feminine and neuter genders by adding *a* and *um* to the root of the masculine; as, *bonus,* root *bon,* fem. *bona,* neut. *bonum ; piger,* gen. *pigri,* root *pigr,* fem. *pigra,* neut. *pigrum.*

The masculine in *us* is declined like *dominus ;* that in *er* like *gener* or *ager ;* the feminine like *musa ;* and the neuter like *regnum.*

Bonus, *good.*

Singular.

Masc.	Fem.	Neut.
N. bo′-nus,	bo′-na,	bo′-num,
G. bo′-ni,	bo′-næ,	bo′-ni,
D. bo′-no,	bo′-næ,	bo′-no,
Ac. bo′-num,	bo′-nam,	bo′-num,
V. bo′-ne,	bo′-na,	bo′-num,
Ab. bo′-no,	bo′-nâ,	bo′-no.

Plural.

	Masc.	Fem.	Neut.
N.	bo′-ni,	bo′-næ,	bo′-na,
G.	bo-nŏ′-rum,	bo-nā′-rum,	bo-nŏ′-rum,
D.	bo′-nis,	bo′-nis,	bo′-nis,
Ac.	bo′-nos,	bo′-nas,	bo′-na,
V.	bo′-ni,	bo′-næ,	bo′-na,
Ab.	bo′-nis,	bo′-nis,	bu′-nis.

In like manner decline

Al′-tus, *high.*	Fi′-dus, *faithful.*	Lon′gus, *long.*
A-vā′-rus, *covetous.*	Im′-prŏ-bus, *wicked.*	Ple′-nus, *full.*
Be-nig′-nus, *kind.*	In-ī′-quus, *unjust.*	Tac′-I-tus, *silent.*

Like *bonus* are also declined all participles in *us*.

Tener, *tender.*

Singular.

	Masc.	Fem.	Neut.
N.	te′-ner,	ten′-ĕ-ra,	ten′-ĕ-rum,
G.	ten′-ĕ-ri,	ten′-ĕ-ræ,	ten′-ĕ-ri,
D.	ten′-ĕ-ro,	ten′-ĕ-ræ,	ten′-ĕ-ro,
Ac.	ten′-ĕ-rum,	ten′-ĕ-ram,	ten′-ĕ-rum,
V.	te′-ner,	ten′-ĕ-ra,	ten′-ĕ-rum,
Ab.	ten′-ĕ-ro,	ten′-ĕ-râ,	ten′-ĕ-ro,

Plural.

	Masc.	Fem.	Neut.
N.	ten′-ĕ-ri,	ten′-ĕ-ræ,	ten′-ĕ-ra,
G.	ten-e-rŏ′-rum,	ten-e-rā′-rum,	ten-e-rŏ′-rum,
D.	ten′-ĕ-ris,	ten′-ĕ-ris,	ten′-ĕ-ris,
Ac.	ten′-ĕ-ros,	ten′-ĕ-ras,	ten′-ĕ-ra,
V.	ten′-ĕ-ri,	ten′-ĕ-ræ,	ten′-ĕ-ra,
Ab.	ten′-ĕ-ris,	ten′-ĕ-ris,	ten′-ĕ-ris.

In like manner are declined

As′-per, *rough.*	La′-cer, *torn.*	Pros′-per, *prosperous.*
Ex′-ter, *foreign.*	Li′-ber, *free.*	Sa′-tur, *full.*
Gib′-ber, *crook-backed.*	Mi′-ser, *wretched.*	Sem′-I-fer, *half-wild.*

Most other adjectives in *er* drop *e* in declension.

7

Piger, *slothful.*

Singular.

	Masc.	Fem.	Neut.
N.	pi'-ger,	pi'-gra,	pi'-grum,
G.	pi'-gri,	pi'-græ,	pi'-gri,
D.	pi'-gro,	pi'-græ,	pi'-gro,
Ac.	pi'-grum,	pi'-gram,	pi'-grum,
V.	pi'-ger,	pi'-gra,	pi'-grum,
Ab.	pi'-gro,	pi'-grâ,	pi'-gro,

Plural.

N.	pi'-gri,	pi'-græ,	pi'-gra,
G.	pi-gro'-rum,	pi-grā'-rum,	pi-gro'-rum,
D.	pi'-gris,	pi'-gris,	pi'-gris,
Ac.	pi'-gros,	pi'-gras,	pi'-gra,
V.	pi'-gri,	pi'-græ,	pi'-gra,
Ab.	pi'-gris,	pi'-gris,	pi'-gris.

In like manner decline

Æ'-ger, *sick.*	In'-tĕ-ger, *entire*	Ru'-ber, *red.*
A'-ter, *black.*	Ni'-ger, *black.*	Sa'-cer, *sacred.*
Cre'-ber, *frequent.*	Pul'-cher, *fair.*	Si-nis'-ter, *left.*

Unus, *one.*

Singular.

	Masc.	Fem.	Neut.
N.	u'-nus,	u'-na,	u'-num,
G.	u-ni'-us,	u-ni'-us,	u-ni'-us,
D.	u'-ni,	u'-ni,	u'-ni,
Ac.	u'-num,	u'-nam,	u'-num,
V.	u'-ne,	u'-na,	u'-num,
Ab.	u'-no,	u'-nâ,	u'-no.

The plural is regular, like that of *bonus.*

In like manner decline

Nul'-lus, *no one.*	To'-tus, *the whole.*
So'-lus, *alone.*	Ul'-lus, *any.*

REMARK. — *Alius* has *aliud* in the nominative and accusative singular neuter, and in the genitive *alīus* contracted for *aliīus*

ADJECTIVES OF THE THIRD DECLENSION.

Some adjectives of the third declension have three terminations in the nominative singular; some two; and others only one.

I. Those of three terminations end in *er*, masc.; *is*, fem.; and *e*, neut.; and are thus declined : —

Acer, *sharp.*

Singular.

	Masc.	Fem.	Neut.
N.	a'-cer,	a'-cris,	a'-cre,
G.	a'-cris,	a'-cris,	a'-cris,
D.	a'-cri,	a'-cri,	a'-cri,
Ac.	a'-crem,	a'-crem,	a'-cre,
V.	a'-cer,	a'-cris,	a'-cre,
Ab.	a'-cri,	a'-cri,	a'-cri,

Plural.

	Masc.	Fem.	Neut.
N.	a'-cres,	a'-cres,	a'-cri-a,
G.	a'-cri-um,	a'-cri-um,	a'-cri-um,
D.	ac'-ri-bus,	ac'-ri-bus,	ac'-ri-bus,
Ac.	a'-cres,	a'-cres,	a'-cri-a,
V.	a'-cres,	a'-cres,	a'-cri-a,
Ab.	ac'-ri-bus,	ac'-ri-bus,	ac'-ri-bus.

In like manner are declined the following : —

Al'-a-cer, *cheerful.*	Pe-des'-ter, *on foot.*
Cel'-e-ber, *famous.*	Sa-lu'-ber, *wholesome.*
E-ques'-ter, *equestrian.*	Sil-ves'-ter, *woody.*
Pa-lus'-ter, *marshy.*	Vol'-u-cer, *winged.*

REMARK. — The nominative singular masculine sometimes ends in *is*, like the feminine; as, *saluber* or *salubris.*

II. Adjectives of two terminations end in *is* for the masculine and feminine, and *e* for the neuter, except comparatives, which end in *or* and *us*.

Mitis, *mild.*

	Singular.		*Plural.*	
	M. & F.	*N.*	*M. & F.*	*N.*
N.	mi'-tis,	mi'-te,	mi'-tes,	mit'-i-a,*
G.	mi'-tis,	mi'-tis,	mit'-i-um,*	mit'-i-um,
D.	mi'-ti,'	mi'-ti,	mit'-ĭ-bus,	mit'-ĭ-bus,
Ac.	mi'-tem,	mi'-te,	mi'-tes,	mit'-i-a,
V.	mi'-tis,	mi'-te,	mi'-tes,	mit'-i-a,
Ab.	mi'-ti,	mi'-ti,	mit'-ĭ-bus,	mit'-ĭ-bus.

In like manner decline

Ag'-ĭ-lis, *active.*	Dul'-cis, *sweet.*	In-col'-ŭ-mis, *safe.*
Bre'-vis, *short.*	For'-tis, *brave.*	Mi-rab'-ĭ-lis, *wonderful.*
Cru-dē'-lis, *cruel.*	Gra'-vis, *heavy.*	Om'-nis, *all.*

Tres, three, is declined like the plural of *mitis.*

All comparatives except *plus,* more, are declined like

Mitior,* *milder.*

Singular.

	M. & F.	*N.*
N.	mit'-i-or,	mit'-i-us,
G.	mit-i-ō'-ris,	mit-i-ō'-ris,
D.	mit-i-ō'-ri,	mit-i-ō'-ri,
Ac.	mit-i-ō'-rem,	mit'-i-us,
V.	mit'-i-or,	mit'-i-us,
Ab.	mit-i-ō'-re *or* ri,	mit-i-ō'-re *or* ri,

Plural.

N.	mit-i-ō'-res,	mit-i-ō'-ra,
G.	mit-i-ō'-rum,	mit-i-ō'-rum,
D.	mit-i-or'-ĭ-bus,	mit-i-or'-ĭ-bus,
Ac.	mit-i-ō'-res,	mit-i-ō'-ra,
V.	mit-i-ō'-res,	mit-i-ō'-ra,
Ab.	mit-i-or'-ĭ-bus,	mit-i-or'-ĭ-bus.

In like manner decline

Al'-ti-or, *higher.*	Fe-lic'-i-or, *happier.*	Gra'-vi-or, *heavier.*
Bre'-vi-or, *shorter.*	For'-ti-or, *braver.*	U-be'-ri-or, *more fertile.*

* Pronounced *mish'-e-um,* etc.

Plus, *more*, is thus declined : —

Singular.		*Plural.*	
N.		*M. & F.*	*N.*
N. plus,		N. plu'-res,	plu'-ra, *rarely* plu'-ri-a.
G. plu'-ris,		G. plu'-ri-um,	plu'-ri-um,
D. ———		D. plu'-rĭ-bus,	plu'-rĭ-bus,
Ac. plus,		Ac. plu'-res,	plu'-ra,
V. ———		V. ———	———
Ab. ———		Ab. plu'-rĭ-bus,	plu'-rĭ-bus.

III. Adjectives of one termination increase in the genitive, and are declined like

Felix, *happy.*

Singular.

M. & F.	*N.*
N. fe'-lix,	fe'-lix,
G. fe-lĭ'-cis,	fe-lĭ'-cis,
D. fe-lĭ'-ci,	fe-lĭ'-ci,
Ac. fe-lĭ'-cem,	fe'-lix,
V. fe'-lix,	fe'-lix,
Ab. fe-lĭ'-ce *or* -ci,	fe-lĭ'-ce *or* -ci,

Plural.

N. fe-lĭ'-ces,	fe-lic'-i-a,*
G. fe-lic'-ĭ-um,*	fe-lic'-i-um,
D. fe-lic'-ĭ-bus,	fe-lic'-ĭ-bus,
Ac. fe-lĭ'-ces,	fe-lic'-i-a,
V. fe-lĭ'-ces,	fe-lic'-i-a,
Ab. fe-lic'-ĭ-bus,	fe-lic'-ĭ-bus.

Præsens, *present.*

Singular.

M. & F.	*N.*
N. præ'-sens,	præ'-sens,
G. præ-sen'-tis,	præ-sen'-tis,
D. præ-sen'-ti,	præ-sen'-ti,
Ac. præ-sen'-tem,	præ'-sens,
V. præ'-sens,	præ'-sens,
Ab. præ-sen'-te *or* -ti,	præ-sen'-te *or* -ti,

---

* Pronounced *fe-lish'-e-um*, etc.

Plural.

N. præ-sen'-tes,	præ-sen'-ti-a,*
G. præ-sen'-ti-um,	præ-sen'-ti-um,
D. præ-sen'-tĭ-bus,	præ-sen'-tĭ-bus,
Ac. præ-sen'-tes,	præ-sen'-ti-a,
V. præ-sen'-tes.	præ-sen'-ti-a,
Ab. præ-sen'-tĭ-bus,	præ-sen'-tĭ-bus.

In like manner decline

Au'-dax, -ācis, *bold.*　　Par'-tĭ-ceps, -ĭpis, *participant.*
Fe'-rox, -ōcis, *fierce.*　　Sol'-lers, -tis, *shrewd.*
In'-gens, -tis, *huge.*　　Sos'-pes, -ĭtis, *safe;* gen. pl. -um.

All present participles are declined like *præsens.*

(*Here learn Exercises* XXXIV., XXXV., XXXVI.)

NUMERAL ADJECTIVES.

Numeral adjectives are those which denote number. They are divided into three principal classes, — *Cardinal, Ordinal,* and *Distributive.*

Cardinal numbers are those which simply denote the number of things, in answer to the question, " How many ? " as, *unus,* etc.

Ordinal numbers are such as denote order or rank; as, *primus,* etc.

Distributive numbers are those which indicate an equal division among several persons or things; as, *bini,* two by two, *or* two to each.

	Cardinal.	Ordinal.
1.	Unus, *one.*	Primus, *first.*
2.	Duo, *two,* etc.	Secundus, *second,* etc.
3.	Tres.	Tertius.
4.	Quatuor.	Quartus.
5.	Quinque.	Quintus.
6.	Sex.	Sextus.
7.	Septem.	Septĭmus.
8.	Octo.	Octāvus.
9.	Novem.	Nonus.

* Pronounced *prĕ-sen'-she-a,* etc.

10.	Decem.	Decĭmus.
11.	Undĕcim.	Undecĭmus.
12.	Duodĕcim.	Duodecĭmus.
13.	Tredĕcim.	Tertius decĭmus.
14.	Quatuordĕcim.	Quartus decĭmus.
15.	Quindĕcim.	Quintus decĭmus.
16.	Sedĕcim or sexdĕcim.	Sextus decĭmus.
17.	Septendĕcim.	Septĭmus decĭmus.
18.	Octodĕcim.	Octāvus decĭmus.
19.	Novendĕcim.	Nonus decĭmus.
20.	Vĭginti.	Vicesĭmus or vigesĭmus.
21.	{ Viginti unus or unus et viginti.	Vicesĭmus primus.
22.	{ Viginti duo or duo et viginti, etc.	Vicesĭmus secundus.
30.	Triginta.	Tricesĭmus or trigesĭmus.
40.	Quadraginta.	Quadragesĭmus.
50.	Quinquaginta.	Quinquagesĭmus.
60.	Sexaginta.	Sexagesĭmus.
70.	Septuaginta.	Septuagesĭmus.
80.	Octoginta.	Octogesĭmus.
90.	Nonaginta.	Nonagesĭmus.
100.	Centum.	Centesĭmus.
200.	Ducenti, -æ, -a.	Ducentesĭmus.
300.	Trecenti.	Trecentesĭmus.
400.	Quadringenti.	Quadringentesĭmus.
500.	Quingenti.	Quingentesĭmus.
600.	Sexcenti.	Sexcentesĭmus.
700.	Septingenti.	Septingentesĭmus.
800.	Octingenti.	Octingentesĭmus.
900.	Nongenti.	Nongentesĭmus.
1000.	Mille.	Millesĭmus.
2000.	Duo millia or bis mille.	Bis millesĭmus.

Duo is thus declined : —

Plural.

	Masc.	Fem.	Neut.
N.	dŭ'-o,	dŭ'-æ,	dŭ'-o,
G.	du-ō'-rum,	du-ā'-rum,	du-ō'-rum,
D.	du-ō'-bus,	du-ā'-bus,	du-ō'-bus,
Ac.	dŭ'-os or dŭ'-o,	dŭ'-as,	dŭ'-o,
V.	dŭ'-o,	dŭ'-æ,	dŭ'-o,
Ab.	du-ō'-bus,	du-ā'-bus,	du-ō'-bus.

Ambo, both, is declined like duo.

The cardinal numbers, from four to a hundred inclusive, are indeclinable.

Those denoting hundreds are declined like the plural of *bonus*.

Ordinal numbers are declined like *bonus*.

(Here learn Exercises XXXVII., XXXVIII.)

COMPARISON OF ADJECTIVES.

The comparison of an adjective is the expression of its quality in different degrees.

There are three degrees of comparison, — the *positive*, the *comparative*, and the *superlative*.

The positive simply denotes a quality, without reference to other degrees of the same quality; as, *altus*, high; *mitis*, mild.

The comparative denotes that a quality belongs to one of two objects, or sets of objects, in a greater degree than to the other; as, *altior*, higher; *mitior*, milder.

The superlative denotes that the quality belongs to one of several objects or sets of objects, in a greater degree than to any of the rest; as, *altissimus*, highest; *mitissimus*, mildest.

The comparative and superlative in Latin, as in English, are denoted either by peculiar terminations, or by certain adverbs prefixed to the positive.

The terminational comparative ends in *ior*, masc.; *ior*, fem.; *ius*, neut.; — the terminational superlative in *issimus, issima, issimum*.

These terminations are added to the root of the positive; as, *altus, altior, altissimus*; high, higher, highest; — *mitis, mitior, mitissimus*; mild, milder, mildest; — *felix*, gen. *felicis, felicior, felicissimus*; happy, happier, happiest.

In like manner compare

Arc'-tus, *straight.*	Cru-dē'-lis, *cruel.*
Ca'-pax, *capacious.*	Cle'-mens, *gen.* -tis, *merciful.*
Ca'-rus, *dear.*	In'-ers, *gen.* -tis, *sluggish.*

IRREGULAR COMPARISON.

Adjectives in *er* form their superlative by adding *rĭmus* to that termination; as, *acer*, active; gen. *acris*; comparative, *acrior*; superlative, *acerrĭmus*.

Six adjectives in *lis* form their superlative by adding *lĭmus* to the root: —

Facĭlis,	facilior,	facillĭmus,	*easy.*
Difficĭlis,	difficilior,	difficillĭmus,	*difficult.*
Gracĭlis,	gracilior,	gracillĭmus,	*slender.*
Humĭlis,	humilior,	humillĭmus,	*low.*
Simĭlis,	similior,	simillĭmus,	*like.*
Dissimĭlis,	dissimilior,	dissimillĭmus,	*unlike.*

REMARK. — Imbecillus *or* imbecillis, *weak*, has two forms, — imbecillissĭmus *and* imbecillĭmus.

These five have regular comparatives, but irregular superlatives: —

Dexter,	dexterior,	dextĭmus,	*right.*
Extĕra, (*fem.*)	exterior,	extrēmus *or* extĭmus,	*outward.*
Postĕra, (*fem.*)	posterior,	postrēmus *or* postŭmus,	*hind.*
Infĕrus,	inferior,	infĭmus *or* imus,	*low.*
Supĕrus,	superior,	suprēmus *or* summus,	*high.*

The following are very irregular in comparison: —

Bonus,	melior,	optĭmus,	*good,*	*better,*	*best.*
Malus,	pejor,	pessĭmus,	*bad,*	*worse,*	*worst.*
Magnus,	major,	maxĭmus,	*great,*	*greater,*	*greatest.*
Parvus,	minor,	minĭmus,	*little,*	*less,*	*least.*
Multus,	———	plurĭmus,			
Multa,	———	plurĭma,	*much,*	*more,*	*most.*
Multum,	plus,	plurĭmum,			
Nequam,	nequior,	nequissĭmus,	*worthless.*		
Frugi,	frugalior,	frugalissĭmus,	*frugal.*		

REMARK. — All these form their comparatives and superlatives from obsolete adjectives, or from other words of similar signification, except *magnus*, whose regular forms are contracted.

DEFECTIVE COMPARISON.

Seven adjectives want the positive: —

Citerior, citĭmus, *nearer.*
Deterior, deterrĭmus, *worse*
Interior, intĭmus, *inner.*
Ocior, ocissĭmus, *swifter.*

Prior, primus, *former.*
Propior, proxĭmus, *nearer.*
Ulterior, ultĭmus, *farther.*

The comparative and superlative may also be formed by prefixing to the positive the adverbs *magis*, more, and *maxĭmè*, most; as, *idoneus*, fit; *magis idoneus*, more fit; *maxĭmè idoneus*, most fit.

(Here learn Exercises XXXIX., XL.)

PARTICLES.

Particles are those parts of speech which are neither declined nor conjugated.

They are adverbs, prepositions, conjunctions, and interjections.

ADVERBS.

An adverb is a particle used to modify or limit the meaning of a verb, an adjective, or another adverb; as, bene *et* sapienter *dixit*, he spoke *well* and *wisely*.

COMPARISON OF ADVERBS.

Adverbs derived from adjectives with the terminations *e* and *ter*, and most of those in *o*, are compared like their primitives.

The comparative ends in *ius*, and the superlative in *ĭme*; as, *facĭle, facilius, facillĭme*.

PREPOSITIONS.

A preposition is a particle which expresses the relation between a noun or pronoun and some preceding word; as, *eo* ad *te*, I go *to* thee.

CONJUNCTIONS.

A conjunction is a particle which connects words or propositions.

Conjunctions, according to their different uses, are

divided into two general classes, — *coördinate* and *subordinate*.

I. Coördinate conjunctions are such as join similar constructions ; as, *Luna* et *stellæ fulgēbant*, the moon *and* stars were shining.

REMARK. — This class includes *copulative, disjunctive, adversative, illative,* and most of the *causal* conjunctions.

II. Subordinate conjunctions are such as join *dissimilar* constructions ; as, Edo *ut vivam*, I eat that I may live.

REMARK. — This class includes all those connectives which unite subordinate or dependent clauses.

These are the *concessive, illative, final, conditional, interrogative,* and *temporal* conjunctions, and the *causals,* — *quod, quum, quoniam,* etc.

To these may be added the *relatives,* whether pronouns, adjectives, or adverbs.

Conjunctions, in respect to their signification, are either *copulative, disjunctive, concessive, comparative, adversative, causal, illative, final, conditional, temporal,* or *interrogative.*

Copulatives connect things that are to be considered jointly ; as, *ac, atque, et, etiam, –que, quoque,* and *nec* or *neque.*

Disjunctives connect things that are to be considered separately ; as, *aut, seu, sive, –ve,* and *vel.*

Concessives denote a concession ; comparatives, a comparison ; adversatives, opposition ; causals, a cause or reason ; illatives, an inference ; finals, a purpose or result ; conditionals, a condition ; temporals, time ; and interrogatives, a question.

INTERJECTIONS.

An interjection is a particle used in exclamation, and expressing some emotion of the mind.

(Here learn Exercises XLI., XLII.)

PRONOUNS.

A pronoun is a word which supplies the place of a noun.

There are eighteen simple pronouns : —

E*g*o, *I.*	Hic, *this, the latter.*	Suus, *his, her, its, their.*
Tu, *thou.*	Is, *that* or *he.*	Cujus ? *whose ?*
Sui, *of himself,* etc.	Quis ? *who ?*	Noster, *our.*
Ille, *that, the former.*	Qui, *who.*	Vester, *your.*
Ipse, *himself.*	Meus, *my.*	Nostras, *of our country.*
Iste, *that, that of yours.*	Tuus, *thy.*	Cujas ? *of what country ?*

Pronouns are divided into two classes, — substantives and adjectives.

Three — *ego, tu,* and *sui* — are substantives ; the remaining fifteen, and all the compound pronouns, are adjectives.

The substantive pronouns take the gender of the objects which they denote.

Ego is of the first person, *tu* of the second, and *sui* of the third.

SUBSTANTIVE PRONOUNS.

The substantive pronouns are thus declined : —

Singular.

N.	e′-go, *I ;*	tu, *thou ;*	———————
G.	me′-i, *of me ;*	tu′-i, *of thee ;*	{ su′-i, *of himself, her-self, itself ;*
D.	mi′-hi, *to me ;*	tib′-i, *to thee ;*	sib′-i, *to himself,* &c.
Ac.	me, *me ;*	te, *thee ;*	se, *himself,* &c.
V.	———————	tu, *O thou ;*	
Ab.	me, *with me ;*	te, *with thee ;*	se, *with himself,* &c.

Plural.

N.	nos, *we ;*	vos, *ye* or *you ;*	———————
G.	{ nos′-trûm or nos′-tri, } *of us ;*	.ves′-trûm or ves′-tri, } *of you ;*	su′-i, *of themselves ;*
D.	no′-bis, *to us ;*	vo′-bis, *to you ;*	sib′-i, *to themselves ;*
Ac.	nos, *us ;*	vos, *you ;*	se, *themselves ;*
V.	———————	vos, *O ye* or *you ;*	———————
Ab.	no′-bis, *with us.*	vo′-bis, *with you.*	se, *with themselves.*

ADJECTIVE PRONOUNS.

Adjective pronouns may be divided into the following classes : — *demonstrative, intensive, relative, interrogative, indefinite, possessive,* and *patrial.*

DEMONSTRATIVE PRONOUNS.

Demonstrative pronouns are such as specify what object is meant.

They are *ille, iste, hic,* and *is,* and their compounds, and are thus declined : —

Singular,

	M.	F.	N.
N.	il'-le,	il'-la,	il'-lud,
G.	il-li'-us,	il-li'-us,	il-li'-us,
D.	il'-li,	il'-li,	il'-li,
Ac.	il'-lum,	il'-lam,	il'-lud,
V.	il'-le,	il'-la,	il'-lud,
Ab.	il'-lo,	il'-lâ,	il'-lo,

Plural.

N.	il'-li,	il'-læ,	il'-la,
G.	il-lo'-rum,	il-lä'-rum,	il-lo'-rum,
D.	il'-lis,	il'-lis,	il'-lis,
Ac.	il'-los,	il'-las,	il'-la,
V.	il'-li,	il'-læ,	il'-la,
Ab.	il'-lis,	il'-lis,	il'-lis.

Iste is declined like *ille.*

Singular.

	M.	F.	N.
N.	hic,	hæc,	hoc,
G.	hu'-jus,	hu'-jus,	hu'-jus,
D.	huic,*	huic,	huic,
Ac.	hunc,	hanc,	hoc,
V.	hic,	hæc,	hoc,
Ab.	hoc,	hac,	hoc,

* Pronounced *hike.*

8

Plural.

N.	hi,	hæ,	hæc,
G.	ho'-rum,	ha'-rum,	ho'-rum,
D.	his,	his,	his,
Ac.	hos,	has,	hæc,
V.	hi,	hæ,	hæc;
Ab.	his,	his,	his.

Singular.

	M.	F.	N.
N.	is,	e'-a,	id,
G.	e'-jus,	e'-jus,	e'-jus,
D.	e'-i,	e'-i,	e'-i,
Ac.	e'-um,	e'-am,	id,
V.	——	——	——
Ab.	e'-o,	e'-â,	e'-o,

Plural.

N.	i'-i,	e'-æ,	e'-a,
G.	e-ō'-rum,	e-ā'-rum,	e-ō'-rum,
D.	i'-is *or* e'-is,	i'-is *or* e'-is,	i'-is *or* e'-is,
Ac.	e'-os,	e'-as,	e'-a,
V	——	——	——
Ab.	i'-is *or* e'-is,	i'-is *or* e'-is,	i'-is *or* e'-is.

The compound pronoun *idem*, the same, is thus declined : —

Singular.

	M.	F.	N.
N.	i'-dem,	e'-ă-dem,	i'-dem,
G.	e-jus'-dem,	e-jus'-dem,	e-jus'-dem,
D.	e-ī'-dem,	e-ī'-dem,	e-ī'-dem,
Ac.	e-un'-dem,	e-an'-dem,	i'-dem,
V.	——	——	——
Ab.	e-ō'-dem,	e-ā'-dem,	e-ō'-dem.

Plural.

N.	i-ī'-dem,	e-æ'-dem,	e'-ă-dem,
G.	e-o-run'-dem,	e-a-run'-dem,	e-o-run'-dem,
D.	e-is'-dem *or* i-is'-dem,	e-is'-dem *or* i-is'-dem,	e-is'-dem *or* i-is'-dem,
Ac.	e-os'-dem;	e-as'-dem,	e'-ă-dem,
V.	——	——	——
Ab.	e-is'-dem *or* i-is'-dem,	e-is'-dem *or* i-is'-dem,	e-is'-dem *or* i-is'-dem.

INTENSIVE PRONOUNS.

Intensive pronouns are such as serve to render an object emphatic.

To this class belongs *ipse*, which is thus declined:—

Singular.

M.	F.	N.
N. ip'-se,	ip'-sa,	ip'-sum,
G. ip-si'-us,	ip-si'-us,	ip-si'-us,
D. ip'-si,	ip'-si,	ip'-si,
Ac. ip'-sum,	ip'-sam,	ip'-sum,
V. ip'-se,	ip'-sa,	ip'-sum,
Ab. ip'-so,	ip'-sâ,	ip'-so,

Plural.

M.	F.	N.
N. ip'-si,	ip'-sæ,	ip'-sa,
G. ip-sō'-rum,	ip-sā'-rum,	ip-sō'-rum,
D. ip'-sis,	ip'-sis,	ip'-sis,
Ac. ip'-sos,	ip'-sas,	ip'-sa,
V. ip'-si,	ip'-sæ,	ip'-sa,
Ab. ip'-sis,	ip'-sis,	ip'-sis.

RELATIVE PRONOUNS.

Relative pronouns are such as relate to a preceding noun or pronoun.

They are *qui*, who, and the compounds *quicumque* and *quisquis*, whoever.

Qui is thus declined:—

Singular.

M.	F.	N.
N. qui,	quæ,	quod,
G. cu'-jus,	cu'-jus,	cu'-jus,
D. cui,*	cui,	cui,
Ac. quem,	quam,	quod,
V. ——	——	——
Ab. quo,	quâ,	quo,

* Pronounced *ki.*

Plural.

	M.	F.	N.
N.	qui,	quæ,	quæ,
G.	quo'-rum,	qua'-rum,	quo'-rum,
D.	qui'-bus,	qui'-bus,	qui'-bus,
Ac.	quos,	quas,	quæ,
V.	———	———	———
Ab.	qui'-bus,	qui'-bus,	qui'-bus.

INTERROGATIVE PRONOUNS.

Interrogative pronouns are such as serve to inquire which of a number of objects is intended. They are

Quis ?	*who ?*			Cujus, *whose ?*	
Quisnam ?	*what ?*	Ecquis ?		Cujas, *of what*	
Qui ?	*which ?*	Ecquisnam ?	*is any one ?*	*country ?*	
Quinam ?	*what ?*	Numquis ?			
		Numquisnam ?			

Quis and its compounds are used substantively; *qui* and its compounds adjectively. *Qui* is declined like *qui* the relative.

Quis is thus declined : —

Singular.

	M.	F.	N.
N.	quis,	quæ,	quid,
G.	cu'-jus,	cu'-jus,	cu'-jus,
D.	cui,	cui,	cui,
Ac.	quem,	quam,	quid,
V.	———	———	———
Ab.	quo,	quâ,	quo,

Plural.

	M.	F.	N.
N.	qui,	quæ,	quæ,
G.	quo'-rum,	qua'-rum,	quo'-rum,
D.	qui'-bus,	qui'-bus,	qui'-bus,
Ac.	quos,	quas,	quæ,
V.	———	———	———
Ab.	qui'-bus,	qui'-bus,	qui'-bus.

INDEFINITE PRONOUNS.

Indefinite pronouns are such as denote an object in a general manner, without indicating a particular individual. They are, —

Aliquis, *some one.*   Quisquam, *any one.*   Quidam, *a certain one.*
Siquis, *if any.*   Quispiam, *some one.*   Quilibet, } *any one you*
Nequis, *lest any.*   Unusquisque, *each.*   Quivis, } *please.*
Quisque, *every one.*   Aliquipiam, *any, some.*

Aliquis is thus declined : —

Singular.

	M.	F.	N.
N.	al'-ĭ-quis,	al'-ĭ-qua,	al'-ĭ-quod *or* -quid,
G.	al-i-cŭ'-jus,	al-i-cŭ'-jus,	al-i-cŭ'-jus,
D.	al'-ĭ-cui,	al'-ĭ-cui,	al'-ĭ-cui,
Ac.	al'-ĭ-quem,	al'-ĭ-quam,	al'-ĭ-quod *or* -quid,
V.	———	———	———
Ab.	al'-ĭ-quo,	al'-ĭ-quâ,	al'-ĭ-quo,

Plural.

N.	al'-ĭ-qui,	al'-ĭ-quæ,	al'-ĭ-qua,
G.	al-i-quŏ'-rum,	al-i-quā'-rum,	al-i-quŏ'-rum,
D.	a-liq'-uĭ-bus,*	a-liq'-uĭ-bus,	a-liq'-uĭ-bus,
Ac.	al'-ĭ-quos,	al'-ĭ-quas,	al'-ĭ-qua,
V.	———	———	———
Ab.	a-liq'-uĭ-bus,	a-liq'-uĭ-bus,	a-liq'-uĭ-bus.

Siquis and *nequis* are declined in the same manner.

POSSESSIVE PRONOUNS.

The possessive are derived from the substantive pronouns, and from *quis*, and designate something belonging to their primitives.

They are *meus, tuus, suus, noster, vester,* and *cujus.*

Meus, tuus, and *suus,* are declined like *bonus.*

Meus has in the vocative singular masculine *mi*, and very rarely *meus.*

PATRIAL PRONOUNS.

Patrial pronouns are such as relate to one's country.
These are *nostras* and *cujas.*
They are declined like adjectives of one termination ; as, *nostras, nostrātis.*

* Pronounced *a-lĭk'-we-bus.*

8*

REFLEXIVE PRONOUNS.

Reflexive pronouns are such as relate to the subject of the proposition in which they stand.

The reflexives of the third person are *sui* and *suus*. *Meus, tuus, noster,* and *vester,* are also used reflexively, when the subject of the proposition is of the first or second person.

(*Here learn Exercises XLIII., XLIV.*)

SYNTAX.

Syntax treats of the construction of sentences.

A sentence is a thought expressed in words; as, *Canes latrant,* the dogs bark.

It may consist either of one proposition or of two or more propositions connected together.

A proposition consists of a *subject* and a *predicate*.

The *subject* of a proposition is that of which something is affirmed.

The *predicate* is that which is affirmed of the subject.

Thus, in the proposition, *Equus currit,* The horse runs, *equus* is the subject, and *currit* is the predicate.

Propositions are either *principal* or *subordinate*.

A *principal* proposition is one which makes complete sense by itself; as,

Phocion fuit perpetuo pauper, *quum ditissimus esse posset, Phocion was always poor,* though he might have been very rich.

A *subordinate* proposition is one which, by means of a subordinate conjunction, is made to depend upon or limit some part of another proposition; as,

Phocion fuit perpetuus pauper, quum ditissimus esse posset, Phocion was always poor, *though he might have been very rich.*

A sentence consisting of one proposition is called a *simple* sentence; as,

Cadunt folia, The leaves fall.

A sentence consisting of a principal and one or more subordinate propositions is called a *complex* sentence; as,

Qui fit, ut nemo contentus vivat ? How happens it, that no one lives content ?

A sentence consisting of two or more principal propositions, either alone or in connection with one or more subordinate propositions, is called a *compound* sentence ; as,

Spirant venti et cadunt folia, The winds blow and the leaves fall.

The propositions composing a complex or a compound sentence are called its *members* or *clauses ;* the principal proposition is called the *leading clause,* its subject the *leading subject,* and its verb the *leading verb.*

SUBJECT.

The subject also is either *simple, complex* or *compound.*

The *simple* subject, which is also called the *grammatical* subject, is either a noun or some word standing for a noun ; as,

Aves volant, Birds fly ; *Mentiri est turpe, To lie* is base.

The *complex* subject, called also the *logical* subject, consists of the simple subject with its *modifications ;* as,

Conscientia bene actæ vitæ est jucundissima, The consciousness of a well spent life is very pleasant. Here *conscientia* is the grammatical, and *conscientia bene actæ vitæ* the complex, subject.

The *compound* subject consists of two or more simple or complex subjects to which a single predicate belongs ; as,

Luna et stellæ fulgebant, *The moon* and *stars* were shining.

NOTE. — Words are said to *modify* or *limit* other words when they serve to explain, define, or otherwise qualify their meaning.

Every sentence must contain a subject and a predicate.

PREDICATE.

The predicate, like the subject, is either *simple*, *complex*, or *compound*.

The *simple* predicate, which is also called the *grammatical* predicate, is either a single finite verb, or the copula *sum* with a noun, adjective, and rarely with an adverb; as,

Sol lucet, The sun *shines.* Brevis est *voluptas,* Pleasure *is brief.*

The *complex* predicate, called also the *logical* predicate, consists of the simple predicate with its modifications; as,

Scipio fudit Annibălis copias, Scipio *routed the forces of Hannibal.* Here *fudit* is the grammatical, and *fudit Annibălis copias* the logical, predicate.

The *compound* predicate consists of two or more simple or complex predicates belonging to the same subject; as,

Probĭtas laudatur *et* alget, Honesty *is praised* and *neglected.*

The members of a *compound* sentence are connected by coördinate conjunctions; those of a *complex* sentence by some relative word, or by a subordinate conjunction.

Agreement is the correspondence of one word with another in gender, number, case, or person.

A word is said to *govern* another, when it requires it to be put in a certain case or mood.

A word is said to *depend* on another, when its case, gender, number, mood, tense, or person, is determined by that word.

A word is said to *follow* another, when it depends upon it in construction, whatever may be its position in the sentence.

ANALYSIS AND PARSING.

The analysis of a simple sentence consists in distinguishing the subject from the predicate, and in pointing out their several modifiers, if any.

The analysis of a complex or a compound sentence consists in dividing it into its several component propositions, and pointing out their relation to each other.

Parsing consists in resolving a proposition into the parts of speech of which it is composed, tracing the derivation of each word, and giving the rules of formation and construction applicable to it.

RULES FOR PARSING.

1. Name the part of speech to which each word belongs.

2. If it is an inflected word : —

(1.) Name its root, and decline, compare, or conjugate it.

(2.) If a verb, tell what kind, and its voice, mood, tense, number, person, and subject.

(3.) If a noun or pronoun, tell its gender, number, and case; also its verb, or the word on which its case depends.

(4.) If an adjective, adjective pronoun, or participle, tell the word which it modifies.

3. If a conjunction, tell its class, and what it connects.

4. If a preposition, tell the words whose relation is expressed by it.

5. If an adverb, tell what it qualifies.

6. Prove the correctness of each step of the process by quoting the definition or rule of formation or construction on which it depends.

EXAMPLES OF ANALYSIS AND PARSING.

1. *Tempus veniet,* The time will come.

ANALYSIS.

This is a simple sentence. Its *subject* is *tempus;* its *predicate* is *veniet,* and each of them is simple.

PARSING.

Tempus is a common noun, of the third declension, neuter gender, [Decline it,] in the singular number, and is nominative to *veniet.* [See under *Cases,* on page 58, and repeat the Rule, 33.]

Veniet is a neuter verb, of the fourth conjugation. [Repeat the principal parts, as found in the dictionary.] It is formed in the active voice, from the first root, [Repeat the parts formed from this root, as in *audio,*] in the indicative mood future tense, [Repeat the persons of this tense,] third person singular number, agreeing with *tempus.* [Repeat the Rule, 34.]

NOTE. — The questions to be asked in parsing *tempus* are such as these : — Why is *tempus* a noun? Why a *common* noun? Why of the *third* declension? Why *neuter?* etc. In parsing *veniet,* the questions are : — Why is *veniet* a verb? Why a *neuter* verb? Why of the fourth conjugation? Which are the *principal parts* of a verb? Of what does the *first root* of a verb consist? What parts of a verb are derived from the *first root?* etc.

The answer in each case may be found by consulting the etymological rules and definitions.

2. *Sola laurus fulmine non icitur,* The laurel alone is not struck by lightning.

ANALYSIS.

This is a simple sentence.

Its subject is *sola laurus*, the laurel alone; its predicate *fulmine non icitur ;* both of which are *complex*.

The grammatical subject is *laurus*, the laurel; this is modified by *sola*, alone.

The grammatical predicate is *icitur*, is struck; this is modified by two independent modifiers, — *non*, not, and *fulmine*, by lightning.

PARSING.

Sola is an adjective, of the feminine gender, from *solus*, of the first and second declensions, [Decline it in the feminine gender, page 74,] in the singular number, nominative case, agreeing with *laurus*. [Repeat the Rule, 1.]

Laurus is a common noun, of the second declension, feminine gender, [Decline it,] in the nominative case to *icitur*. [Repeat the Rule, 33.]

Fulmine is a common noun, of the third declension, neuter gender, [Decline it,] in the singular number, ablative case after *icitur*. [Repeat the Rule, 68.]

Non is an adverb modifying *icitur*.

Icitur is an active verb, of the third conjugation. [Repeat its principal parts.] It is formed in the passive voice, from the first root, [Repeat the parts formed from this root,] in the indicative mood, present tense, [Repeat the persons,] third person, singular, agreeing with *laurus*. [Repeat the Rule, 34.]

8. *Urbs, quam Romŭlus condĭdit, vocabātur Roma*, The city which Romulus built was called Rome.

ANALYSIS.

This is a complex sentence, consisting of two members. The principal proposition is, *Urbs vocabātur Roma*, the city was called Rome. The subordinate proposition is, *Quam Romŭlus condĭdit*, which Romulus built.

The leading clause has a simple subject, *urbs*, and a complex predicate, *vocabātur Roma*, in which *vocabātur* is the grammatical predicate, modified by *Roma*. The subordinate proposition, which is connected to the leading clause by the relative *quam*, has also a simple subject, *Romŭlus*, and a complex predicate, *quam condĭdit*, in which *condĭdit* is the grammatical predicate, modified by *quam*.

PARSING.

Urbs is a common noun, of the third declension, feminine gender, [Decline it,] in the nominative case to *vocabātur*. [Repeat the Rule, 33.]

Quam is a relative pronoun, of the feminine gender, from *qui, quæ, quod,* agreeing with its antecedent *urbs*, [Repeat the Rule, 1, Rem. 8.] [Decline it in the feminine,] in the accusative after *condĭdit*. [Repeat the Rule, 54.]

Romŭlus is a proper noun, of the second declension, masculine gender, [Decline it,] in the nominative case to *condĭdit*. [Repeat the Rule 33.]

Condĭdit is an active verb, of the third conjugation. [Repeat the principal parts.] It is formed in the active voice, from the second root, [Repeat the parts formed from this root,] in the indicative mood, perfect indefinite tense, [Repeat the persons,] third person, singular, agreeing with *Romŭlus*. [Repeat the Rule, 34.]

Vocabātur is an active verb, of the first conjugation. [Repeat the principal parts.] It is formed in the passive voice, from the first root, [Repeat the parts formed from this root,] in the indicative mood, imperfect tense, [Repeat the persons of this tense,] third person, singular, agreeing with *urbs*. [Rule.]

Roma is a proper noun, of the first declension, feminine gender, [Decline it,] in the nominative case after *vocabātur*. [Repeat the Rule, 35.]

ARRANGEMENT.

In a Latin sentence, after *connectives*, are placed, first, the *subject* and its modifiers; then the *oblique cases*, and other words which depend upon or modify the verb; and last of all, the *verb*.

Connectives generally stand at the beginning of a clause.

Oblique cases precede the words upon which they depend, but they follow prepositions.

Infinitives precede the verbs on which they depend.

Relatives are commonly placed after their antecedents, and as near to them as possible.

The emphatic word is placed before the word or words connected with it.

RULES FOR TRANSLATING CERTAIN FORMS AND IDIOMS.

IMPERSONAL VERBS.

The English subject of an impersonal verb in the passive voice may be either the agent in the ablative, expressed or understood, or an abstract noun formed from the verb; as,

Pugnatum est ab nobis, (*ab illis*, &c.,) or simply *pugnatum est*, we, (they, etc.) fought; or, like *pugna pugnata est*, the battle was fought.

Sometimes the English subject of an impersonal verb is, in Latin, an oblique case of a noun or pronoun following the verb; as,

Miseret me tui, I pity you. *Favetur tibi*, Thou art favored.

PARTITIVE GENITIVE.

Nihil, a neuter adjective of quantity, or a neuter pronoun, followed by a partitive genitive, is often to be translated by an adjective agreeing with its noun; as,

Nihil præmii, No reward. *Tantum fidei*, So much fidelity. *Id temporis*, That time.

9

COMPARATIVE DEGREE.

The comparative degree may sometimes be translated by the positive with *too* or *rather ;* as,

Liberius vivēbat, He lived too freely.   *Tristior fuit,* He was rather sad.

SUPERLATIVE DEGREE.

The superlative degree may often be translated by the positive with *very ;* as,

Amicus carissimus, A very dear friend.

ABLATIVE ABSOLUTE.

When the ablative absolute denotes *time,* it may sometimes be translated by a clause beginning with *when, while, after,* etc., and sometimes by turning the participle or adjective into a corresponding noun limited by the other noun ; as,

Romŭlo regnante, While Romulus reigned; or, In the reign of Romulus.

When the act denoted by a perfect passive participle was performed by the subject of the leading clause, it may be translated by an active participle agreeing with such subject, or by a clause having its verb in the active voice ; as,

Galli, re cognĭtâ, obsidiōnem relinquunt, The Gauls *learning* (or, *having learned*) the fact, raise the siege; or, When the Gauls had learned the fact, etc.

PARTICIPLES.

1. The present participle is sometimes used to express a *state* or *condition,* where, in English, a substantive is employed with a preposition ; as,

Ignorans, from ignorance ; *consulatum petens,* in his suit for the consulship ; *flens,* in tears.

2. The future participle in *–rus* is commonly translated *about* or *going,* with the present infinitive ; as,

Scripturus, About to write ; or, Going to write.

3. The participle in *–rus*, especially with verbs of motion, often denotes *intention* or *purpose*, and is to be translated by the present infinitive active; as,

Pergit consultūrus, He goes to consult.

4. The participle in *–rus* is also used where, in English, a clause connected by *since, when, although*, etc. is employed; as,

Plura locutūros *abīre nos tussit*, When *or* although we intended to say more, etc.

5. The perfect passive participle is commonly translated by the English participles of the passive voice; as,

Amātus, Loved, being loved, or, having been loved.

6. The perfect passive participle is often to be translated by a present active participle; as,

Pectus percussa, Striking her breast.

7. The perfect passive participle may sometimes be translated by a verbal noun; as,

Ante Romam condĭtam, Before the building of Rome.

8. The participle in *–dus* is commonly translated by the present infinitive passive; as, *amandus*, to be loved: but when joined to *sum*, it is translated *must be*, or *ought to be*.

9. The participle in *–dus* may sometimes be translated by a verbal noun; as,

Consilia urbis delendœ, Plans for destroying, *or* for the destruction of the city.

10. The participle in *–dus* also denotes a purpose passively, when joined with verbs signifying *to give, to deliver, to agree for, to have, to receive, to undertake*, etc.; as,

Testamentum tibi tradit legendum, He delivers his will to you to read. *Muros dirŭtos reficiendos curāvit, —* ordered to be restored.

11. The present and perfect participles, in addition to their literal translation, may sometimes take the particles *while, when, because, though, if,* etc.; as,

Mihi scribenti, To me while writing, etc.

12. Sometimes the present and perfect participles may be translated by a relative clause, or by a clause containing a noun or pronoun with some particle prefixed, as,

Mihi scribenti, To me, who was writing; or, To me, while I was writing, etc.

GERUNDS AND SUPINES.

After *ad* a gerund or gerundive may be translated by the infinitive active; as,

Ad pœnitendum propĕrat, He hastens to repent.

Supines in *u* are translated by the present infinitive, either active or passive; as,

Mirabile dictu, Wonderful to tell, or, to be told.

SUBJUNCTIVE MOOD

1. In dependent sentences the present subjunctive is often to be translated by *might, could, would,* or *should,* instead of *may.*

2. In indirect questions the subjunctive is commonly translated by the indicative; as,

Quis ego sim, me rogas? Do you ask me who I *am?*

3. After adverbs of time, the subjunctive is commonly translated by the indicative; as,

Quum sciret, When he knew.

4. The subjunctive denoting a *result* is commonly translated by the indicative or the infinitive; as,

In Alpibus tantum est frigus, ut nix ibi nunquam liquescit, The cold in the Alps is so great, that the snow never melts there.

5. The subjunctive denoting a *purpose* or *object* is translated by the potential or the infinitive; as,

Edo, ut vivam, I eat to live; or, that I may live.

ADJECTIVES, ADJECTIVE PRONOUNS, AND PARTICIPLES.

Rule 1.

Adjectives, adjective pronouns, and participles agree with their nouns in gender, number, and case ; as,

Bonus vir, A good man.	*Bonos viros*, Good men.
Benigna mater, A kind mother.	*Vanœ leges*, Useless laws.
Triste bellum, A sad war.	*Hœc res*, This thing.

REMARK 1.—An adjective may belong to each of two or more nouns, and in such case is put in the plural ; and if the nouns are of the same gender, the adjective agrees with them in gender ; as, *Lupus et agnus siti* compulsi, A wolf and a lamb, constrained by thirst.

When the nouns are of different genders :—

(1.) If they denote *living things*, the adjective is masculine rather than feminine ; as,

Pater mihi et mater mortui *sunt*, My father and mother are dead.

(2.) If they denote things *without life*, the adjective is generally neuter ; as,

His *genus, œtas, eloquentia prope* æqualia *fuēre ;* Their family, age, and eloquence, were nearly equal:

Exc. The adjective often agrees with the nearest noun, and is understood with the rest ; as,

Sociis et rege recepto, (Our) companions and king having been recovered.

REM. 2.—An adjective qualifying a *collective* noun is often put in the plural, taking the gender of the individuals which the noun denotes ; as, *Pars certāre* parāti, A part prepared to contend.

REM. 3.—An adjective is often used alone, the noun with which it agrees being understood ; as, Boni *sunt rari*, sc. *homĭnes ;* Good (men) are rare. *Dextra*, sc. *manus ;* The right (hand.)

REM. 4.—Neuter adjectives are very often used alone; when the word *thing* is to be supplied in English ; as, *Bonum*, a good thing; *malum*, a bad thing, or an evil.

REM. 5. — Imperatives, infinitives, adverbs, clauses, and words considered merely as such, may be used substantively, and take a neuter adjective in the singular number ; as, Suprēmum vale *dixit*, He pronounced a last farewell. *Nunquam est utĭle peccāre*, To do wrong is never useful.

9*

Rem. 6. — Adjectives and adjective pronouns, instead of agreeing with their nouns, are sometimes put in the neuter gender, with a partitive signification, and their nouns in the genitive; as, *multum temporis,* for *multum tempus,* much time.

Rem. 7. — The first part, last part, middle part, etc., of any place or time are generally expressed in Latin by the adjectives *primus, medius, ultĭmus, extrēmus, infĭmus, infĭmus, ĭmus, summus, suprēmus, relĭquus,* and *cetĕra;* as, *Media nox,* The middle of the night. *Summa arbor,* The top of a tree.

RELATIVES.

Rem. 8. — Relatives agree with their antecedents in gender, number, and person; but their case depends on the construction of the clause to which they belong; as, *Puer* qui *legit,* The boy who reads. *Aedificium quod exstruxit,* The house which he built. *Litĕrœ* quas *dedi,* The letter which I gave.

(1.) Sometimes the antecedent is a proposition, and then the relative is commonly neuter.

(2.) A relative or demonstrative pronoun referring to a *collective* noun is often put in the plural, taking the gender of the individuals which the noun denotes.

(3.) *Qui,* at the beginning of a sentence, is often translated like a demonstrative; as, Quæ *quum ita sint,* Since *these* (things) are so.

POSSESSIVES.

Rem. 9. — The possessive pronouns are often omitted, especially when used as reflexives; as, *Quò revertar ? in patriam ?* sc. meam; Whither shall I return? to (my) country?

CASES AFTER ADJECTIVES.

GENITIVE.

Rule 2.

A noun limiting the meaning of an adjective is put in the objective genitive, to denote the relation expressed in English by *of, in,* or *in respect to* ; as,

Avĭdus laudis, Desirous *of praise. Appĕtens* gloriæ, Eager *for glory. Memor* virtūtis, Mindful *of virtue. Plena* timōris, Full *of fear. Egēnus* aquæ, Destitute *of water. Doctus* fandi, Skilful *in speaking.*

Rule 3.

Adjectives and adjective pronouns, denoting a part, are followed by a genitive denoting the whole; as,

Nulla sorōrum, No one of the sisters. *Aliquis philosophōrum,* Some one of the philosophers. *Quis mortalium ?* Who of mortals? *Major juvĕnum,* The elder of the youths. *Doctissĭmus Romanōrum,* The most learned of the Romans. *Multum pecuniœ,* Much (of) money. . (Compare Rules 12 and 30.)

DATIVE.

Rule 4.

A noun limiting the meaning of an adjective is put in the dative, to denote the *object* to which the quality is directed; as,

Utĭlis agris, Useful to the fields. *Jucundus amicis,* Agreeable to (his) friends. *Inimĭcus quiĕti,* Unfriendly to rest.

ACCUSATIVE.

Rule 5.

Adjectives are sometimes followed by an accusative denoting the *part* to which their signification relates; as,

Nudus membra, Bare as to (his) limbs. (Compare Rule 59.)

Note. — This construction is usually called SYNECDOCHE, or the *limiting,* or *Greek accusative.*

Rule 6.

The adjectives *propior* and *proxĭmus* are often joined with the accusative; as,

Ipse propior montem *suos collŏcat.* (Compare Rule 14.)

ABLATIVE.

Rule 7.

Dignus, indignus, contentus, præditus, and *fretus,* are followed by the ablative of the object; as,

Dignus laude, Worthy of praise.   *Vox populi* majestāte *indigna,* A speech unbecoming the dignity of the people.

Rule 8.

An adjective may be followed by the ablative, denoting *in what respect* its signification is taken; as,

Jure *peritus,* Skilled in law.   *Anxius* animo, Anxious in mind. Pedĭbus *æger,* Lame in his feet.   (Compare Rules 32 and 72.)

NOTE. — For the ablative of *cause, manner, means,* and *instrument,* after adjectives, see under Rule 68.

Rule 9.

Adjectives of *plenty* or *want* are sometimes limited by the ablative; as,

Domus plena servis, A house full of servants.   *Dives* agris, Rich in land.   *Inops* verbis, Deficient in words.   *Orba* fratrĭbus, Destitute of brothers.

Rule 10.

The comparative degree, when *quàm* is omitted, is followed by the ablative of that with which the comparison is made; as,

Nihil est virtūte *formosius,* Nothing is more beautiful than virtue. *Quis* C. Lælio *comĭor?* Who (is) more courteous than C. Lælius?

REMARK 1. — *Plùs, mĭnùs,* and *ampliùs,* are often used without *quàm,* and yet are commonly followed by the same case as if it were expressed; as, *Hostium plùs quinque* millia *cæsi eo die,* More than five thousand of the enemy were slain that day.

REM. 2. — The *degree of difference* between objects compared is expressed by the ablative; as, *Minor uno* mense, Younger by one month.   Quanto *sumus superiōres,* tanto *nos submissiùs gerāmus;* The more eminent we are, the more humbly let us conduct ourselves. Multo *doctior es patre,* Thou art (by) much more learned than thy father.

ADVERBS.
Rule 11.

Adverbs modify or limit the meaning of verbs, adjectives, and sometimes of other adverbs; as,

Bene mones, You advise well. *Fortissìmè urgentes,* Most vigorously pressing on. *Longè dissimìlis,* Far different. *Valde bene,* Very well.

CASES AFTER ADVERBS.

GENITIVE.
Rule 12.

Adverbs denoting a part are followed by a genitive denoting the whole; as,

Satis eloquentìæ, Enough of eloquence. *Ubinam gentium sumus?* Where on earth are we? (Compare Rules 3 and 30.)

DATIVE.
Rule 13.

Some adverbs derived from adjectives are followed by the dative of the object; as,

Proxĭme castris, Very near to the camp. *Congruenter natūræ,* Agreeably to nature.

ACCUSATIVE.
Rule 14.

The adverbs *propius* and *proxĭme* are often joined with the accusative; as,

Proxĭme Hispaniam. (Compare Rule 6.)

GENITIVE OR ACCUSATIVE.
Rule 15.

Pridie and *postridie* are followed by a genitive or an accusative; as,

Pridie ejus diei, On the day before that day, i. e., The day before. *Pridie eum diem.*

CONJUNCTIONS.

Rule 16.

Copulative, disjunctive, and other coördinate conjunctions connect similar constructions; as,

Pulvis *et* umbra *sumus*, We are dust and shade.   Clarus *et* honorātus *vir*, An illustrious and honorable man.   *Quum ad oppidum* accessisset, *castráque ibi* ponēret; When he had approached the town, and was pitching his camp there

CASES AFTER PREPOSITIONS.
ACCUSATIVE.

Rule 17.

Twenty-six prepositions are followed by the accusative.   These are, —

ad,	extra,	post,
adversùs *or* adversùm,	infra,	prætcr,
ante,	inter,	prope,
apud,	intra,	propter,
circa *or* circum,	juxta,	secundum,
circiter,	ob,	supra,
cis *or* citra,	penes,	trans,
contra,	per,	ultra ; as,
crga,	pone,	

Ad templum, To the temple.   *Adversùs hostes*, Against the enemy.
Cis Rhenum, This side the Rhine.   *Intra muros*, Within the walls.
Penes reges, In the power of kings.

Rule 18.
ACCUSATIVE OR ABLATIVE.

In, *sub*, *super*, *subter*, and *clam*, are followed by the accusative or ablative.

REMARK 1. — *In* and *sub*, denoting *motion* or *tendency*, are followed by the accusative ; denoting *situation*, they are followed by the ablative ; as, *Via ducet in* urbem, The way conducts into the city.   *Exercĭtus sub* jugum *missus est*, The army was sent under the yoke.   *Medĭâ in* urbe, In the midst of the city.   *Bella sub Iliăcis* mœnĭbus *gerĕre*, To wage war under the Trojan walls.

Rem. 2. — *Super*, when denoting *place* or *time*, is followed by the accusative, and sometimes poetically by the ablative; but when it signifies *on*, *about*, or *concerning*, it takes the ablative; as, *Super labentem* culmĭna *tecti*, Gliding over the top of the house. *Super tenĕro prosternit* gramĭne *corpus*, He stretches (his) body on the tender grass. *Multa super* Priămo *rogĭtans super* Hectŏre *multa*, ... concerning Priam, &c.

Rem. 3. — *Subter* generally takes the accusative, but sometimes, in poetry, the ablative; as, *Subter* terras, Under the earth. *Subter densâ* testudĭne.

Rem. 4. — *Clam* is followed by either the accusative or the ablative; as, *Clam* vos, Without your knowledge. *Clam* vobis.

ABLATIVE.

Rule 19.

Eleven prepositions are followed by the ablative. These are, —

a, ab, *or* abs,	cum,	palam,	sine,
absque,	de,	præ,	tenus ; as,
coram,	e *or* ex,	pro,	

Ab illo tempŏre, From that time. *A scribendo*, From writing. *Cum exercĭtu*, With the army. *Certis de causis*, For certain reasons. *Ex fugâ*, From flight.

THE INFINITIVE MOOD.

SUBJECT—ACCUSATIVE.

Rule 20.

The subject of the infinitive mood is put in the accusative; as,

Molestè Pompeium *id ferre* constābat, That Pompey took that ill, was evident. *Miror te ad me nihil scribĕre*, I wonder that you do not write to me.

THE INFINITIVE AS THE SUBJECT OF A VERB.

Rule 21.

The infinitive, either with or without a subject-accusative, may be the *subject* of a verb; as,

Numquam est utĭle peccāre, To do wrong is never useful.

THE INFINITIVE AS THE OBJECT OF A VERB.

Rule 22.

The infinite, either with or without a subject-accusative, may be the *object* of a verb ; as,

Hæc vitāre *cupĭmus*, We desire to avoid this.   *Spero te* valēre, I hope that you are well.

REMARK 1. — The infinitive alone may also depend upon an adjective, and sometimes upon a noun ; as, *Sollers ornāre*, Skilful to adorn. *Dignus amāri*, Worthy to be loved. Tempus *est hujus libri* facĕre *finem*, It is time to finish this book.

REM. 2. — The infinite, without a subject-accusative, is used after verbs denoting *ability, obligation, intention,* or *endeavor ;* after verbs signifying *to begin, continue, cease, abstain, dare, fear, hesitate,* or *be wont ;* and after the passive of verbs of *saying, believing, reckoning,* &c. ; as, *Hæc vitare cupimus*, These things we desire to avoid.

REM. 3. — The infinitive with a subject-accusative follows verbs of *saying, thinking, knowing, perceiving,* and the like ; as, Vidēbat, *id non posse fiĕri*, He saw that that could not be done.

REM. 4. — The accusative with the infinitive is sometimes rendered into English by a similar form ; as, *Si vis* me flere, If you wish *me to* weep ; but the dependent clause is more frequently connected to the verb of saying, &c., by the conjunction *that,* and the infinitive translated by the indicative or potential mood ; as, *Sentĭmus nivem esse album*, We perceive *that snow is white.*   .

PARTICIPLES.

Rule 23.

Participles are followed by the same cases and constructions as their verbs ; as,

Quidam, poēta *nominātus ;* A certain one, called a poet.   Catulōrum *oblīta leœna*, The lioness forgetful of her whelps. Tendens *palmas*, Extending (his) hands.

REMARK 1. — The participle in *rus,* especially with verbs of motion, often denotes intention or purpose ; as, *Pergit consultŭrus,* He goes to consult.

REM. 2. — The participle in *dus,* when agreeing with the subject of a sentence, denotes necessity or propriety ; as, *Is venerandus a nobis est,* He should be worshipped by us. *Dolendum est ipsi tibi,* You yourself must grieve.

GERUNDS AND GERUNDIVES.

Rule 24.

Gerunds are governed like nouns, and are followed by the same cases as their verbs ; as,

Metus parendi sibi, Fear of obeying him. *Parcendo* victis, By sparing the vanquished.

REMARK 1. — The participle in *dus* is called a gerundive when it is used instead of a gerund.

REM. 2. — The *genitive* of gerunds and gerundives may follow either nouns or adjectives ; as, *Amor habendi*, The love of possessing. *Insuētus navigandi*, Unaccustomed to navigating.

REM. 3. — The *dative* of gerunds and gerundives is used after adjectives which govern a dative, especially after those which signify *usefulness* or *fitness;* and also after certain verbs and phrases to denote a *purpose;* as, *Charta inutĭlis* scribendo, Paper not useful for writing. *Locum oppĭdo* condendo capĕre, To choose a place for building a town.

REM. 4. — The *accusative* of gerunds and gerundives follows the prepositions *ad* or *inter*, and sometimes *ante, circa*, or *ob;* as, *Ad pœnitendum propĕrat*, He makes haste to repentance. *Inter bibendum*, While drinking.

REM. 5. — The *ablative* of gerunds and gerundives follows the prepositions *a, ab, de, e, ex*, or *in;* or it is used without a preposition as the ablative of *cause, manner*, or *means;* as, *A scribendo*, From writing. *Crescit eundo*, It increases by going.

SUPINES.

Rule 25.

Supines in *um* are followed by the same cases as their verbs ; as,

Non Graiis servitum matrĭbus ibo, I shall not go to serve Grecian matrons.

Rule 26.

Supines in *um* follow verbs of motion, and serve to denote the purpose of the motion ; as,

Te admonĭtum venio, I come to admonish you.

Rule 27.

The supine in *u* is used to limit the meaning of adjectives signifying *wonderful, agreeable, easy* or *difficult, worthy* or *unworthy, honorable* or *base,* and a few others ; as,

Mirabile dictu ! Wonderful to tell, *or* to be told !

REMARK. — The supine in *u* is used also after the nouns *fas, nefas,* and *opus ;* as, *Nefas dictu !* Shameful to relate !

CASES AFTER NOUNS.

APPOSITION.

Rule 28.

A noun annexed to another noun or to a pronoun, and denoting the same person or thing, is put in the same case ; as,

Roma urbs, the city Rome.   *Nos consŭles,* we consuls.

REMARK 1. — A noun in apposition to two or more nouns is usually put in the plural ; as, *M. Antonius, C. Cassius* tribūni *plebis ;* Mark Antony (and) Caius Cassius, tribunes of the people.

REM. 2. — The principal noun or pronoun in the answer to a question must be in the same case as the corresponding interrogative word ; as, Quis *herus est tibi ?* Amphitruo, scil. *est ?* Who is your master ? Amphitruo, (is.) Quid *quæris ?* Librum, scil. *quæro.* What are you looking for ? A book.

GENITIVE.

Rule 29.

A noun which limits the meaning of another noun, denoting a different person or thing, is put in the genitive ; as,

Amor gloriæ, Love of glory.   *Vitium iræ,* The vice of anger.

Arma Achillis, The arms of Achilles.   *Nemŏrum custos,* The guardian of the groves.

Pater patriæ, The father of the country.   *Amor habendi,* Love of possessing.

REMARK 1. — The genitive is called *subjective* when it denotes the *subject* of the action, feeling, etc., implied in the noun which it limits. It is called *objective* when it denotes the *object* affected by such action, or toward which such feeling is directed ; as,

Subjective.	*Objective.*
Facta virōrum, Deeds of men.	*Odium vitii*, Hatrèd of vice.
Dolor anĭmi, Grief of mind.	*Amor virtūtis*, Love of virtue.
Junōnis ira, The anger of Juno.	*Desiderium otii*, Desire of leisure.

REM. 2. (*a*.) A substantive pronoun in the genitive, limiting the meaning of a noun, is commonly objective; as, *Cura mei*, Care for me. *Pars tui*, Part of thee.

(*b*.) Instead of the *subjective* genitive of a substantive pronoun, the corresponding adjective pronoun is commonly used; as, *Liber meus*, not *liber mei*, my book.

REM. 3. — The dative is sometimes used like the genitive; as, *Exitium* pecŏri, A destruction to the flock. Cui *corpus porrigĭtur*, For whom the body (*i. e.* whose body) is extended.

REM. 4. — When the limiting noun denotes a *property*, *character*, *quality*, or *condition*, it has an adjective agreeing with it, and is put either in the genitive or ablative; as, *Vir exempli recti*, A man of correct example. *Adolescens summæ audaciæ*, A youth of the greatest boldness. *Fossa pedum viginti*, A ditch of twenty feet, (*i. e.* in width.) Pulchritudĭne eximiâ *femĭna*, A woman of exquisite beauty. Maxĭmo natu *filius*, The eldest son. Magno *timore* sum, I am in great fear.

REM. 5. — When the noun on which the genitive depends is a general word denoting *a person, an animal*, etc., or signifying *part*, *property*, *duty*, *office*, *business*, *characteristic*, etc., it is often omitted after the verb *sum*; as, *Thucydĭdes, qui ejusdem ætatis fuit* scil. *homo*, Thucydides, who was of the same age. *Temerĭtas est florentis ætātis, prudentia senectūtis;* Rashness is (the characteristic) of youth, prudence of old age. *Adolescentis est majōres natu reverēri*, It is (the duty) of a youth to reverence the aged.

Rule 30.

Nouns denoting a part are followed by a genitive denoting the whole; as,

Pars civitātis, A part of the state. (Compare Rules 3 and 12.)

ABLATIVE.

Rule 31.

Opus and *usus*, signifying *need*, usually take the ablative of the thing needed; as,

Auctoritāte *tuâ nobis opus est,* We need your authority. *Naves,* quibus *consūli usus non esset;* Ships, for which the consul had no occasion.

Rule 32.

A noun may be followed by the ablative, denoting *in what respect* its signification is taken; as,

Pietāte filius, consilio *parens;* In affection a son, in counsel a parent. *Reges* nomĭne *magìs quàm* imperio, Kings in name rather than in authority. (Compare Rules 8 and 72.)

VERBS.

SUBJECT—NOMINATIVE.

Rule 33.

The noun or pronoun which is the subject of a finite verb is put in the nominative; as,

Ego lego, I read.	*Nos legĭmus,* We read.
Tu scribis, Thou writest.	*Vos scribĭtis,* You write.
Equus currit, The horse runs.	*Equi currunt,* Horses run.

NOTE. — A verb in any mood except the infinitive is called a *finite* verb.

REMARK 1. — The nominatives *ego, tu, nos, vos,* are seldom expressed; as, *cupio,* I desire; *vivis,* thou livest; *habēmus,* we have. The nominative of the third person also is often omitted.

REM. 2. — The subject of the verb is sometimes an infinitive or a neuter participle (either alone or with other words), one or more propositions, or an adverb.

REM. 3. — The relative *qui* may refer to an antecedent either of the first, second, or third person; and its verb takes the person of the antecedent; as, *Ego qui* lego, I who *read.* *Tu qui* scribis, Thou who *writest.* *Equus qui* currit, The horse which *runs.*

REM. 4. — A collective noun has sometimes a plural verb; as, *Pars epŭlis* onĕrant *mensas,* Part load the tables with food.

REM. 5. — Two or more nominatives singular, not in apposition, generally have a plural verb; as, Furor irāque *mentem* præcipĭtant, Fury and rage hurry on (my) mind.

REM. 6. — If the nominatives are of different persons, the verb is of the first person rather than the second or third, and of the second rather than the third; as, *Si tu et Tullia* valētis, *ego et Cicĕro* valēmus; If you and Tullia *are well,* Cicero and I *are well.*

Rule 34.

A verb agrees with its subject nominative in number and person. (See examples under Rule 33.)

REMARK.—A verb in the singular is often used after several nominatives singular, especially if they denote things without life.

CASES AFTER VERBS.

PREDICATE—NOMINATIVE. '

Rule 35.

A noun in the predicate, after a verb neuter or passive, is put in the same case as the subject, when it denotes the same person or thing ; as,

Ira furor *brevis est*, Anger is a short madness. *Ego vocor* Lyconĭdes, I am called Lyconides. *Ego incēdo* regīna, I walk a queen. Judĭcem *me esse volo*, I wish to be a judge.

REMARK.—Adjectives, adjective pronouns, and participles, standing in the predicate after verbs neuter or passive, and relating to the subject, agree with it in gender, number, and case ; as, *Lupus obambŭlat nocturnus.*

GENITIVE.

Rule 36.

Sum, and verbs of *valuing*, are followed by a genitive denoting *degree of estimation ;* as,

A me argentum, quanti *est sumĭto ;* Take of me so much money as (he) is worth. Magni *æstimābat pecuniam,* He valued money greatly.

Rule 37.

Misereor and *miseresco* are followed by a genitive of the object in respect to which the feeling is exercised ; as,

Miseremĭni sociōrum, Pity the allies. *Miserescĭte regis*, Pity the king.

Rule 38.

Satăgo is sometimes followed by a genitive denoting *in what respect ;* as,

Is *satăgit* rerum *suārum*, He is busily occupied with his own affairs.

Rule 39.

Refert and *intĕrest* are followed by a genitive of the person or thing whose concern or interest they denote; as,

Humanitātis *refert*, It concerns human nature. *Intĕrest* omnium rectè *facĕre*, It concerns all to do right.

REMARK. — Instead of the genitive of the substantive pronouns, the adjective pronouns *mea, tua, sua, nostra,* and *vestra,* are used ; as Mea *nihil refert*, It does not concern me.

Rule 40.

Many verbs which are usually otherwise construed, are sometimes followed by a genitive.

This rule includes, —

1. Certain verbs denoting an affection of the mind.

2. Some verbs denoting *to fill, to abound, to want* or *need, to free ;* also *potior,* and some others.

GENITIVE OR ACCUSATIVE.

Rule 41.

Recordor, memĭni, reminiscor, and *obliviscor,* are followed by a genitive or accusative of the object remembered or forgotten ; as,

Omnes gradus *ætātis recordor tuæ,* I call to mind all the periods of your life. *Memĭni* vivōrum, I am mindful of the living. Numĕros *memĭni,* I remember the measure.

GENITIVE AND ACCUSATIVE.

Rule 42.

The impersonal verbs of feeling, *misĕret, pœnĭtet, pudet, tœdet, piget, miserescit, miserētur,* and *pertœsum est,* are followed by a genitive of the object in respect to which the feeling is exercised, and an accusative of the person exercising the feeling; as,

Tui me *misĕret,* I pity you.

Rule 43.

Verbs of *accusing, convicting, condemning,* and *acquitting,* with the accusative of the person, are followed by a genitive denoting the *crime;* as,

Arguit me furti, He charges me with theft. Altĕrum *accūsat* probri, He accuses another of villany.

Rule 44.

Verbs of *admonishing,* with the accusative of the person, are followed by a genitive of the person or thing respecting which the admonition is given; as,

Milĭtes tempŏris *monet,* He admonishes the soldiers of the occasion.

DATIVE.

Rule 45.

A noun limiting the meaning of a verb is put in the dative, to denote the *object to* or *for* which any thing is, or is done; as,

Mea domus tibi *patet,* My house is open *to you.* Tibi *seris,* tibi metis; You sow *for yourself,* you reap *for yourself.* *Licet* nemĭni, It is not lawful *for any one. Hoc* tibi *promitto,* I promise *you* this.

REMARK. — Many verbs have, with the dative, an accusative, expressed or understood.

Rule 46.

Many verbs signifying to *favor, please, trust, assist,* and their contraries, also to *command, obey, serve, resist, threaten,* and *be angry,* take a dative of the object; as,

Illa tibi *favet,* She favors you.

Rule 47.

Many verbs compounded with these eleven prepositions, *ad, ante, con, in, inter, ob, post, præ, pro, sub,* and *super,* are followed by the dative; as,

Annue cœptis, Be favorable to (our) undertakings. Romānis equitĭbus *litĕræ afferuntur,* Letters are brought to the Roman knights. *Antecellĕre* omnĭbus, To excel all.

Rule 48.

Some verbs of *repelling* and *taking away* (most of which are compounds of *ab, de,* or *ex*), are sometimes followed by the dative, though more commonly by the ablative; as,

Nec mihi *te eripient,* Nor shall they take you from me.

Rule 49.

Verbs compounded with *satis, bene,* and *malĕ,* are followed by the dative; as,

Et natūræ *et* legĭbus *satisfēcit,* He satisfied both nature and the laws. *Pulchrum est benefacĕre* reipublĭcæ, It is honorable to benefit the state.

Rule 50.

Verbs in the passive voice are sometimes followed by a dative of the agent; as,

Neque cernĭtur ulli, Nor is he seen by any one.

Rule 51.

The participle in *dus* is followed by a dative of the agent; as,

Adhĭbenda est nobis *diligentia,* We must use diligence. *Unda* omnĭbus *enaviganda,* The wave over which (we) all must pass.

Rule 52.

Est is followed by a dative denoting a *possessor;* the thing possessed being the subject of the verb.

REMARK.—*Est* thus used may generally be translated by the verb *to have*, with the dative as its subject; as, *Est* mihi *domi pater,* I have a father at home. *Sunt* nobis *mitia poma,* We have mellow apples.

Rule 53.

Sum, and several other verbs, are followed by two datives, one of which denotes the *object to which,* and the other the *end for which,* any thing is, or is done; as,

Mihî *maxĭmœ est* curœ, It is a very great care to me. *Spero* nobis *hanc conjunctiōnem* voluptāti *fore,* I hope this union will afford us pleasure.

ACCUSATIVE.

Rule 54.

The object of a transitive verb is put in the accusative; as,

Legātos *mittunt,* They send ambassadors. *Anĭmus movet* corpus, The mind moves the body. *Da* veniam *hanc,* Grant this favor. Eum *imitāti sunt,* They imitated him.

REMARK 1.—An infinitive, or one or more clauses, may supply the place of the accusative; as, *Da mihi* fallĕre, Give me to deceive.

REM. 2. — *Juvat, delĕctat, fallit, fugit, prœtĕrit,* and *decet,* with their compounds, take an accusative of the person; as, *Te hilări anĭmo esse valdê* me *juvat,* That you are in good spirits greatly delights me.

Rule 55.

Verbs signifying to *name* or *call,* to *choose, render,* or *constitute,* to *esteem* or *reckon,* are followed by two accusatives, one of the *object,* and the other of the *predicate;* as,

Urbem Antiochĭam *vocāvit,* He called the city Antioch.

REMARK.—Many other verbs beside their proper accusative take a second, denoting a *purpose, time, character,* etc.; as, *Filiam tuam* mihi uxorem *posco,* I demand your daughter for my wife.

Rule 56.

Verbs of *asking, demanding*, and *teaching*, and *celo*, (to conceal,) are followed by two accusatives, one of the person, and the other of the thing; as,

Posce deos veniam, Ask favor of the gods. *Quis* musĭcam *docuit* Epaminondam? Who taught Epaminondas music? *Antigŏnus* iter omnes *celat*, Antigonus conceals his route from all.

REMARK 1. — When a verb which, in the active voice, takes an accusative both of the person and of the thing, is changed to the passive form, the accusative of the person becomes the nominative, and the accusative of the thing is retained; as, *Rogātus est* sententiam, He was asked his opinion.

REM. 2. — Many active verbs with the accusative of the person take also an accusative denoting *in what respect* or *to what degree* the action of the verb is exerted; as, Eos hoc *moneo*, I admonish them of this.

Rule 57.

Some *neuter* verbs are followed by an accusative of kindred signification to their own; as,

Vitam *jucundam vivĕre*, To live a pleasant *life*. Istam pugnam *pugnābo*, I will fight *that battle*.

Rule 58.

Many verbs are followed by an accusative depending upon a preposition with which they are compounded; as,

Omnem equitātum pontem *transdūcit*, He leads all the cavalry over the bridge. *Magĭcas accingier* artes, To prepare one's self for magic arts.

Rule 59.

Verbs and perfect participles are sometimes followed by an accusative denoting the *part* to which their signification relates; as,

Tremit artus. Anĭmum *incensus*. (Compare Rule 5.)

ABLATIVE.

Rule 60.

Many verbs compounded with *a, ab, abs, de, e, ex,* and *super,* are followed by an ablative depending upon the preposition ; as,

Abesse urbe, To be absent from the city. *Detrūdunt naves* scopŭlo, They push the ships from the rock.

Rule 61. ·

Utor, fruor, fungor, potior, vescor, and their compounds, are followed by the ablative ; as,

His vocĭbus *usa est,* She addressed these words. *Frui* voluptāte, To enjoy pleasure. *Fungĭtur* officio, He performs (his) duty.

Rule 62.

Nītor, innītor, fido, and *confīdo,* may be followed by the ablative without a preposition ; as,

Hastâ *innixus,* Leaning on his spear.
REMARK. — *Fido* and *confīdo* often take the dative.

Rule 63.

Misceo. with its compounds, takes, with the accusative of the object, the ablative of the thing mingled with ; as,

· *Miscēre aquas* nectăre, To mingle water with nectar.
REMARK. — *Misceo, admisceo,* and *permisceo,* often take the dative.

Rule 64.

Assuesco, assuefacio, consuesco, insuesco, and sometimes *acquiesco,* take either the dative or the ablative of the thing ; as,

Aves sanguĭne *et* prædâ *assuetæ,* Birds accustomed to blood and prey. *Corvus assuefactus* sermōni.

Rule 65..

Vivo and *epŭlor*, "to live" or "feast upon," are followed by the ablative ; as,

Lacte *atque* pecŏre *vivunt,* They live upon milk and cattle.

Rule 66.

Sto, when it signifies "to be filled with," or "to cost," is followed by the ablative without a preposition; when it signifies "to persevere in," and the like, by the ablative either with or without *in.* *Consto,* "to consist of," or "to rest upon," is followed by the ablative alone, or with *ex, de,* or *in.*

Rule 67.

Perfect participles denoting *origin* are often followed by the ablative of the *source* without a preposition; as,

Nate deâ! O son of á goddess ! Tantâlo *prognătus,* Descended from Tantalus. *Satus* Nereîde, Sprung from a Nereid.

ABLATIVE OF CAUSE, ETC.

Rule 68.

Nouns denoting the *cause, manner, means,* and *instrument,* after adjectives and verbs, are put in the ablative without a preposition.

1. The *cause.* (1.) Adjectives which have a passive signification, as denoting a state or condition produced by some external cause, may take such cause in the ablative ; as, Prœlio *fessi lassique,* Weary and faint with the battle.

(2.) Neuter verbs expressing an action, state, or feeling of the subject originating in some external cause, may take that cause in the ablative ; as, *Interiit* fame, He perished with hunger. *Lætor tua* dignităte, I rejoice in your dignity.

2. The *manner.* *Cum* is regularly joined with the ablative of manner, when expressed simply by a noun not modified by any other word ; and also when an adjective is joined with the noun, provided *an additional circumstance,* and not merely an essential

character of the action, is to be expressed; as, Cum voluptāte *aliquem* *audīre*, To hear one with pleasure. *Verres Lampsacum venit cum* *magna* calamitate *civitātis*. But *modus, ratio, mos,* etc., signifying manner, do not take *cum;* and it is omitted in some expressions with other substantives; as, Hoc modo *scripsi,* I wrote in this manner. Silentio *audītus est,* He was heard in silence.

3. The *means* and *instrument.* An ablative is joined with verbs of every kind, and also with adjectives of a passive signification, to express the means or instrument; as, *Amicos* observantia *rem parsi-* monia retinuit, He retained his friends by attention, his property by frugality. *Trabs saucia* secūri, A tree cut with the axe.

Remark. — The voluntary agent of a verb in the passive voice is put in the ablative with *a* or *ab;* as, (in the active voice,) *Clodius* *me diligit,* Clodius loves me; (in the passive,) A Clodio *diligor,* I am loved by Clodius.

Rule 69.

A noun denoting the means by which the action of a verb is performed is put in the ablative after verbs signifying to *affect* in any way, to *fill, furnish, load, array, equip, endow, adorn, reward, enrich,* and many others; as,

Instruxēre epŭlis *mensas,* They furnished the tables with food. *Naves onĕrant* auro, They load the ships with gold. *Cumŭlat altaria* donis, He heaps the altars with gifts. *Terra se* gramĭne *vestit,* The earth clothes itself with grass.

Rule 70.

A noun denoting that in *accordance* with which any thing is, or is done, is often put in the ablative without a preposition; as,

Nostro more, According to our custom. Instĭtūto *suo Cæsar copias* *suas eduxit;* Cæsar, according to his practice, led out his forces.

Rule 71.

The ablative denoting *accompaniment* is usually joined with *cum;* as,

Vagāmur egentes cum conjŭgĭbus *et* libĕris, Needy, we wander with (our) wives and children.

Rule 72.

A verb may be followed by the ablative, denoting *in what respect* its signification is taken ; as,

Anĭmo *angi,* To be troubled in mind.   (Compare Rules 8 and 32.)

Rule 73.

Verbs signifying to *abound,* and to be *destitute,* are followed by the ablative ; as,

Scatentem belluis *pontum,* The sea abounding in monsters.   *Urbs redundat* milital̄ibus, The city is full of soldiers.   (Compare Rule 40.)

Rule 74.

A noun denoting that of which any thing is *deprived* or from which it is *freed, removed,* or *separated,* is often put in the ablative without a preposition ; as,

Nudantur arbŏres foliis, The trees are stripped of leaves.   *Hoc me libĕra* metu, Free me from this fear.

REMARK. — This construction occurs after verbs signifying to *deprive, free, debar, drive away, remove, depart,* and others which imply *separation.*

ABLATIVE ABSOLUTE.

Rule 75.

A noun and a participle are put in the ablative, called *absolute,* to denote the *time, cause,* or *concomitant* of an action, or the *condition* on which it depends ; as,

Pythagŏras, Tarquinio regnante, *in Italiam venit ;* Pythagoras came into Italy in the reign of Tarquin.   *Lupus,* stimulante fame, *captat ovile ;* Hunger inciting, the wolf seeks the fold.

REMARK 1. — A noun is put in the ablative absolute only when it denotes a different person or thing from any in the leading clause.

REM. 2. — As the verb *sum* has no present participle, two nouns, or a noun and an adjective, are put in the ablative absolute without a participle ; as, *Quid* adolescentŭlo *duce, efficĕre possent ;* What they could do under the guidance of a youth.   *Romam venit,* Mario consŭle ; *He came to Rome in the consulship of Marius.*

PRICE.

GENITIVE.

Rule 76.

Sum and verbs of valuing are joined with the genitive, when the value is expressed in *a general* or *indefinite* manner. (Compare Rule 86.)

ABLATIVE.

Rule 77.

The *price* or *value* of a thing is put in the ablative, when it is a definite sum, or is expressed by a substantive; as,

Vendidit hic auro *patriam*, This one sold (his) country for gold.

TIME.

ACCUSATIVE OR ABLATIVE.

Rule 78.

Nouns denoting *duration of time* are put, after adjectives and verbs, in the accusative, and sometimes after verbs in the ablative; as,

Appius cæcus multos annos *fuit*, Appius was blind many years. Annos *natus viginti septem*, Twenty-seven years old. *Vixit* annis undetriginta. (Compare Rule 84.)

ABLATIVE.

Rule 79.

A noun denoting the time *at* or *within* which any thing is said to be, or to be done, is put in the ablative without a preposition; as,

Die *quinto decessit*, He died on the fifth day. *Hoc tempore*, At this time.

PLACE.

GENITIVE.

Rule 80.

The name of a town *in which* any thing is said *to be* or *to be done*, if of the first or second declension and singular number, is put in the genitive ; as,

Habitat Milēti, He lives at Miletus. *Quid* Romæ *faciam?* What can I do at Rome?

REMARK. — The genitives *domi, militiæ, belli,* and *humi,* are construed like names of towns ; as, *Tenuit se* domi, He staid at home. *Unà semper* militiæ *et* domi *fuimus,* We were always together, both at home and in the camp.

ACCUSATIVE.

Rule 81.

After verbs expressing or implying motion, the name of the town *in which the motion ends* is put in the accusative without a preposition ; as,

Regŭlus Carthagĭnem *rediit,* Regulus returned to Carthage. Capuam *flectit iter.* He turns (his) course to Capua.

REMARK. — *Domus* in both numbers, and *rus* in the singular, are put in the accusative, like names of towns ; as, *Ite* domum, Go home. Rus *ibo,* I will go into the country.

ABLATIVE.

Rule 82.

The name of a town *in which* any thing is said *to be,* or *to be done,* if of the third declension or plural number, is put in the ablative without a preposition ; as,

Alexander Babylōne *est mortuus,* Alexander died at Babylon. Thebis *nutrītus an* Argis, Whether brought up at Thebes or at Argos. So also *terra marique,* By land and by sea.

REMARK. — Before the names of countries, and of all other places in which any thing is said to be or to be done, except those of towns, and *domus* and *rus,* the preposition *in* is commonly used.

Rule 83.

After verbs expressing or implying motion, the name of a town *whence* the motion proceeds is put in the ablative without a preposition ; as,

Brundisio *profecti sumus*, We departed from Brundisium. Corintho *arcessivit colōnos*, He sent for colonists from Corinth.

REMARK. — The ablatives *domo*, *humo*, and *rure* or *ruri*, are used like names of towns, to denote the place whence the motion proceeds ; as, Domo *profectus*, Having set out from home. *Surgit* humo *juvĕnis*, The youth rises from the ground.

SPACE.

ACCUSATIVE OR ABLATIVE.

Rule 84.

Nouns denoting *extent of space* are put, after adjectives and verbs, in the accusative, and sometimes after verbs in the ablative ; as,

Duas fossas quindĕcim pedes *latas perduxit*, He extended two ditches fifteen feet broad. (Compare Rule 78.)

CASES AFTER INTERJECTIONS.

NOMINATIVE.

Rule 85.

The interjections *en*, *ecce*, and *O*, are sometimes followed by the nominative ; as,

En Priămus ! Lo Priam ! *Ecce* homo Catiēnus !

DATIVE.

Rule 86.

Certain interjections are followed by the dative of the object ; as,

Hei mihi ! Ah me ! *Vae* mihi ! Woe is me ! (Compare Rule 13.)

11*

ACCUSATIVE.

Rule 87.

In exclamations, the noun or pronoun which marks the *object of the feeling* is put in the accusative, either with or without the interjections *O, ah, heu, eheu, ecce, en, hem, pro,* or *vae;* as,

En quatuor *aras! ecce* duas *tibi Dáphni!* Behold four altars! lo, two for thee, Daphnis!

VOCATIVE.

Rule 88.

The vocative is used, either with or without an interjection, in addressing a person or thing; as,

O formôse puer! O beautiful boy! Fili *mi,* My son.

RULES FOR THE SUBJUNCTIVE MOOD.

Rule 89.

The subjunctive mood is used to express an action or state simply as conceived by the mind.

NOTE. — The tenses of the subjunctive are, in general, not limited in regard to time, like the corresponding tenses of the indicative.

1. The subjunctive is sometimes to be translated by the indicative, particularly in *indirect questions,* in clauses expressing a *result,* and after adverbs of *time;* as,

Rogas me quid tristis *sim,* You ask me why I am sad. *Stellarum tanta est multitŭdo, ut numerāri non* possint; The multitude of stars is so great that they cannot be counted. *Quum Cœsar* esset *in Gallia,* When Cæsar was in Gaul.

2. The subjunctive is used to express what is contingent or hypothetical, including *possibility, power, liberty, will, duty,* and *desire.*

REMARK. — The present subjunctive is often used to express a *wish,* an *exhortation, asseveration, request, command,* or *permission;* as, Moriar, *si,* etc.; May I die, if, etc. *In media arma* ruāmus, Let us rush into the midst of arms. *Ne me* attingas, Do not touch me. Faciat *quod lubet,* Let him do what he pleases.

SUBJUNCTIVE AFTER PARTICLES.

Rule 90.

A clause denoting the *purpose, object,* or *result* of a preceding proposition takes the subjunctive after *ut, ne, quò, quin,* and *quomĭnus;* as,

Ea, non ut te institŭĕrem, *scripsi;* I did not write that in order to instruct you. *Irrĭtant ad pugnandum,* quò fiant *acriōres;* They stimulate them to fight, that they may become fiercer.

REMARK. — *Ut* is often omitted before the subjunctive, after verbs denoting *willingness* and *permission;* also after verbs of *asking, advising, reminding,* etc., and the imperatives *dic* and *fac.*

Rule 91.

The subjunctive is used after particles of *wishing;* as, *utĭnam, uti, O!* and *O! si;* as,

Utĭnam minùs vitœ cupĭdi fuissēmus! O that we had been less attached to life!

Rule 92.

Quamvis, however; *licèt,* although; *tamquam, tamquam si, quasi, ac si, ut si, velut, velut si, velúti, sicúti* and *ceu,* as if; *mòdo, dum* and *dummŏdo,* provided, — take the subjunctive; as,

Quamvis *ille felix* sit, tamen, etc.; However happy he may be, still, etc. *Verĭtas* licèt *nullum defensōrem* obtineat, Though truth should obtain no defender.

REMARK. — *Quamquam,* "although," is sometimes joined with the subjunctive.

Rule 93.

After *antĕquam* and *priusquam,* the imperfect and pluperfect tenses are usually in the subjunctive; the

present and perfect may be either in the indicative or
subjunctive ; as,

Ea causa ante *mortua est*, quàm *tu* natus esses ; That cause was
dead before you were born.

Rule 94.

Dum, donec, and *quoad,* signifying *until,* are followed by the subjunctive, if they refer to the attainment
of an object ; as,

Dum *hic* venīret, *locum relinquĕre noluit ;* He was unwilling to leave
the place until he (Milo) should come.

Rule 95.

Quum, or *cùm,* when it signifies a *relation of time,*
takes the indicative ; when it denotes a *connection of
thought,* the subjunctive ; as,

Qui non defendit injuriam quum potest, *injuste facit ;* He who does
not avert an injury *when* he can, does unjustly.   Quum *tot* sustineas
et tanta negotia, peccem, si morer tua tempŏra ; Since you are burdened
with so many and so important affairs, I should do wrong if I should
occupy your time.

REMARK. — In narration, *quum* (even when it relates to time,) is
usually joined with the imperfect and pluperfect subjunctive, when
a historical perfect stands in the principal clause.

SUBJUNCTIVE AFTER QUI.

Rule 96.

Relatives require the subjunctive, when the clauses
connected by them express merely a conception ; as,
for example, a *consequence,* an *innate quality,* a *cause,
motive,* or *purpose.*

1. When the relative *qui* is equivalent to *ut* with a
personal or demonstrative pronoun, it takes the subjunctive ; as,

Quis est tam Lynceūs, qui *in tantis tenēbris nihil* offendat ? i. e. *ut
ille in tantis,* etc. ; who is so quick-sighted that he would not stumble
(or, *as not to stumble*) in such darkness ?

NOTE. — *Qui* is thus used after *tam* with an adjective; *tantus, talis, ejusmŏdi, hujusmŏdi, is, ille, iste,* and *hic,* in the sense of *talis.*

2. When the relative is equivalent to *quanquam is, etsi is,* or *dummŏdo is,* it takes the subjunctive; as,

Laco, consilii quamvis egregii, quod *non ipse* afferret, *inimicus ;* Laco, an opponent of any measure, however excellent, provided he did not himself propose it.

3. *Quod,* in restrictive clauses, takes the subjunctive; as,

Quod sciam, As far as I know. *Quod meminěrim,* as far as I recollect. Quod *sine molestiâ tuâ* fiat, So far as it can be done without troubling you.

4. A relative clause, after the comparative followed by *quàm,* takes the subjunctive; as,

Major sum quàm cui possit *fortŭna nocēre,* i. e. *quàm ut mihi,* etc. ; I am too great for fortune to be able to injure me.

5. A relative clause expressing a *purpose, aim,* or *motive,* and equivalent to *ut* with a personal or demonstrative pronoun, takes the subjunctive; as,

Lacedæmonii legātos Athēnas misērunt, qui *eum absentem* accusārent; i. e. *ut illi eum accusarent ;* The Lacedæmonians sent ambassadors to Athens to accuse him in his absence.

6. A relative clause with the subjunctive after certain *indefinite general expressions,* specifies the circumstances which characterize the individual or class indefinitely referred to in the leading clause; as,

Fuērunt *eâ tempestāte,* qui dicěrent; There were at that time some who said.

The expressions included in the rule are *est, sunt, adest, præsto sunt, existunt, exoriuntur, inveniuntur, reperiuntur,* (scil. *homĭnes,*) *si quis est, tempus fuit, tempus veniet,* etc.

7. A relative clause after a *general negative,* or an *interrogative expression implying a negative,* takes the subjunctive; as,

Nemo est, qui *haud* intellĭgat; There is no one who does not understand. *Quis est,* qui *utilia* fugiat? Who is there that shuns what is useful?

8. A relative clause expressing the *reason* of what goes before takes the subjunctive; as,

Peccavisse mihi videor, qui *a te* discessĕrim; I think I did wrong in leaving you. *Inertiam accūsas adolescentium*, qui *istam artem non* ediscant; You blame the idleness of the young men, because they do not learn that art.

9. After *dignus, indignus, aptus,* and *idoneus*, a relative clause takes the subjunctive; as,

Vidētur, qui *aliquando* impĕret, dignus *esse;* He seems to be worthy at some time to command.

10. The imperfect and pluperfect subjunctive are used in narration after relative pronouns and adverbs, when a repeated action is spoken of; as,

Semper habĭti sunt fortissĭmi, qui *summam imperii* potirentur; Those were always accounted the bravest, who obtained the supreme dominion.

SUBJUNCTIVE IN INDIRECT QUESTIONS.

Rule 97.

Dependent clauses containing an *indirect question* take the subjunctive; as,

Qualis sit *anĭmus, ipse anĭmus nescit;* The mind itself knows not what the mind is.   Quis *ego* sim, *me rogĭtas?* Do you ask me who I am?   *Nec* quid scribam, *habeo;* Nor have I any thing to write.

NOTE. — A question is indirect when its substance is stated in a dependent clause without the interrogative form.

SUBJUNCTIVE IN INSERTED CLAUSES.

Rule 98.

A verb is put in the subjunctive when the clause in which it stands is connected, as an *essential part*, to another clause, whose verb is in the subjunctive, or in the infinitive with the accusative; as,

Quid enim potest esse tam perspicuum, quàm esse aliquod numen, quo hæc regantur? For what can be so clear as that there is some divinity by whom these things are governed?   Here the thing which is stated to be clear is not merely *esse aliquod numen*, that there is a god, but also that the world is governed by him. *Audiam quid sit, quòd Epicūrum non* probes; I shall hear why it is that you do not approve of Epicurus.

Rule 99.

In the *oratio oblīqua*, the main proposition is expressed by the accusative with the infinitive; and dependent clauses, connected with it by relatives and particles, take the subjunctive; as,

Socrātes dicěre solēbat, omnes, in eo quod scirent, *satis esse eloquentes:* Socrates was accustomed to say that "all were sufficiently eloquent in that which they understood."

NOTE. — In the *oratio oblīqua,* "indirect discourse," or "reported speech," the language of another is presented, not as it was conceived or expressed by him, but in the third person. Thus Cæsar said, "I came, I saw, I conquered," is direct; Cæsar said that "he came, saw, and conquered," is indirect discourse.

Rule 100.

A clause connected to another by a relative or causal conjunction takes the subjunctive, (whatever be the mood of the preceding verb,) when it contains not the sentiment or allegation of the writer, but that of some other person alluded to; as,

Socrātes accusātus est, quòd corrumpěret *juventūtem;* Socrates was accused of corrupting the youth, literally, because (as was alleged) he corrupted the youth.

EXERCISES.

I.

Letters, etc.

Write five English words containing diphthongs, and five having successive vowels which are not diphthongs. Write ten English words of more than one syllable, and mark the accented syllable of each with the acute accent.

II.

Orthoëpy — Sounds of the Letters.

Pronounce the following words : — bo'-na, di'-e, mi'-hi, fu'-gĭ-unt, pol'-ў-pus, præ'-mĭ-um, mœ'-nĭ-a, au-dī'-mus, Eu-rō'-pa, mach'-ĭ-na, ge'-ner, a'-gri, ci'-nis, a-mī'-cus, a-mī'-ci, dom'-ĭ-nos, ser-mō'-nes. Write ten English words of one syllable, ten of two, and ten of more than two.

III.

Orthoëpy — Quantity, etc.

Mark the quantity of the penult in the following words : — pen-na, tu-us, vir-tus, di-es, a-cris, post-quam, al-te-ri-us, vic-to-ri-a, in-cen-dit, cau-sa, an-cil-la, pug-nan-dum, di-ver-sus, the-sau-rus, ma-jor, phar-e-tra, lin-gua, cœ-no, ax-is, mo-les-tus, ga-za, vol-u-cres, me-li-or, con-jux.

Give the general rule for the quantity of penna, — of tuus, — of virtus, etc.

Mark the accent on the following words : — mo-nes, lu-dunt, ful-gē-bant, tem-pŏ-ra, ju-rav-é-rat, de-fen-de-bā-tur, fe-lix.

How many syllables has reges ? — rustĭcus ? — pŭ-ĕri ? — monebāmus ? — tempus ? — alĭquis ? — dormie-bātis ? — dixĕras ? — memoria ? — **ambulaverĭmus** ? — ocŭlus ? — exercitationĭbus ?

IV.

Verbs.

What word in each of the following sentences is a verb ? — and why is it a verb ?

Scipio destroyed Carthage.

The bee loves flowers.

Romulus founded Rome.

Life is short.

Roses shine among the lilies.

The dogs will pursue.

Determine which of the following verbs are active, and which are neuter : —

To sit ; to read ; to walk ; to love ; to eat ; to be ; to hear ; to purchase ; to laugh ; to destroy ; to sleep ; to desire.

Determine the voice of each of the following verbs : I love. He is hated. They are despised. We shall be taught. Fortune favors the brave. The brave are favored by fortune. All men desire happiness. The ship is driven by the wind. The horses draw the chariot. He eats and drinks. The provisions were consumed.

What is the verb in each of the following sentences? Why is it a verb ? What kind of verb is it ? And, if an active verb, of which voice is it ? —

Benefits procure friends.

The ripe apple falls.
The eyes are deceived.
A shout is heard.
Care follows money.
Darius was conquered by Alexander.

V.

Moods.

Determine the mood of the verb in each of the following sentences : —

The soul is immortal.
If the king rule.
The apples were falling.
Years glide away.
Do you understand ?
Be ye advised.
I desire to see you.

A clamor was heard.
If the apples should fall.
I will follow thee.
If I have followed thee.
He desired to follow thee.

VI.

Tenses.

Determine the tense of the verb in each of the following sentences : —

The king rules.
The king is ruling.
The king was ruling.
The boys used to read.
He made a law.
He has made a law.
He will lose a day.
He had lost a day.
The soldiers will have slept.

Let the horse run.
The stars were shining.
Dido was founding Carthage.
Overcome anger.
Dido founded Carthage.
Will the time come ?
The shadow had fled.
The sun is shining.

VII.

Conjugation — Roots.

Determine the conjugation of each of the following verbs, and write down its general root. (The present infinitive of each verb is given.) —

Nominăre, *to name.*
Ducĕre, *to lead.*
Amāri, *to be loved.*
Cædi, *to be cut.*
Docēri, *to be taught.*
Legi, *to be read.*

Scīre, *to know.*
Dāri, *to be given.*
Timēre, *to fear.*
Munire, *to fortify.*
Punīri, *to be punished.*
Ostendĕre, *to show.*

Form the first, second, and third roots from the following infinitives : —

Amāre.
Aestimāre.
Cantāre.
Terrēre.

Monēre.
Carpĕre.
Acuĕre.
Statuĕre.

Audire.
Munire.
Mœrēre.
Scīre.

VIII.

The auxiliary verb sum.

Latin to be translated into English.

Sum.
Sim.
Sunt.
Sint.
Eras.
Eris.
Sūmus.
Simus.
Erant.
Erunt.
Fui.
Erāmus.
Erimus.
Es.
Sis.
Fuisti.
Fuĕrant.
Fuĕrunt.

Fuĕrint.
Fuïmus.
Essem.
Fuissem.
Essent.
Fuissent.
Fuistis.
Fuēre.
Erātis.
Erītis.
Esse.
Esto.
Estōte.
Sunto.
Fuisse.
Futūrus.
Futūrus esse.

Fuĕro.
Fuĕrim.
Futūrus fore.
Fuerāmus.
Fuerïmus.
Fuit.
Sit.
Est.
Erat.
Erit.
Fuissētis.
Essētis.
Estis.
Sitis.
Fuerātis.
Fuerītis.
Este.

English to be translated into Latin.

I was.	I might be.
Thou art.	They might have been.
He will be.	He would have been.
They are.	Thou mayst be.
Ye have been.	You may have been.
We were.	We should have been.
I will be.	He could have been.
He may be.	They might have been.
He had been.	Let him be.
Thou wilt be.	Let them be.
He will have been.	To have been.

IX.

REGULAR VERBS.

First Conjugation, Active Voice.

Rogo, *to ask.*

Rogo.	Rogant.	Rogābant.
Rogāre.	Rogent.	Rogābunt.
Rogāvi.	Rogārent.	Rogem.
Rogātum.	Rogavistis.	Rogārem.
Rogāmus.	Rogavissētis.	Rogāte.
Rogēmus.	Rogaverātis.	Rogavīmus.
Rogābas.	Rogaverĭtis.	Rogavissēmus.
Rogābis.	Rogavissent.	Rogavisse.
Rogāvit.	Rogas.	Rogarētis.
Rogavērunt.	Roges.	Rogētis.
Rogavĕrint.	Roga.	Rogatūrus.
Rogāret.	Roganto.	Rogans.
Rogavisset.	Rogāres.	

We ask.	We asked.
I was asking.	He was asking.
I am asking.	You have asked.
He will ask.	Dost thou ask ?
They asked.	They had asked.
We had asked.	Thou wilt have asked.

You will have asked.	He may have asked.
I do ask.	He is asking.
Thou mayst ask.	Let them ask.
He may have asked.	To have asked.
You might ask.	Asking.
They should have asked.	About to ask.

NOTE.—*Do* is a sign of the present tense, *did* of the perfect indefinite; but when it denotes continued or customary action, of the imperfect. These auxiliaries are used especially in interrogations.

A sentence may be changed from the declarative to the interrogative form, by prefixing *an* or *num*, or by annexing the enclitic *ne* to the first word in the clause: as, *amas*, thou lovest; *an amas? num amas?* or *amasne?* dost thou love?

X.

First Conjugation, Passive Voice.

Rogor.	Rogāti simus.	Rogati erīmus
Roger.	Rogātur.	Rogabantur.
Rogābar.	Rogētur.	Rogamĭni.
Rogābor.	Rogarētur.	Rogemĭni.
Rogātus est.	Rogātus erat.	Rogātus eras.
Rogātus sit.	Rogātus esset.	Rogātus eris.
Rogāti sumus.	Rogāti erāmus.	Rogāti estis.

Active and Passive Voices.

Rogāmus.	Rogamĭni.	Rogāti erĭtis.
Rogāmur.	Rogemĭni.	Rogavĕris.
Rogēmur.	Rogārent.	Rogāris.
Rogēmus.	Rogarentur.	Rogēris.
Rogabamĭni.	Rogavisset.	Rogantur.
Rogabimĭni.	Rogātus esset.	Rogantor.
Rogavistis.	Rogātus sis.	Rogans.
Rogāti sitis.	Rogavisti.	Rogātus.
Rogaremĭni.	Rogātus es.	Rogāre.
Rogarētis.	Rogābas.	Rogāri.
Rogāti erātis.	Rogabāris.	Rogandus.
Rogāti erĭtis.	Rogabĕris.	Rogātu.
Rogātis.	Rogāti erātis.	

He is asking.

He is asked.

They were asking.

They should have asked.

Thou mayst ask.

He may be asked.

We may have asked.

They were asked.

We had been asked.

You had asked.

They would have been asked.

I shall have asked.

Thou wilt have been asked.

To be asked.

I should have asked.

Thou mightest be asked.

You might have been asked.

Let him be asked.

Being asked.

To have been asked.

What is the first root of *rogo?* — the second? — the third? Write out the parts of the verb *rogo*, in the active voice, formed from the first root; — from the second; — from the third; — the parts of the passive voice formed from the first root; — from the third.

XI.

Second Conjugation.

Habeo, *to have;* Jubeo, *to order;* (second and third roots irregular, *juss.*)

Habeo.	Habeas.	Habēbant.
Habēre.	Habēres.	Habēbunt.
Habui.	Habēmus.	Habuisses.
Habĭtum.	Habeāmus.	Habuisti.
Habēbat.	Habuistis.	Habuēre.
Habēbit.	Habuissētis.	Habēte.
Habuit.	Habuērunt.	Habens.
Habuĕras.	Habuĕrant.	Habitūrus esse.
Habuĕris.	Habuisset.	Habuisse.
Habes.	Habērent.	

Jubeo.	Jubeor.	Jubēris.
Jubēre.	Jubear.	Jubeāris.
Jussi.	Jubebāris.	Juberēris.
Jussum.	Jubebĕris.	Jussus est.

Jussi sint.	Jubebuntur.	Jussus fuĕro.
Jussi fuĕrant.	Jussus erat.	Jussus fuĕrim.
Jussus esset.	Jussus erit.	Jussi essent.
Jussi fuĕrunt.	Jussi essētis.	Jubebamĭni.
Jussi fuĕrint.	Jussi estis.	Juberētur.
Jubentur.	Jussi sitis.	Jubēre,(*passive*)
Jubeantur.	Jubemĭni.	Jussus.
Jubebantur.	Jubeamĭni.	Jussum iri.
Jussit.	Jussus erat.	Jubēbat.
Jussus sum.	Jubēbant.	Jubes.
Jussēre.	Jubebantur.	Jubeantur.
Jussi sunt.	Jubēbunt.	Jube.
Jussĕrint.	Jubebuntur.	Jubentor.
Jussi sint.	Jubebĭtur.	Jussus esse.
Jussĕrant.		

They have.	You might have.
We had.	They might have had.
Thou hadst.	I may have.
Thou hast.	Thou mayst have had
I have had.	Hast thou ?
Thou hadst had.	Will they have ?
He will have.	Didst thou have ?
We shall have had.	They did have.
I order.	You might be ordered.
Thou art ordered.	They might have been
He was ordered.	ordered.
We had been ordered.	To be ordered.
You will be ordered.	Having been ordered.
They will be ordered.	To have been ordered.
You will have been ordered.	Let him be ordered.
I may be ordered.	Dost thou order ?
He may have been ordered.	Did ye order ?
We might order.	

What is the first root of *habeo*? — the second? — the third? Write out the parts of the verb *habeo*, in the active voice, formed from the first root; — from the second;—from the third;—the parts of the passive voice formed from the first root;—from the third.

XII.

Third Conjugation.

Lego, *to read*, Fugio, *to flee*, (third root *fugit;*) Mitto, *to send.*

Lego.	Legāmus.	Legētis.
Legĕre.	Legisti.	Legātis.
Legi.	Legisses.	Legistis.
Lectum.	Legĕrent.	Legĕro.
Legunt.	Legērunt.	Legĕrim.
Legent.	Legĕrant.	Legisset.
Legant.	Legĕrint.	Legit.
Legĭmus.	Legēbas.	Leget.
Legēmus.	Legĭtis.	Legat.

Fugio.	Fugerātis.	Fugĕres.
Fugĕre.	Fugerĭtis.	Fugĕras.
Fugi.	Fugerētis.	Fugĕris.
Fugĭtum.	Fugiātis.	Fugissēmus.
Fugis.	Fugiētis.	Fugĕrat.
Fugisti.	Fugĭtis.	Fugĕrit.
Fugies.	Fugiunt.	Fugĕret.
Fugias.	Fugient.	Fugisse.
Fugistis.	Fugiant.	Fugiens.

Mitto.	Mittātur.	Missi erunt.
Mittĕre.	Mittebātur.	Missus est.
Misi.	Mitterētur.	Missi sunt.
Missum.	Missi erant.	Mittens.
Mittor.	Missi essent.	Missus.
Mittar.	Mittuntur.	Mitti.
Missus sum.	Mittentur.	Mittĭtor.
Missus sim.	Mittantur.	Misisse.
Mittĭtur.	Mittebantur.	Missum iri.
Mittētur.	Mitterentur.	

Thou readest.
He is reading.
We were reading.
You have read.
They will read.
I had read.

Thou wilt have read.
He may read.
We may have read.
You might read.
They would have read.
Dost thou read ?

He flees.
They are fleeing.
I was fleeing.
He fled.
We had fled.

Thou wilt flee.
They will have fled.
We may flee.
You may have fled.
They might have fled.

They are sent.
We were sent.
You will be sent.
I had been sent.
Thou mayst be sent.
He may send.

We shall be sent.
You will have sent.
They will have been sent.
Being sent.
Having been sent.
To have been sent.

What is the first root of *lego ?* — the second ? — the third ? Write out the parts of the verb *lego*, in the active voice, formed from the first root ; — from the second ; — from the third ; — the parts of the passive voice, formed from the first root ; — from the third. In like manner give the roots of *fugio* and *mitto*, and write out the parts formed from the different roots.

XIII.

Fourth Conjugation.

Venio, *to come,* (second root *ven ;* third root *vent ;*)
Punio, *to punish.*

Venio.
Venire.
Veni.
Ventum.
Venit.

Venïet.
Venïat.
Veniebātis.
Venisti.
Venerātis.

Venerïtis.
Venirētis.
Venissent.
Veniunt.
Venient.

Veniant.
Veniebat.
Venĕrat.
Venĕrit.
Venistis.

Venirētis.
Venērunt.
Venĕrant.
Venĕrint.
Venīrent.

Veniĕbant.
Venisse.
Veniens.
Venturus.

Punio.
Punīre.
Punīvi.
Punītum.
Punītis.
Puniris.
Puniēris.
Puniāris.
Punimĭni.
Puniebamĭni.

Puniemĭni.
Puniamĭni.
Punītus est.
Punītus eras.
Punīti sint.
Punītus esset.
Puniremĭni.
Puniuntur.
Punientur.
Puniantur.

Punīti sunt.
Punītus erit.
Punītus erat.
Puniri.
Puniendus.
Punītus.
Punītus esse.
Punītor.
Punītur.

We come.
They were coming.
Thou hast come.
He came.
We had come.
You will have come.
They might have come.

I may have come.
Thou mayst come.
He might come.
Coming.
To have come.
About to come.
He did come.

He is punished.
They were punished.
You will be punished.
I will punish.
Thou wilt be punished.
He should be punished.
Was he punished?
We may be punished.

You would be punished.
They should have been
  punished.
Let him be punished.
To have been punished.
Being punished.
Let them be punished.

XIV.

The four Conjugations of Regular Verbs.

Voco, *to call;* Doceo, *to teach;* Dico, *to say;* Dormĭo, *to sleep.*

Voco.	Vocăbat.	Vocavissent.
Vocāre.	Vocābit.	Vocāmus.
Vocāvi.	Vocavĕrit.	Vocēmus.
Vocātum.	Vocavisset.	Vocarēmus.
Vocābam.	Vocabāmus.	Voca.
Vocābo.	Vocabĭmus.	Vocavisse.
Vocavĕras.	Vocavisti.	Vocans.
Vocavĕris.	Vocavĕrunt.	Vocatūrus.
Vocat.	Vocavĕrant.	Vocatūrus esse.
Vocet.	Vocavĕrint.	Vocanto.
Vocāret.	Vocārent.	

Doceo.	Doceant.	Docnĕris.
Docēre.	Docērent.	Docuisset.
Docui.	Docuĕrunt.	Doce.
Doctum.	Docuĕrant.	Docuisse.
Docet.	Docuĕrint.	Docens.
Doceat.	Doces.	Doctūrus.
Docuit.	Doceas.	Docento.
Docēbant.	Docēres.	Docturus esse.
Docent.	Docuĕras.	

Dico.	Dicerēmus.	Dicunt.
Dicĕre.	Dicĭmus.	Dicent.
Dixi.	Diximus.	Dicant.
Dictum	Dicēmus.	Dicĕret.
Dicit.	Dicāmus.	Dixerĭtis.
Dicet.	Dicĕrent.	Dixissent.
Dicat.	Dicēbant.	Dixisse.
Dixit.	Dicĕ isset.	Dicens.
Dicebātis.	Dixĕrit.	Dicĭte.
Dixerātis.	Dixĕrat.	Dictūrus.

Dormio.

Dormīre.

Dormīvi.

Dormītum.

Dormiunt.

Dormient.

Dormiant.

Dormiēbat.

Dormiêrunt.

Dormiêrant.

Dormiêrint.

Dormiĕbant.

Dormīrent.

Dormiêre.

Thou callest.

He was calling.

They will call.

We had called.

You will have called.

He may call.

They might have called.

We called.

Did you call?

He will call.

He teaches.

They were teaching.

We taught.

Were they teaching?

He will teach.

You might teach.

We might have been taught.

I was teaching.

He taught.

They have taught.

I say.

Do you say?

He was saying.

They said.

We have said.

You had said.

They may say.

I might have said.

Thou mayst have said.

He might say.

Let them say.

Saying.

Thou art sleeping.

He was sleeping.

We will sleep.

You slept.

They had slept.

I may sleep.

Thou couldst have slept.

He may have slept.

We might sleep.

Let him sleep.

What is the first root of *voco?* — the second? — the third? Write out the parts of the verb *voco*, in the active voice, formed from the first root; — from the second; — from the third; — the parts of the passive voice, formed from the first root; — from the third.

In like manner give the roots of *doceo*, *dico*, and *dormio*, and write out the parts formed from the different roots.

XV.

The Four Conjugations.

Accūso, *to accuse;* Video, *to see,* (second and third roots irregular, *vide, vis*); Duco, *to lead;* Erudio, *to instruct.*

Accūso.	Accusēris.	Accusabĭtur.
Accusāre.	Accusarēris.	Accusāvit.
Accusāvi.	Accusātur.	Accusātus sit.
Accusātum.	Accusētur.	Accusāti sunt.
Accūsor.	Accusarētur.	Accusāret.
Accūser.	Acousātus est.	Accusarētur.
Accusabāris.	Accusāti erunt.	Acousāti essent.
Accusabĕris.	Accusāti erant.	Accusātus.
Accusāris.	Accusabātur.	Accusandus.
Video.	Visus 'est.	Vidēris.
Vidĕre.	Visi erant.	Videāris.
Vidi.	Vĭsi erunt.	Viderēris.
Visum.	Videātur.	Videbamĭni.
Videor.	Vidētur.	Videbimĭni.
Videar.	Viderentur.	Visus ero.
Videbātur.	Visus sit.	Visĭ sint.
Videbĭtur.	Visi essent.	Videremĭni.
Vidit.		
Duco.	Ducti erunt.	Ducemĭni.
Ducĕre.	Ducebantur.	Ducamĭni.
Duxi.	Ducerentur.	Duceremĭni.
Ductum.	Ducĭtur.	Ducti erant.
Ducor.	Ducētur.	Ducti essent.
Ducĕris.	Ducātur.	Ductus fuĕrat.
Ducēris.	Ductus erat.	Ductus fuĕrit.
Ducāris.	Ducti sunt.	Ducĭtor.
Ducerēris.	Ducti sint.	Ducuntor.
Duxit.	Ductus esset.	Ductus.
Ductus est.	Ductus erit.	Ductus esse.
Ducti erant.	Ducimĭni.	

Erudio.　　　　　　Erudītus eris.　　　　Erudiāris.
Erudīre.　　　　　　Erudiebāris.　　　　　Erudirēris
Erudīvi.　　　　　　Erudītur.　　　　　　Erudītus esses.
Erudītum.　　　　　Erudiētur.　　　　　　Erudimīni.
Erudior.　　　　　　Erudiātur.　　　　　　Erudiemīni.
Erudiar.　　　　　　Erudītus es.　　　　　Erudiamīni.
Erudiebantur.　　　 Erudīti sumus.　　　　Erudīri.
Erudītus est.　　　　Erudīti sitis.　　　　Erudītum iri.
Erudīti sint.　　　　Erudīris.　　　　　　 Erudītus.
Erudīti estis.　　　　Erudiēris.

He is accused.
Thou wast accused.
We were accused.
You will be accused.
They may be accused.
I might accuse.
Thou mayst be accused.

He might be accused.
We may have been accused.
They might have been accused.
Let him be accused.
Having been accused.

They are seen.
I was seen.
Thou hast been seen.
He had been seen.
We shall be seen.
You will have seen.
They will have been seen.
I might be seen.

Thou mayst be seen.
He may have been seen.
We might have been seen.
Let them be seen.
Being seen.
To have been seen.

He is led.
Thou wast led.
We have been led.
You will be led.
They had been led.

I may be led.
They might have been led.
Having been led.

I am instructed.
Thou hast been instructed.
He will have been instructed.
We might be instructed.

You may have been instructed.
They were instructed.
Being instructed.
About to be instructed.

What is the first root of *accūso?* — the second? — the third?

Write out the parts of the verb *accūso*, in the active voice, formed from the first root; — from the second; — from the third; — the parts of the passive voice, formed from the first root; — from the third.

In like manner give the roots of *video, duco,* and *erudio,* and write out the parts formed from the different roots.

XVI.

Verbal Roots.

The following table contains the first roots of certain regular verbs, from which the student is to form their present and perfect indicative and their former supine. Those which belong to the second conjugation add *ui* and *ĭtum*. The figure prefixed denotes the conjugation.

2. Hab-	2. Noc-	2. Plac-	1. Nomĭn-
1. Accus-	1. Regn-	1. Nunti-	2. Mer-
4. Aud-	4. Pun-	3. Duc-	3. Indu-
3. Acu-	4. Erud-	4. Sc-	4. Nutr-
2. Tac-	2. Terr-	3. Tribu-	1. Prob-
1. Invĭt-	1. Impĕr-	3. Metu-	2. Mon-
4. Mun-	3. Carp-	3. Argu-	3. Carp-
3. Ru-	4. Moll-	4. Fin-	4. Vest-
1. Loc-			

What tenses of the indicative mood, active and passive voices, are formed from the first root? — of the subjunctive mood in both voices?

What mood is wholly formed from the first root in both voices? What part of the infinitive in both voices is formed from the first root? What active participle? What passive participle? What other part of the active voice comes from the first root?

In which voice is the second root used? What

parts of the active voice are formed from the second root?

What parts of the active voice are formed from the third root? What parts of the passive voice are formed from the third root?

XVII.

Verbal Terminations.

NOTE. — The student should be exercised on the terminations of verbs, in each conjugation, voice, mood, tense, person, and number, till he can give the required termination of any part.

Give the verbal terminations, first in the active voice and then in the passive: —

Of the indicative mood, present tense, in the first conjugation; — in the second; — in the third; — in the fourth.

Of the indicative mood, imperfect tense, in the first conjugation; — in the second; — in the third; — in the fourth.

Of the indicative mood, future tense, in the first conjugation; — in the second; — in the third; — in the fourth.

Of the subjunctive mood, present tense, in the first conjugation; — in the second; — in the third; — in the fourth.

Of the subjunctive mood, imperfect tense, in the first conjugation; — in the second; — in the third; — in the fourth.

Of the imperative mood, in the first conjugation; — in the second; — in the third; — in the fourth.

Of the infinitive mood, present tense, in the first conjugation; — in the second; — in the third; — in the fourth.

Give the verbal terminations: —

Of the present active participle, in the first conjugation; — in the second; — in the third; — in the fourth.

Of the future passive participle, in the first conjugation; — in the second; — in the third; — in the fourth.

Of the gerund in the first conjugation; — in the second; — in the third; — in the fourth.

Give the terminations of the active voice, indicative mood, perfect tense; — pluperfect tense; — future perfect tense.

Of the subjunctive mood, perfect tense; — pluperfect tense.

Of the infinitive perfect.

Give the verbal terminations of the passive voice, indicative mood, perfect tense.

Of the passive voice, indicative mood, pluperfect tense.

Of the passive voice, indicative mood, future perfect tense.

Of the passive voice, subjunctive mood, perfect tense.

Of the passive voice, subjunctive mood, pluperfect tense.

Of the passive voice, infinitive mood, perfect tense.

Of the perfect passive participle; — of the infinitive future active; — of the future active participle; — of the future infinitive passive; — of the former and latter supines.

XVIII.

Deponent, Impersonal, and Neuter Passive Verbs.

Miror, *to admire;* polliceor, *to promise;* utor, *to use;* sequor, *to follow;* audeo, *to dare;* delectat, *it delights;* decet, *it becomes;* contingit, *it happens;* pugnatur, *it is fought.*

Miror.	Miratus est.	Mirentur.
Mirarisne?	Mirati sunt.	Mirantur.
Miratur.	Mirabitur.	Miratus sit.
Mirabantur.	Mirabatur.	Mirati essent.

13*

Mirarentur.

Mirāri.

Mirans.

Mirandus.

Polliceor.

Pollicētur.

Utor.

Utītur.

Utebantur.

Usus est.

Utētur.

Utātur.

Sequor.

Secūtus est.

Sequebātur.

Sequĭtur.

Sequuntur.

Audeo.

Audet.

Audebāmus.

Ausus est.

Delectat.

Delectābit.

Delectābat.

Decet.

Decuit.

Decēbit.

Contingit.

Continget.

Contingat.

Contigisset.

Contingēbat.

Contingĕret.

Pollicebantur.

Pollicĭtus est.

Pollicĭtus sit.

Pollicerentur.

Polliceantur.

Uterentur.

Usus sit.

Usi essent.

Usi sunt.

Utuntur.

Utentur.

Sequentur.

Sequantur.

Sequātur.

Secūti sunt.

Sequerētur.

Audēbit.

Audeat.

Audērem.

Delectet.

Delectāret.

Delectāvit.

Decēbat.

Deceat.

Decuĕrit.

Pugnātur.

Pugnētur.

Pugnabātur.

Pugnātum est.

Pugnātum erat.

Pollicēbor.

Pollicebātur.

Pollicĭtus erit.

Pollicĭtus erat.

Pollicĭti erĭmus.

Usus sum.

Utens.

Uti.

Usus.

Usūrus.

Usus ero.

Secūtus erat.

Secūti sumus.

Secūtus esset.

Sequens.

Ausus sit.

Ausi essēmus.

Audesne?

Delectavisset.

Delectāre.

Decuisse.

Decuĕrat.

Pugnabĭtur.

Pugnarētur.

Pugnātum esse.

Pugnātum iri.

Pugnāri.

We admire.
He was admiring.
They admired.
Do you admire?
You promised.
We had promised.
They will promise.
He used.
They were using.
You might use.

We might have used.
I will use.
They follow.
We followed.
You were following.
He will follow.
Thou mayst follow.
They might have followed.

He dares.
We were daring.
They dared.
I had dared.
Thou wilt dare.
He will have dared.

We may dare.
You may have dared.
They might dare.
He might have dared.
Darest thou?
He did dare.

It delights.
It delighted.
It will delight.
It may delight.
It may have delighted.
It happened.
It may happen.

It might have happened.
It becomes.
It might become.
It would have become.
It was fought.
It may be fought.
It had been fought.

XIX.

First Declension. — Terminations and Roots.

What are the terminations of the several cases of Latin nouns of the first declension, in the singular number? — in the plural?

What is the termination of the nominative singular? — of the nominative plural? — of the genitive singular? — of the genitive plural? — of the dative singular? — of the dative plural? — of the accusative singular? — of the accusative plural? — of the vocative singular? — of the vocative plural? — of the ablative singular? — of the ablative plural?

What cases in the singular end in *a?* — in *æ?*
What case in *am?* What cases in the plural end in
æ? — in *is?* What cases in *ārum?* — in *as?* What
case ends in *m?* — in *s?*

What is the root of *musa? — aula? — cura? —
galea? — machina? — penna? — sagitta?*

XX.

First Declension. — Syntax, Rules 33, 34.

Note. — The pupil will here begin to make use of the Vocabulary; and before proceeding further with the Exercises, he should learn what is a *proposition*, its *subject* and *predicate*. The Rules of Syntax referred to should be committed to memory, and applied in this and the following Exercises.

Musa canit.	Faveat fortūna.	Filia amat.
Musæ canunt.	Corōna data est.	Filiæ amabuntur.
Insülæ defecĕrant.	Corōnæ datæ sunt.	Porta pandītur.
Aquíla volābat.	Stellæ fulgēbant.	Portæ panduntur.
Aquílæ volūbunt.	Insüla defēcit.	Roma condīta
Litĕra missa est.	Luna emicuit.	erat.
Fama fugit.	Hora venĕrat.	Troja eversa fuit.
Stella fulget.	Copiæ devictæ	Æneas aufūgit.
Litĕræ missæ sunt.	erant.	

Note. — The English exercises are to be translated into Latin. They are generally *literal* translations, rather than the best English. The corresponding Latin words, a little varied, will be found in the preceding Latin exercises, so that an English vocabulary is not necessary.

The muses sing.	The moon shines forth.
The stars shine.	The hour will come.
The island revolted.	Daughters are loved.
An eagle was flying.	The gates are opened.
Letters are sent.	Rome was founded.
Crowns had been given.	The hour is coming.

XXI.

Second Declension. — *Terminations and Roots.*

What are the terminations of masculine Latin nouns of the second declension in the nominative singular? What is the termination of neuter Latin nouns of the second declension in the nominative singular? Give the terminations in the singular number of the several cases of masculines of the second declension in *us* ; — of nouns of the second declension in *er* ; — of all masculines of this declension in the plural. Give the terminations of neuters of the second declension in the several cases of the singular; — of the plural. What cases of neuters of the second declension have the same terminations as masculines? What cases of neuters of the second declension have different terminations from those of masculines? In what class of nouns of the second declension is the vocative singular unlike the nominative? What cases of the second declension always end in *o?* — in *s?*

What three cases of neuters end alike in the singular? — in the plural?

How in the second declension do these cases end in the singular? — in the plural?

What is the root of *anĭmus?* — *clipeus?* — *corvus?* — *gladius?* — *numĕrus?* — *puer?* — *socer?* — *aper?* — *faber?* — *magister?* — *antrum?* — *bellum?* — *negotium?*

XXII.

Second Declension. — *Rules* 33, 34.

Legātus venit.	Puer ludit.
Legāti veniunt.	Puĕri ludent.
Nuncius missus est.	Amīcus adjuvābit.
Nuncii mittuntur.	Amīci adjŭvent.
Equus currit.	Fata vocant.
Equi currēbant.	Oppĭdum est munītum.

Vir festīnat.
Festinavitne vir?
Viri festinābant.
Magister erŭdit.
Magistri erudiēbant.

Oppĭda erant munīta.
Vicus incendĭtur.
Vici incensi sunt.
Locus munītur.
Loca munīta sunt.

Embassadors were sent.
Messengers came.
Horses were running.
The men hasten.
Teachers can instruct.
Boys play.

Friends assisted.
The town is fortified.
The villages were burned.
We came.
He was sent.
Are the boys playing.

XXIII.

First and Second Declensions. — Syntax, Rule 54.

Legātus littĕras tradĭdit.
Ariovistus legātos misit.
Nuncius captīvos revŏcat.
Epistŏlam accēpi.[a]
Accepistine [a] epistŏlam?
Copiæ fugātæ sunt.
Legātus auxilium rogāvit.
Effŭgit [a] invidïam.

Bella geruntur.
Patriam vindicāvit.
Regnum adeptus est.
Agros divīsit.
Provincias vexābat.
Castella communīvit.
Copias traduxit.
Pericŭlum timuērunt.

The embassadors delivered the letters.
The messengers recalled the troops.
They escaped envy.
He feared danger.
They fortified the castle.

The embassadors sought aid.
War was carried on.
The troops had been put to flight.
The provinces are vexed.
The castles were fortified.

XXIV.

Third Declension. — Terminations and Roots.

What terminations of nouns of the third declension are masculine? — what are feminine? — what are neuter?

a Rule 33, Rem. 1.

What is the termination of the nominative, accusative, and vocative plural of masculines and feminines of the third declension? — of the genitive singular of all nouns of the third declension? — of the genitive plural? — of the dative singular? — of the dative plural? — of the ablative singular? — of the ablative plural? — of the nominative, accusative, and vocative plural of neuter nouns of the third declension?

What two cases of all nouns of the third declension and singular number are alike? What three cases of all neuter nouns are alike in the singular? What three cases of all nouns of the third declension are alike in the plural? What two other cases are alike in the plural? What is the termination of these two cases? What case in the singular number of masculines and feminines of the third declension ends in *m?* — in *i?* — in *e* or *i?* Where, in the plural of masculines and feminines of the third declension, is the termination *es* found? How do the same cases end in neuters? In what cases of the plural of neuters of the third declension is *s* final found? In what case of the plural of masculines and feminines is final *s* not found?

What is the root of *poëma?* — *stemma?* — *ancile?* — *aquilo?* — *regio?* — *formido?* — *ferrugo?* — *animal?* — *Titan?* — *carcer?* — *agmen?* — *tibicen?* — *frater?* — *piëtas?* — *rupes?* — *miles?* — *seges?* — *quies?* — *classis?* — *flos?* — *nepos?* — *opus?* — *trabs?* — *ars?* — *vox?* — *lex?* — *apex?*

XXV.

Third Declension. — *Rules* 33, 34, 54.

Tempus venit.
Opinio manēbat.
Pontem fecit.
Custōdes relīquit.
Hostis vicit

Potestatem retinuĕrat.
Consŭles hostes vicērunt
Pacem petēbant.
Cadunt adolescentes.
Cæsar fœdus violābat.

Classem cepit.
Urbem clausit.
Lex data erat.
Navem conscendit.
Urbes delēvit.
Pacem conciliāvit consul.
Consul nomĭna conscrībit.
Clamor audītus est.
Naves mersæ sunt.
Milĭtes victi erant.
Urbs est spoliāta.
Pacem fecit.
Classem comparāvit.

Milĭtes urbem custodiē-
    bant.
Arbŏres stratæ sunt.
Classis est devicta.
Tempestas orta est.
Cadit adolescens.
Milĭtes exaudient clamō-
    rem.
Hortātus est custōdes.
Classis capta est.
Urbes spoliātæ erant.
Hostem conspexit.
Plebs urbem relīquit.

They left a guard.
The soldiers heard a clamor.
The enemy were conquered.
The soldiers plundered the cities.
The consul made peace.

A fleet was prepared.
Cities were destroyed.
Laws were given.
They made a bridge.
He enrolled the names.

XXVI.

First, Second & Third Declensions.—Rules 33, 34, 54.

Fossam complent.
Murum subruunt.
Portas succēdunt.
Hostes terga vertunt.
Concilium dimittit.
Fines propagāvit.
Anĭmam efflāvit.
Prodĭtōres percŭlit.
Conjuratiōnem fecērunt.
Tela conjiciēbant.
Copias deduxērunt.

Castra movent.
Homĭnes misit.
Legatiōnem suscēpit.
Filiam misit.
Honōres petēbat.
Pontem rescindit.
Insŭlam devīcit.
Luxuria reprimerētur.
Præsidium datur.
Conjuratio facta est
Urbs claudĭtur.

They filled the ditches.
The wall was undermined.

The islands were con-
quered.

The troops were led forth.
They seek honor.
Honors were sought.
They broke down the bridges.

The council had been dismissed.
The boundaries were extended.
The bridges were broken down.

XXVII.

Fourth and Fifth Declensions. — Terminations and Roots.

What is the termination of the nominative and vocative singular of masculines and feminines of the fourth declension? — of the nominative, accusative and vocative plural? — of the dative singular? — of the dative plural? — of the ablative singular? — of the ablative plural? — of the genitive singular of all nouns of the fourth declension? — of the genitive plural? — of the nominative singular of neuter nouns of the fourth declension? — of their nominative, accusative, and vocative plural? What cases of neuter nouns of the fourth declension are like the nominative singular?

What is the root of *cantus?* — *currus?* — *exercitus?* — *veru?*

What are the terminations of the several cases of nouns of the fifth declension in the singular? — in the plural? — of the nominative and vocative singular? — of the nominative, accusative and vocative plural? — of the genitive singular? — of the genitive plural? — of the dative singular? — of the dative plural? — of the ablative singular? — of the ablative plural?

What is the root of *fides?* — *spes?* — *facies?*

XXVIII.

Fourth and Fifth Declensions. — Rules 33, 34, 54.

Cursum direxit.
Exercitus devictus est.
Dies venit.

Exercitum reduxit.
Aciem instruit.
Impětus tardātus est.

Manum comparāvit.
Res (acc. pl.) constituit.
Impĕtum fecit.
Diem constituērunt.

Fidem dant.
Equitātum præmittit.
Aciem instruēbat.

Promiscuous Examples on the Declensions.

Fortūna conversa est.
Agros populabantur.
Hostes fūgērunt.
Fremĭtus oriebātur.
Acies cernĭtur.
Amicitia confirmāta est.

Præsidia disponit.
Rex leges abrogāvit.
Milĭtes impĕtum sustin-
uērunt.
Res cecidĕrat.

The day had come.
An armed force was pre-
pared.
An attack was made.
A day was appointed.
The army was led back.

The cavalry was sent for-
ward.
The attack was sustained.
The army was drawn up
in battle array.

XXIX.

The Declensions. — Rule 29.

Vim hostium sustinuērunt.
Scipio fudit Annibālis copias.
Effūgit civium invidiam.
Copias Thracum fugāvit.
Rex anĭmi magnitudĭnem admirātus est.
Honōris corōna data est.
Copiæ Atheniensium devictæ sunt.
Popŭli amicitiam appetīvit.
Hortātus est pontis custōdes.
Helvetii Cæsăris adventum exspectābant.
Spes victoriæ milĭtes delectat.
Senātûs beneficia commemorāvit.

Promiscuous Examples.

(Applying the Rules previously introduced.)

Princĭpes fidem violābant.
Ariovistus aciem instruxit.
Exercĭtus hostium victus est.
Legāti missi sunt.
Cæsar misit nuncios.
Regis provincias vexābat.
Veniam dedit.
Græcia liberāta est.
Conjuratiōnem nobilitātis fecit.
Urbem delēvit.
Castra hostium cepit.
Deus mundum regit.

The camps of the enemy were taken.
They destroyed the cities of the province.
He escaped the envy of the king.
The friendship of the people was earnestly desired.
The soldiers conquered the army of the enemy.
A conspiracy of the nobility was formed.
The enemy's troops were put to flight.
He vexed the king's provinces.
They waited for (expected) the approach of the soldiers.
Crowns of honor had been given.

XXX.

The Declensions.—Rule 45.

Agros civĭbus divīsit.
Insidias hostĭbus fecērunt.
Tempus litĕris Persārum dedit.
Memoriæ prodĭdit.
Thrasybūlo honōris corōna data est.
Locum castris delĭgit.
Cæsāri nunciātum est.
Civitatĭbus libertātem reddĭdit.

Promiscuous Examples.

Semirămis Babylōnem condĭdit.
Divitiăcus copias Æduōrum ducēbat.
Laus virtūti debētur.
Alexander Darium fugāvit.
Scipio fudit Hannibălis copias.
Honorĭbus opĕram dedit.
Otium insūlæ conciliāvit.
Lumĭna oculōrum amīsit.
Ventus agit nubes.
Legātis respondit.
Fines imperii propagāvit.
Diem consilio constitnērunt.
Milĭtes hostium phalangem perfregērunt.
Prædam militĭbus donat.

He divided the booty among (to) the soldiers.
He gave the fields to the citizens.
They selected a place for the camps.
He laid an ambush for the embassador.
He appointed a time for a council.
He procured peace to the empire.
They gave (to) Thrasybulus a crown of honor.
It had been announced to Cæsar.
Praise was due to the soldiers.

XXXI.

The Declensions. — Rule 68.

Armis dimicandum est.
Fugâ pericŭlum evitāvit.
Interiit fame.
Parītur pax bello.
Dolo castra hostium cepit.
Adventu Cæsăris hostes terrentur.
Telis hostium interfectus est.
Darīus virtūte regnum est adeptus.

Justitiæ famâ floruit.
Gladiis impĕtum fecērunt.
Matris scelĕre amīsit uxōrem.
Ferro interemptus est.

Promiscuous Examples.

Utĭcam patriæ restituit.
Ferrum rubīgo consūmit.
Invidiâ virtūtis laudem òbterĕbant.
Belli finem fecērunt.
Filio regnum tradĭdit.
Loca castellis communīvit.
Causam capĭtis dixit.
Rem arbitrio permisērunt Hannibălis.
Æquitāte res constituit.
Scipio Carthagĭnem delevit.
Cæsar prædam sociis dabăt.
Urbem operĭbus clausit.
Princĭpes fidem violābant.
Ariovistus aciem instruxit.
Exercĭtus hostium victus est.

The king was killed with the sword of a soldier.
They avoided danger by flight.
Peace can be procured by the sword.
He obtained the kingdom by bravery.
The camps of the enemy were taken by stratagem.
The place was fortified with castles.

XXXII.

The Declensions. — Promiscuous Examples.

Copiæ hostium silvas occupābant.
Legātus auxilium rogāvit.
Leges abrogātæ sunt.
Auxilium rogātum est.
Copiæ revocantur.

14*

Milītes revocabuntur.
Legáti mittuntur.
Hostes vincentur.
Castella munīta erant.
Præsidia disponebantur.
Milītes hortabātur.
Imperātor aciem instruxit.
Legātus exercītum ducēbat.
Nuncius sermōnem consūlis laudāvit.
Æduōrum oppīda occupābant.
Gloria virtūtem sequītur.
Milītes gloriam persequuntur.
Miles vulnerātus est.
Bella gesta fuĕrant.
Exercītus pulsus erat.
Res Cæsāri enunciāta erat.
Dies colloquio constitūtus est.
Hostes telis repulsi sunt.

They appointed a day for a conference.
The army of the enemy were occupying the woods.
The messenger announced the thing to Cæsar.
The army was occupying the towns of the Ædui.
The soldiers pursued the enemy.
The consul exhorted the soldiers.
Messengers followed the embassadors.
The commander was wounded with a spear.

XXXIII.

The Declensions. — Promiscuous Examples.

Res diligentiam requirēbat.
Dat signum prœlii.
Agros populabantur.
Hostium acies cernītur.
Milītes impĕtum hostium sustinuērunt.
Navium copiam pollicebantur.
Defensōres oppīdo deliguntur.

Milĭtum virtūte servantur.
Civitāti imperium provinciæ pollicētur.
Litĕras Cæsāri remittit.
Popŭli jussu bellum gessit.
Militĭbus signum dedit.
Gladiis pugnātum est.[a]
Principĭbus pecunias pollicētur.
Legiōni auxilium misit.
Morbo consumptus est.
Hostium acies cernebātur.
Civitāti renunciāvit.
Urbem incendio delēvit.
Montium altitudĭne tegebantur.
Arbŏrum tractu equitātus hostium impediebātur.
Miltiădi honor tribūtus est.
Popŭlus largitiōne magistratuum corruptus est.
Statuam Demetrio decrevērunt.
Insūlas bello persecūtus est.
Classem Miltiădi dedērunt.
Insŭlas vi expugnāvit.

The signal for (of) battle was given to the soldiers.
They see the army of the enemy (in battle array.)
The town is preserved by the bravery of the defend-
ers.
He promised (to) the people the government of the
province.
The cities of the province were destroyed with fire.
The enemy's cavalry were covered by the height of
the mountains.

XXXIV.

Adjectives. — Rules 1 *and* 35, *Rem.* (*with* 33, 34, 54.)

Bonus puer discit.
Boni puĕri discunt.
Puĕrum bonum amat.
Puĕros bonos amāmus.

---

a See Rules for translating Impersonal Verbs.

Pulchra puella delectat.
Puellam pulchram laudat.
Puellas pulchras laudant.
Bonum exemplum est utile.[a]
Bona exempla sunt utilia.[a]
Exemplum bonum æmŭlor.
Exempla bona æmulāmur.

Clarus vir laudātur.
Clari viri laudantur.
Virum clarum laudāmus.
Viros·claros laudabĭmus.
Urbs antīqua fuit.
Multæ urbes antīquæ delētæ sunt.
Urbem antīquam delēvit.
Urbes antīquas delevērunt.
Bellum dirum parātur.
Bella dira parabantur.
Bellum dirum parant.
Bella dira parābant.

Miles fortis pugnat.
Milītes fortes pugnābunt.
Omnis dux amat fortem milītem.
Omnes duces cupiunt fortes milītes.
Sapiens est felix.[a]
Sapientes sunt felīces.[a]
Equus velox currit.
Equi velōces currunt.
Equum velōcem incitābat.
Equos velōces incĭtant.
Bellum atrox gerĭtur.
Bella atrocia gerebantur.
Bellum atrox gerunt.
Bella atrocia gessērunt.

A good boy learns.
He loves good boys.
Beautiful girls please.

a Rule 35, Remark.

They praised the beautiful girl.
Good examples are useful.[a]
We should emulate a good example.
An illustrious man will be praised.
W.e will praise illustrious men.
There was an ancient city.
They have destroyed many ancient cities.
The brave soldiers were fighting.
Every general desires brave soldiers.
The wise are happy.[a]
He spurs on (his) swift horse.
The swift horses were running.
A fierce war was carried on.
They carry on fierce wars.

XXXV.

Adjectives Continued. — (*Applying the same Rules as in Exercise No.* 34.)

Anĭma immortālis est.
Frigĭda nox fuit.
Dulcis est libertas.
Vera virtus nobilĭtat.
Humāna consilia cadunt.
Litĕra scripta manet.
Ver erat æternum.
Voluptas nimia nocet
Nix alta jacet.
Æstas torrĭda venĕrat.

Magnam prudentiam habēbat.
Belgæ vicos multos habent.
Magnas res gessit.
Incŏlæ bella magna gerunt.
Nuncius velox venit.
Incŏlæ bella atrocia gerunt.

a Rule 35, Remark.

Equĭtes velōces festīnant.
Atrox prœlium pugnātum est.
Princĭpes poteutes convocāvit.
Alcibiădes fuit dives, laboriōsus, patiens, liberālis, blandus, affabĭlis.
Epaminondas fuit modestus, prudens, gravis.

Many are rich, laborious, patient.
Few are liberal, kind, affable, modest, prudent, great.
Swift messengers came.
A fierce battle had been fought.
They had many villages.
The inhabitants carried on dreadful wars.
A swift horseman hastened.

XXXVI.

Adjectives Continued. — (Applying the same Rules as in Exercise No. 34.)

Mors est certa.
Boni auctōres leguntur.
Magnam relīquit famam.
Equitātum omnem præmittit.
Effŭgit nova pericŭla.
Certos misit homĭnes.
Exercĭtum reduxit incolŭmem.
Totam insŭlam devīcit.
Multa bella administrāvit.
Nulla spes relicta est.
Mare tutum reddĭdit.
Magnas copias fugāvit.
Nonnullæ insŭlæ defecĕrant.
Princĭpes fortes prœlium atrox redintegrăbant.

Promiscuous Examples.

(Applying the Rules introduced in previous Exercises.)

Tutum iter fecērunt.

Magnam corpŏris dignitātem habuit.

Bona militĭbus dispertīvit.

Hannĭbal magnas res gessit secundâ fortūnâ.

Habēbat magnam prudentiam juris civīlis.

Otium toti insŭlæ conciliāvit.

Loca castellis idonea communīvit.

Pausanias magnam belli gloriam turpi morte maculā-
vit.

Omnia oppĭda restĭtuit patriæ.

Pari felicitāte cetēras insŭlas redēgit.

He sent forward the whole army.

They escaped great danger.

All the islands were subdued.

He fortified a suitable place with castles.

They put to flight all the forces.

He led back all the cavalry.

He obtained peace for the whole island.

He restored all the islands to the country.

XXXVII.

Numeral Adjectives.

Belgæ unam partem incŏlunt, Celtæ tertiam.

Duo legiōnes conscrĭbit.

Consul legiōnem decĭmam redūcit.

Decem prætōres creant.[a]

Tres exercĭtus comparāvit.

Ducentārum navium[b] classem cepit.

Mille equĭtes capti sunt.

Centum milītes cecidērunt.

Duodĕcim naves mersæ sunt.

Classem quingentārum navium[b] comparāvit.

a Rule 33, Rem. 1.   *b* Rule 29, Rem. 4.

Tres legāti missæ sunt.
Naves quinque misit.
Præmittit quatuor legiōnes.
Sex legiŏnes pugnavērunt.
Oppĭda viginti novem cepērunt.
Undĕcim naves amissæ sunt.

Promiscuous Examples

Timĭdi lepŏres fugiunt.
Velōces canes sequuntur.
Magna erant onĕra captivōrum.
Fessus viātor sedēbat.
Præda multa militĭbus divīsa est.
Omnes.copiæ revocabantur.
Defensōres oppĭdo idonei deliguntur.
Superbi homĭnes cadunt.
Humĭles casæ stabunt.
Magnis itinerĭbus pervēnit.
Æquitāte summâ res constituit.

They fortified two castles.
He enlisted three legions.
He sent forward seven ships.
A thousand soldiers fell.
A hundred horsemen were captured.
The consul led back eight legions.
He distributed much booty among (to) the soldiers.
The burdens of the captives were great.

XXXVIII.

Cases after Adjectives. — Rules 2 to 10.

Consilii plenus erat.
Prudens rei militāris erat.
Vivo carus amīcis.[a]
Omnĭbus ignōtus navem conscendit.

a Rule 1, Rem. 9.

Nemīni erat dubium.[a]
Nudus membra fuit.
Insŭla erat referta divitiis.
Nihil est virtūte formosius.
Pœnâ dignus ducebātur.
Fuit rei mīlitāris perītus.
Multum[b] superĕrat munitiōnis.
Civĭtas mille misit milĭtum.
Omni ætāti mors est commūnis.
Domo fuit contentus.
Helvetii relĭquos Gallos virtūte præcēdunt.
Omnes fortūnâ expertes sumus.
Leges adversas plebi abrogāvit.
Jure perītus fuit.
Propior montem suos[c] collŏcat.
Dives agris fuit.

Dilīgens erat imperii.
Pauci Themistŏcli pares arbitrantur.
Fortis manu erat.
Res multas memoriâ dignas gessĭt.
Veritātis dilīgens erat.
Hostium multa millia concīdit.
Multum[b] tempŏris perdĭdit.
Consilia patriæ inimīca capiēbat.
Milĭtum virtūte fretus conflixit.
Nulla vox est audīta popŭli Romāni majestāte
    indigna.
Habēbat equĭtum viginti millĭa.
Anxius est anĭmo.
Canis simĭlis lupo est.

Vetĕres Romāni erant laudis avĭdi.
Consimĭlis fugæ profectio videbātur.
Fronte lætus fuit.
Sidĕre pulchrior est.

---

a Rule 1, Rĕm. 3 and 4.
b Rule 1, Rem. 6, and Rules for translating partitive genitive.
c Supply milĭtes, Rule 1, Rem. 3.

Militĭbus fretus conflixit.
Ferax secŭlum bonis artĭbus erat.
Dux est delectus belli imperĭtus.
Quantum[a] hostes uno prœlio auctoritātis essent[b] con-
secūti, sentiēbat.
Crassus proxĭmus mare Oceănum hiemārat.[c]
Nemo Alcibiădi par fuit.
Fessus erat corpŏre.
Romāno popŭlo periculōsum[d] videbātur.
Cupĭdus rerum novārum fuit.

Promiscuous Examples.

Legis pœnam inflixit.
Pecuniæ talenta quinquginta civĭbus donat.
Angustos habēbant fines.
Frumentum omne combūrunt.
Oppĭda omnia incendunt.
Magnis itinerĭbus festīnant.
Nullĭus rei cupĭdus fuit.
Pauca[d] memoriâ digna evenēre.
Popŭlus acer, suspĭcax, mobĭlis, invĭdus potentiæ, Ti-
motheum revŏcat.
Locum fossâ mūnīvit.
Commūnis infĭmis, par principĭbus videbātur.
Ducenta pedĭtum millia misit.
Multum[a] frumenti præbet.
Fretus numĕro copiārum conflixit.
Dives agris fuit.
Laude dignus erat.

No one was equal to Themistocles.
He was skilled in war
The islands were full of riches.

\ Rule 1, Rem. 6, and Rules for translating, partitive genitive.
l Syntax, Rule 97, and Rules for translating the subjunctive, 2.
c See Remark under Conjugation, page 17.
d Rule 1, Rem. 4.

The Helvetii excelled the rest of the Gauls in
    bravery.

They were accounted worthy of punishment.

Relying on the bravery of the soldiers, he fought.

Thou art worthy of praise.

It seemed dangerous to the people.

They were fond of praise.

He is anxious in mind.

Much time was lost.

The state sent ten thousand footmen.

XXXIX.

Comparison of Adjectives.

Romāni ampliōres copias exspectābant.

Cæsar maxĭmas[a] copias comparāvit.

Hostes loca superiōra occupābant.

Hannĭbal bellicosissĭmas gentes subēgit.

Regio putabātur locupletissĭma.[b]

Mons altissĭmus impendēbat.

Ferociōrem reddĭdit civitātem.

Ornatissĭmum habēbat exercĭtum.

Regem certiōrem fecit.

Tres exercĭtus maxĭmos comparāvit.

Amicior omnium libertāti fuit.

Amicissĭmus erat Bruto.

Nemo fuit carior.[b]

Altĕra via longior[b] fuit, altĕra periculosior.[b]

Antonii inimīci erant potentissĭmi.

Themistŏcles peritissĭmos belli navālis fecit Athe-
    nienses.

Maxĭmas gentes subēgit.

Legātos nobilissĭmos mittunt.

Nemo fuit major.

a See Rules for translating, superlative degree.
b Rule 35, Rem.

Invitissimi sunt secūti.

Præcipuam habēbat laudem pulcherrimæ corpŏris formæ.

Altĕra via brevior fuit, altĕra tutior.

Antĭochus fuit poteutissimus.

Promiscuous Exercises.

Multōrum[a] obtrectatio devicit unīus[a] virtūtem.

Pharnabāzo summa imperii tradīta est.

Romānus popŭlus omnes gentes virtūte superāvit.

Cupidissĭmus litterārum fuit.

Dion erat intĭmus Dionysio priōri.

Laude dignus ducebātur

Industria multum[b] voluptātis habet.

Major natu est.

Locum altissimo muro muniĕrant.

The Romans were expecting larger forces.

The enemy occupied a higher place.

He subdued very many nations.

They prepared very great forces.

He was dearer to Brutus.

The king was very powerful.

They have most beautiful forms.

One way is very long, the other very dangerous.

One way is shorter, the other safer.

They are very fond of literature (letters).

The place was fortified with a very high wall.

XL.

Cases after Adjectives, continued. — Rules 8 and 10.

Omnium formosissĭmus erat.

Gallōrum omnium fortissĭmi sunt Belgæ.

Turpis fuga morte est pejor.

Omnium potentissĭmus rex Antiŏchus fuit.

a Rule 1, Rem. 3. *b* Rule 1, Rem. 6.

Auri avidissĭma gens erat.

Existimatĭōne nihil habēbat carius.

Suevōrum gens est bellicosissĭmus Germanōrum.

Minor uno mense[a] fuit.

Civītas mille misit milĭtum.

Turris fuit altior muro.

Hannĭbal fortĭssĭmus erat omnium Carthaginiensium.

Nemo Hannibāle fortior fuit.

Cicĕro erat oratōrum Romanōrum eloquentissĭmus.

Cicerōne nemo fuit eloquentior.

Socrātes erat philosophōrum Græcōrum sapientissĭmus.

Theophrastus elegantissĭmus philosophōrum erat.

Promiscuous Examples.

Hostium anĭmos timor præoccupavĕrat.

Omnes splendōre superāvit vitæ.

Finitīmas regiōnes vexābat.

Quærit. quid[b] causæ sit.[c]

Multum pecuniæ perdĭdit.

Perpetui impĕrii cupĭdus fuit.

Æger erat vulnĕribus.

Civitāti fuit carissĭmus.

Libertas est carior vitâ.

Omnium civium ditissĭmus fuit.

Habēbat equĭtum viginti millia.

Socrates was very wise.

Socrates was the wisest of the Grecian philosophers.

Nothing is dearer than reputation.

Cicero was very eloquent.

Cicero was the most eloquent of Roman orators.

No one was more eloquent than Cicero.

She was one month younger.

---

a Rule 10, Rem. 2.   *b* Rules for translating, partitive genitive.
c Syntax, Rule 97, and rules for translating the subjunctive, 2.

XLI.

Adverbs. — *Rules* 11, 12, 13, 14, 15.

Eo confŭgit.
Maxĭmè florēbat.
Non effŭgit invidiam.
Non longè abfuit.
Ibi castra posuit.
Milĭtes fortĭter pugnant.
Minùs timebātur.
Pejùs res administrāta est.
Postridie Calendārum equĭtes misit.
Satis præsidii dedit.
Omnium optĭmè loquĭtur.
Habēbat satis eloquentiæ.
Obviàm hostĭbus venērunt.
Proxĭmè Hispaniam Mauri sunt.

Conjunctions. — *Rule* 16.

Rogo et oro.
Obsĭdes et arma poposcit.
Incŏlæ bella magna et atrocia gerunt.
Diu et acrĭter milĭtes pugnābant.
Et proditōres percŭlit, et hostes profligāvit.
Nec melior vir fuit, nec clarior.
Dicit liberiùs*ᵃ* atque audaciùs.
Superbè respondēbat et crudelĭter imperābat.

Promiscuous Examples.

Mirabilĭter vulgi mutāta est voluntas.
Hamilcăris arbitrio rem ultrò permisērunt.
Ut virtutĭbus, sic vitiis est obrŭtus.
Non salūtis, quàm fidei, fuit cupidior.

---

a See Rules for translating. comparative degree.

Epaminondas erat adeò veritãtis dilĭgens, ut ne joco quidem mentirētur.ᵃ

Proxĭmi sunt Germānis.

Ætāte proxĭmus erat.

Fortūnâ non contentus erat.

Alcibiădes et potentior et major quàm privātus, existimabãtur.

Nihil dulcius est libertãte.

Obviàm Cæsãri proficiscĭtur.

Non satis præsidii dedit.

Helvetiōrum longè nobilissĭmus et ditissĭmus fuit Orgetŏrix.

They were not far distant.

He did not escape envy.

We fled thither.

The inhabitants carried on great and fierce wars.

The enemy fought long and bravely

They went to meet Cæsar.

They speak too freely and boldly

He had sufficient eloquence.

He spoke the best of all.

A sufficient guard is given.

They came to meet the enemy.

XLII.

Prepositions. — *Rules* 17, 18, 19.

Ad senectūtem vixit.

E civitāte ejectus est.

Philippus a Pausaniâ juxta theātrum occisus est.

Ex classe copias eduxit.

Cæsar a lacu ad montem murum perduxit.

In morbum incĭdit.

Pontem fecit in flumĭne.

Conon in vincŭla conjectus est.

ᵃ Syntax, Rule 90, and Rules for translating the subjunctive, 4.

Cum patre a puĕro in exercitĭbus fuĕrat versātus.

Aristīdes cum Themistŏcle de principātu contendit.

Conon cum navĭbus in patriam venit.

In prœlio cecĭdit.

Hasdrubălis post mortem Hannĭbal ab exercĭtu accēpit imperium.

Demoĕrĭtus causam explĭcat, cur ante lucem galli
canant.[a]

Multùm in judiciis privātis versabātur.

Attĭcus sepultus est juxta viam Appiam.

Præter opiniōnem res cecidĕrat.

In aciem pedĭtum centum perduxit.

Milĭtes Cæsăris sub montem succēdunt.

Est ingens gelĭdum lucus prope amnem.

De Themistŏclis morte multimŏdis apud plerosque
scriptum est.

Pacem inter duas potentissĭmas cīvitātes fecit.

De instantĭbus[b] verissĭmè judicābat, et de futūris cal-
lidissĭmè conjiciēbat.

Copias c navĭbus eduxit.

Exercĭtus in campum deduxit.

Rosæ fulgent inter lilia.

Promiscuous Examples.

Uno concursu barbarōrum maxĭmam vim prostrāvit.

Ariovistus ad Cæsărem legātos mittit.

Cæsar prædam milĭtĭbus sociisque dabat.

Ut virtutĭbus [c] eluxit, sic vitiis est obrŭtus.

Equestrem obtinuit dignitātem.

In armis plurĭmum studii consumēbat.

Non multum superĕrat munitiōnis.

In navem omnĭbus ignōtus ascendit.

Perītus belli fuit Epaminondas.

Non pater quidem carior fuit aut familiarior.

---

a Rule 97, and Rules for translating, subjunctive mood, 2. b Rule 1, Rem.
4. c Rule 1, Rem. 9.

Accēpit gravissĭmum vulnus morte filii.
Nihil carior est existimatiōne.
Suevōrum gens est longe bellicosissĭma Germanōrum
  omnium.
In primam aciem processit.
In arâ consēdit.
Filium eò cum exercĭtu mittit.
Par principĭbus videbātur.
Bonâ fortūnâ non erat contentus.
Ibi tria castella communīvit.

He came with the ships to his native land.
From a boy, he was employed in the army with his
  father.
He was put in prison.
They became sick (fell into disease).
They extended a wall from the lake to the mountain.
Phillip was killed near the theatre.
Peace was made between two most powerful nations.

XLIII.

Pronouns.

Ego lego.
Tu audis.
Ille videt.
Nos scribĭmus.
Vos studētis.
Illi ludunt.
Vos, non nos, laudāvit.
Hic puer est bonus, ille ignāvus.
Ista tua filia est pulchra.
Ego te tradam magistratui.
Magnam relīquit sui[a] famam.
Bellum inter se gerunt.
Id tibi misit.
Ii omnes inter se diffĕrunt.
Se ad Cæsărem recipiunt.

a Rule 29, Rem. 2.

Se ipse reprehendit.
Nemo ei par fuit.
Fidem inter se dant.
Eos ab se dimīsit.
Sese ei dedidērunt.
Id tam illi, quàm cetĕris, non erat apertum.
Huic ille, "nulla," inquit, "mora est."
Ipse sibi mortem conscīvit.
Fugæ sese mandârunt.
Legātos ad eum mittunt.
Idem Cæsar fecit.
Eădem secrētò ab aliis quærĭt.
Equitātum omnem ante se mittit.
Eōrum agros populabantur.
Ei filiam suam in matrimonium dat.

Thraces eas regiōnes tenēbant.
Suas copias deduxērunt.
Hos fugat.
Ea civĭtas mille misit milĭtum.
Hanc legatiōnem suscēpit.
Eōrum classem fugāvit.
Talis honos huic uni ante hoc tempus contĭgit.
Hoc consilio pacem conciliāvit.
Cæsar suas copias in proxĭmum collem subdūcit.
E castris utrisque copias suas edūxit.
Vir bonus virtūtem per se amat.
Alii aliam in partem ferebantur.
Eo ipse dux cecīdit prœlio.
Se suāque omnia Cæsāri dedidērunt.
Sui cuique mores fingunt fortūnam.
Mihi necesse fuit.
Non ea res illum fefellit.

Promiscuous Examples.

Non effūgit civium suōrum invidiam.
Postŭlat, ut sibi urbem tradant.[a]
Neque minus in eâ re prudentiâ, quàm felicitate, adjūtus est.
Cetĕras insŭlas sub ejus potestātem redēgit.
Amicior omnium libertāti, quàm suæ fuit dominationi.
Non solùm spem in eō habēbant maxĭmam, sed etiam timōrem.
Timebātur non minus, quàm diligebātur.
Ex Asiâ in Africam trajēcit.
Is locus abest circĭter sex millia passuum.
Peritissĭmos belli navālis fecit Athenienses.
Non quicquam fecit fide suâ indignum.
Postrĭdie ejus diēi in fines Suessiōnum exercĭtum duxit.
Legāti de pace ad Cæsărem venērunt.
Intra oppĭda murosque compelluntur.
His obviàm universa civĭtas venit.
Ex eo oppĭdo, pons ad Helvetios pertĭnet.
Non satis in eo loco præsidii putabātur.

I write.
Thou seest.
He hears.
We read.
You play.
They study.
He praised me, not you (thee).
They sent (to) us these things.
They all differ among themselves.
He surrendered himself to them.
To him this was evident.
He laid violent hands on himself.
Those states sent ten thousand soldiers.
He led his forces upon the nearest hill.

---

[a] See Rule 90, and Rules for translating the subjunctive, 4.

They were driven from that town.

Some were borne in one direction (part), and others in another.

The general himself fell in that battle.

They did nothing unworthy of themselves.

XLIV.

Relative Pronouns. — Rule 1, Rem. 8.

Is amīcus est, qui juvat[a] in rebus adversis.

Legāti missi sunt, qui consulĕrent[b] oracŭlum.

Incīdit in eandem invidiam, quam pater suus.

Ea, quæ suprà dixĭmus, prædicârunt.

Is inter Thrasybūlum et eos, qui urbem tenēbant, fecit pacem.

Ingrātus est homo, qui non beneficium reddit.

Ea, quæ apportāvit, abstulērunt.

Civis est is, qui patriam suam dilĭgit.

Id, quod pollicĭtus erat, præstĭtit.

Pecuniæ quinquaginta talenta, quæ a Pharnabāzo accepĕrat, civĭbus suis donat.

Legatiōnes, quæ essent[b] illustriōres, per Diōnem administrabantur.

Multitudĭnem, quam secum duxĕrat, in agris collocāvit.

Pontem, qui erat ad Genēvam, rescindunt.

Equitātum, qui sustinēret[b] hostium impĕtum, misit.

In fines Ambianōrum pervēnit, qui se suāque omnia sine morâ dedidērunt.

Ex loco superiōre, quæ res in nostris castris gerebantur, conspicātus est.

Flumen est Arar, quod in Rhodănum influit.

Publius Considius, qui rei militāris peritissĭmus habebātur, cum exploratorĭbus præmittĭtur.

Pompeius, qui a Cæsăre victus est, fugit ad Ægyptum.

---

a Rule 33, Rem. 3.   *b* Rule 96 and subdivision 5, and Rules for translating the subjunctive, 5.

Celerĭter, quod habuērunt, consumpsērunt.
Bellum, quod suscepĕrat, gessit.
Non id, quod petīvit, consecūtus est.
Id, quod erat difficillĭmum, efficiēbat.
Proxĭmi sunt Germānis, qui trans Rheaum incŏlunt.

Promiscuous Examples.

Vive memor senectūtis et mortis.
Non recūsat quò minùs legis pœnam persolveret.[a]
Quo plus[b] habent, eo plus cupiunt.
Præcĭpuus ei honos habĭtus est.
Bellum exitiōsum impendet.
Locam vallo fossâque munīvit.
Neoptolēmus apud Lycomēdem erat educātus.
Qua pugnâ nihĭl adhuc est nobilior.
Furor et ira præcipĭtant anĭmum.
Mora non tuta est.
Litĕras exspecto quas scripsisti.
Dion fretus nou tam suis copiis, quam odio tyranni
  profectus est.
A primâ ætāte me philosophia delectāvit.
Hic fuit omnium potentissĭmus.

They sent ambassadors who should consult (to con-
  sult) the oracle.
They performed what they had promised.
He gave (to) the soldiers the money which he had
  received.
He made peace with those who occupied the city.
Dion conducted the embassies which were most
  renowned.
He took away all that they had brought.

a See Syntax, Rule 90, and Rules for translating, subjunctive mood, 4.
b Rule 10, Rem. 2.

16

XLV. •

Infinitive Mood. — Rules 20, 21, 22.

Necesse est pugnare.[a]
Confligĕre cupiĕbant.
Spero te valēre.[b]
Turpe est fugere.[a]
Resistĕre ausi non sunt.
Ille dignus est amāri.[c]
Difficīle est omnia[a] persĕqui.[a]
Illi dixĕrant sese deditūros.[d]
Illos retinēri jussit.
Vidit tumultu civitātem esse perturbātam.
Cæsar Divitiăcum ad se vocāri jubet.
Dixit sese cum iis pacem esse factūrum.
Obsĭdes dari jussit.
Cur timet flavum Tibĕrim tangĕre?
Tempus est hujus libri facĕre[c] finem.

Ipse ibīdem manēre decrēvit.
Turpe est violāre[a] fidem[a] suam.[a]
Portas claudī jussit.
Miror tuum fratrem non scribĕre.
Dixit, scire se illa esse vera.
Respondit, se ad cum ventūrum esse.
Existĭmant, Romānos discedĕre.
Dixit, hostes consedisse.
Dicit, montem ab hostĭbus tenēri.
Non sunt ausi manēre.

Cupit discĕre.
Miror te non scire.
Illa fuit digna amāri.[c]
Sequi gloria non appĕti debet.
Credo regem amāre pacem.

---

a Rule 1, Rem. 5, and Rule 33, Rem. 2.   b Rule 22, Rem. 4.
c Rule 22, Rem. 1.   d Supply *esse.*

Statuērunt belli finem facere.
Necesse ·est, si in·conspectum venĕris,[a] venerāri[b] te[b] regem.[b]
Illud[c] dignum est cogitāri.[d]
Se legātos ad eos missūros dixērunt.
Bellum cum Germānis gerĕre constituit.
Dixit sese Æduōrum injurias non neglectūrum.
Ex castris equitātum edūci jubet.

It is necessary to fight.
He did not dare to resist.
They are worthy to be loved.
He said that he was about to make peace.
It is time to finish (to make an end of) the war.
He saw that the mountain was held by the enemy.
He wonders that you have not come.
She is·worthy of being (to be) loved.
He said that he would (was about to) send embassadors to them.
They said that they would not neglect the injuries of the soldiers.
He commanded the army to be led out of the camp.

XLVI.

Learn or review the Irregular and Defective Verbs, and apply the same rules as in the preceding Exercise.

Id facĕre possum.
Colōnos mittĕre volēbat.
Adīre nolēbat.
Redīre noluit.
Decĭpi non potĕrat.
Id facĕre potes.
Discĕre vult.
Parēre noluērunt.

a Rule 80.   b Rule 1, Rem. 5, and Rule 33, Rem. 2.   c Rule 1, Rem. 4.
d Rule 22, Rem. 1.

Perīre maluit.
Eum clam interficĕre volēbat.

Pedem referre cœpērunt.
Iter patefiĕri volēbat.
Maluit se dilĭgi quam metui.
Quid fiĕri velit[a], edŏcet.
Id cetĕri facĕre noluērunt.
Quod[b] multi voluērunt, pauci potuērunt ab uno
    tyranno patriam liberāre.
Violāre clementiam, quàm regis opes minui, maluit.
Universos[c] pares esse posse aiēbat.
Non vult regi.
Diutius nostrōrum milītum impĕtum hostes ferre non
    potuērunt.

Satis[d] est, unam rem, exempli causâ, proferre.
Milĭtes ex oppĭdo exīre jussit.
Popŭlus maluit eum innoxium plecti, quàm se diutius
    esse in timōre.
Et obesse plurĭmùm et prodesse potĕrat.
Aut prodesse volunt, aut delectāre poëtæ.
Ad montem se recipĕre cœpērunt.
Quid fiĕri velit[a], ostendit.
Reprehendebātur, quòd parum odisse malos cives
    viderētur.[e]

Promiscuous Examples.

Pauci veniunt ad senectūtem.
Certior factus est, Gallos omnes discessisse.
Vergasillaunus post montem se occultāvit.
Nunciātum est, L. Cassium occīsum esse.
Equĭtes renunciavērunt castra esse munīta.
Sepulcrum Cyri aperīri Alexander jussit.
Codrus se in medios immīsit hostes

a See Rule 97.   b Rule 1, Rem. 8, (1).   c Rule 1, Rem. 3.   d Rule 1, Rem. 5
    and Rule 33 Rem. 2.   e Rule 100.

Audīvi necessitātem esse matrem artium.
Nemo se avārum esse intelligit.
Proba vita via est in cælum.
Existimābant, se eos vi coactūros esse.
Dixit se obsīdes reddītūrum esse.
Reperiēbat, equitātum perterrītum esse.
Aqua Trebiæ flumīnis erat pectorĭbus tenus.

Certior factus est legātos in vincūla conjectos esse.
Animadvertit totum exercĭtum esse peritūrum.
Qui bene latuit bene vixit.
Non hoc præterībo, quamquam nonnullis leve visum
    iri putem.[a]

Tutus ille non est, quem omnes odērunt.
Solem e mundo tollunt, qui amicitiam e vitâ tollunt.
Vinci quam vincĕre maluit.
Ne tentes[b], quod effĭci non potest.
Omnia[c] pecuniâ effĭci non possunt.
Reperiēbat initium fugæ a Dumnorĭge factum esse.
Cæsar negat se posse iter Helvetiis dare.
De digĭto[d] annŭlum detrăho.
Pollicĭtus est se Græciam bello oppressūrum.
Respondit, sibi mirum vidēri quid in Gallia negōtii
    habēret.[e]

Patrem tuum colui, et dilexi.
Mihi verò non est grave, quemvis honōrem habēre
    regi.
Malunt, cum virtūte paucis contenti esse, quàm sine
    eâ multa habēre.
Fretus numĕro copiārum suārum confligĕre cupiēbat.
Constat nihil eo fuisse excellentius.
Sentiēbat, Æduōrum nobilissĭmum et fortissĭmum
    esse Divitiăcum.

a Rule 92, Rem.   b Rule 89, Rem.   c Rule 1, Rem. 4.   d Rule 1, Rem. 9.
e Rule 97.

16*

Satis esse causæ arbitrabantur.
Catilīnæ ferrum de manĭbus extorsīmus.

He can do it.
They were willing to send embassadors.
I was willing to return.
They could not be deceived.
He preferred to be obeyed rather than obey.
We wish to learn.
The enemy began to retreat.
I would rather be loved than feared.
Few have been able to do what many have wished.
They could not withstand.
It is sufficient to mention one example.
It is not grievous to have every respect for the king.

XLVII.

Participles. — Rules 1, 23.

Flens*a* pacem petiit.
Classem devictam cepit.
Germāni, bellum gestūri,*b* deos invocavērunt.
Tempus rei gerendæ*c* non dimīsit.
Flentes pacem petiērunt.
Hostes victi fugērunt.
Athenienses legātos misērunt oracŭlum consultūros.*d*
Ad bellum gerendum ipse dux delectus est.
Fugientem persequĭtur.
Perterrĭti pacem petivērunt.
Cæsar, in Galliam profectūrus, centuriōnes convŏcat.
Murōs dirūtos reficiendos*e* curāvit.
Conantes*f* dicĕre prohibuit.
Sic parātus proficiscĭtur.
Diem delegērunt ad inimīcos opprimĕndos.
Germāni bellum gestūri erant.

a Rules for translating, participles, 1.   *b* Rules for translating, participles, 2.
c   "   "   "   9.   *d*   "   "   "   3.
e   "   "   "   10.   *f*   "   "   "   11.

Cupientĭbus signum dat.

Aciem instructam habuit.

Frumentum omne, præter quod secum portatūrī erant, combŭrunt.

Ad cohortandos milĭtes decucurrit.

Fortissĭmè pugnantes cecidērunt.

Superāti, statuērunt belli finem facĕre.

Sese esse ad bellum gerendum paratissĭmos confirmavērunt.

Ædui legātos ad Cæsărem mittunt, auxilium imploratūros.

Ad eas res conficiendas Orgetŏrix deligĭtur.

Fugientes usque ad flumen persequuntur.

In nostros venientes tela conjiciēbant.

Confecti vulnerĭbus hostes terga vertērunt.

Scipio in Afrĭcam trajēcit, Carthagĭnem deletūrus.[a]

Homĭnes abundantes auro non sunt idcirco curis vacui.

Perītus civitātis regendæ fuit.

Epaminondas studiōsus erat audiendi.

Timotheus belli gerendi fuit perītus.

Nunc confūgi ad te, exagitātus a cunctâ Græciâ, tuam petens amicitiam.

Milĭtes cohortātus, cupientĭbus signum dedit.

Princĭpes, adventu Romanōrum permōti, legātos mittunt.

Magnam multitudĭnem eōrum fugientium[b] concidērunt.

Pacem petentĭbus liberalĭter respondit.

Comĭnus pugnaps telis hostium interfectus est.

Ad classes ædificandas, exercitusque comparandos, quantum pecuniæ quæque civĭtas daret,[c] Aristīdes delectus erat, qui constituĕret.[d]

---

a Rules for translating, participles, 3. *b* Rules for translating, participles, 11. *c* Syntax, Rule 97. *d* Syntax, Rule 96, 5, and Rules for translating, subjunctive, 5.

Legātus repentinâ re perturbātus, centuriōnes convocāvit.

Tempus ejus interficiendi quærēre instituērunt.

Hujus accusandi causâ ille missus est.

Urbes munītas suis tuendas tradit.

Ad eas res conficiendas biennium sibi satis esse dux-
ērunt.

Ille cernens nullum locum sibi tutum in Græciâ, in
Asiam transiit.

Dolo erat pugnandum,[b] quum par non esset[c] armis.

Promiscuous Examples.

Pone montes Rhipæos gens degit felix, quos[d] Hyper-
borēos appellavēre.[e]

Regi fidēlis erat repertus.

Fortissĭmus omnium barbarōrum fuit Datămes.

Stoĭci divisērunt natūram homĭnis in anĭmum et
corpus.

Numquam est utĭle peccāre.

Fidelissĭmi[f] homĭni sunt[g] canis atque equus.

Sæpe est etiam sub palliŏlo sordĭdo sapientia.

Illo nemo fuit fortior.

Matūrat ab urbe proficisci.

Perspicuum est homĭnem e corpŏre animōque con-
stāre.

They, weeping, sought peace.

The barbarians (when) about to carry on war,
invoke the gods.

They did not let the time for doing the thing pass.

They sent embassadors to consult the oracle.

The soldiers pursued the enemy (while) fleeing.

---

a Rule 1, Rem. 3.   *b* Rules for translating, participles, 8; it was necessary
to, or he was obliged to.   *c* Syntax, Rule 95, and Rules for translating,
subjunctive, 4.
  d Rule 1, Rem. 8 (2.)   *e* Supply *homĭnes*.   *f* Rule 1, Rem. 1.
  g Rule 33, Rem. 5.

Cæsar (when) about to go into Gaul, called together
the centurions.
They repaired the overthrown walls.
Embassadors were sent to Cæsar to implore aid.
They captured the vanquished fleet.
Being conquered, they fled.
Having exhorted the soldiers, he gave the signal to
them desiring it.

XLVIII.

Gerunds and Supines. — Rules 24 to 27, and Remarks.

Instābat tempus ad bellum proficiscendi.
Nactus idoneam ad navigandum[a] tempestātem solvit.
Hiemātum exercĭtum reduxit.
Studiōsus audiendi erat.
Nando in tutum pervenērunt.
Difficĭle est factu.
Auxilium postulātum venit.
Incredibĭle est dictu.[b]
Sic se gerendo minĭme est mirandum si vita ejus fuit
secūra.
Mirabĭlĭter flagrābant pugnandi cupiditāte.
Legāti ad Cæsarem gratulātum venērunt.
Aqua utĭlis est bibendo.
Imprīmis dicendo valēbat.
Perfacĭle factu[b] esse ille probat.
Diem ad deliberandum sumit.
Legātos ad Cæsărem mittunt rogātum auxilium.
Cæsar loquendi finem fecit.
Maritĭmos prædōnes consectando mare tutum reddĭdit.
Finem oppugnandi nox fecit.
Mens discendo alĭtur et cogĭtando.
Difficĭle est intellectu.
Phillippus, quum spectātum ludos iret,[c] juxta theā-
trum occīsus est.

---

a Rules for translating, gerunds. *b* Rules for translating, supines. *c* Rule
96, Rem.

Promiscuous Examples.

Amicitia est per se et propter se expetenda.

Miltiades morandi tempus non habens, cursum direxit quò tendēbat.

T. Manlius fuit perindulgens in patrem,

Legatiōnes fidelĭter administrando, crudelissĭmum nomen tyranni suâ humanitāte tegēbat.

Deliberandi sibi spatium relĭquit.

Plato cupiditātem subter præcordia locāvit.

Suevōrum gens est longè maxima et bellicosissĭma Germanōrum omnium.

Nemo melior fuit illo.

Cæsar reperiēbat plerosque Belgas esse ortos ab Germānis.

Cicerōni ex patriâ fugienti sestertiōrum ducenta et quinquaginta millia donāvit.

Eum sibi fidēlem[a] arbitrabātur.

Multo[b] superiōres bello esse cœpērunt.

Post illōrum obĭtum non quisquam dux in illâ urbe fuit dignus memoriâ.

Audaciùs resistĕre ac fortiùs pugnāre cœpērunt.

Pridiè ejus diēi retinēri non potĕrant, quin in nostros tela conjicĕrent.[c]

Erat disertus ut imprīmis dicendo valēret.[c]

Bene sentīre, rectēque facĕre satis est ad bene beatēque vivendum.

Obviàm ei venērunt.

Olim calămus adhibebātur scribendo.

Nemĭnem, nisi victum, dimĭsit.

Ea vidēre ac perspicĕre potestis.

Statim dedit, ne differendo viderētur[c] negāre.

Miltiādes insŭlas, quæ Cyclădes nominantur, sub Atheniensium redēgit potestātem.

---

a Supply *esse.*   *b* Rule 10, Rem. 2.
c Rule 90, and Rules for translating, subjunctive mood, 4.

Legātos ad Cæsărem misērunt orātum ne se in hostium numĕro ducĕret.[a]

Ex Massiliensium classe quinque naves sunt depressæ.

Difficĭle erat intellectu, utrum Attĭcum amīci magis vererentur[a] an amārent.[a]

Ad Cæsărem auxilii ferendi causâ profectūs est.

Finem orandi fecit.

The soldiers were burning with a desire of fighting.

Embassadors were sent to ask aid.

He proved that it was very easy to be done.

He took a day for deliberating.

They came to ask aid.

It is difficult to be done.

Give immediately, lest by delaying you should seem to refuse.

He prevailed especially in speaking.

He found a suitable time for sailing.

He was fond of hearing.

By swimming they came to a safe place.

He made an end of speaking.

He led back his army to pass the winter.

XLIX.

Cases after Nouns. — Rules 28 *to* 32. 35.

Hasdrŭbal, Hannibălis frater, in prœlio cecĭdit.

Maxĭmi erat consilii.[b]

Helĕna causa[c] fuit belli Trojăni.

Omnium rerum principia parva sunt.

Puĕr ingenui pudōris[d] amabĭtur.

Quis huĭc rei[e] testis est?

Magnâ fuit gloriâ.

Invĭdia gloriæ comes[c] est.

---

a Rule 97, and Rules for translating, subjunctive mood, 2. *b* Rule 29, Rem.
4 & 5. *c* Rule 35. *d* Rule 29, Rem. 4. *e* Rule 29, Rem. 3.

Nihil eōrum negāvit.
Nunc virĭbus usus est, nunc manĭbus rapĭdis.
Legātus partem copiārum revocāvit.
Pietāte filius erat, consiliis pater.

Vitæ necisque habēbat potestātem.
Cato, singulāri fuit prudentiâ.[a]
Magna pars plebis urbem relĭquit.
Celĕri ópus est auxilio.
Agesilāus nomĭne, non potestāte fuit rex.
Ejusdem civitātis[b] fuit.
Miles timet sagittam hostis.
Est fortis homĭnis[b] non perturbāri in rebus aspĕris.
Non popŭli Romāni dignitātis[b] esse statuēbat.
Reges nomĭne magis quam imperio erant.

Pontis custōdes relĭquit princĭpes.
Summæ est dementiæ.[b]
Pars civitātis defecĕrat.
Erat oppĭdum nomĭne[c] Bibrax.
Pan deus Arcadiæ erat.
Docet eum magno fore perĭcŭlo.[d]
Neptūnus erat numen aquārum.
Civĭtas inter Belgas magnâ fuit auctoritāte.

Reperiēbat, esse homĭnes magnæ virtūtis.
Juno Jovis conjux erat.
Castra hostium cepit.
Quærĭtur, quid opus[e] sit facto.
Miltiădes regiæ auctoritātis[a] erat.
Critias, dux tyrannōrum, in prœlio cecĭdit.
Aliēnæ erat civitātis.[b]
Non est virtūtis[b] arma tradĕre.
Nunciāvit, quàm celĕri opus[e] esset auxilio.
Orgetorĭgis filia capta est.

Nisus fuit portæ custos.[a]
Consul ipse parvo anĭmo[b] et pravo fuit.
Canis lepŏris vestigia sequĭtur.
Arbĭtror vix ejus[c] fuisse tantam rem suscipĕre.
Calamĭtas virtūtis occasio est.
Secum duxit filium annōrum novem.
Exspectāre, dum hostium copiæ augerentur,[d] summæ
    dementiæ[c] esse judicābat.
Hostĭbus ad consilia capienda nihil[e] spatii dandum
    existimābat.
Ariovistus, rex Germanōrum, tertiam partem agri
    occupāvit.

Erat inter eos dignitāte regiâ.
Res erat multæ opĕris ac labōris.
Navĭbus usus non est.
Hic nomĭne magis quam imperio fuit rex.

The leader, a brother of the king, was slain in the
    battle.
Cato was (a person) of very great wisdom.
He recalled a part of the forces.
The chiefs were left as guards of the town.
There is need of very great wisdom.
It was a work of great labor.
The king had the power of life and death.
He said that this was not (a part) of his design.
Many have been kings in name, rather than in
    power
It would be (the part) of the greatest madness to
    deliver up arms to our enemies.

He was (a man) of remarkable prudence.
There is need of help.

---

a Rule 35. *b* Rule 29, Rem. 4. *c* Rule 29, Rem. 4 and 5. *d* Rule 94. *e* Rules
for translating, partitive genitive.

17

L.

Promiscuous Examples

Dolor in maxĭmis malis ducĭtur.

Perīcŭlum est, ne immodestiâ milĭtum nostrōrum occasio detur[a] Lysandro nostri opprimendı exercĭtus.

Quid hostes consilii capĕrent,[b] exspectābat.

Attĭci quies tantopĕre Cæsări fuit grata; ut huic molestus non fuĕrit.[a]

Inferior copiis, superior omnĭbus prœliis discessit.

Popŭlus invĭdus potentiæ eum revŏcat.

Erat difficillĭmâ natûrâ.[c]

Difficĭle est judicāre, id utrùm ei laboriosius an gloriosius fuerit.[b]

Hic fuit omnium potentissĭmus.

Habēbat satis consiliı.

Pontem qui erat ad Genēvam, jubet rescindi.

Sese omnes flentes Cæsări[d] ad pedes projecērunt.

Turranius fuit homo summâ integritāte.[e]

Nemo illo minus emax fuit.

Comĭnus gladiis pugnātum est.

Eò se suăque omnia contulērunt.

Sperābat se imprudentem hostem oppressūrum.

Ventōrum pater regit navem.

Nunc anĭmis opus est, nunc pectŏre firmo.

Mors omnium malōrum sensum adĭmit.

Aves quædam se in mári mergunt.

Jucunda est memoria præteritōrum malōrum.

Insŭla Delos erat referta divitiis.

His rebus adducti constituĕrunt ea, quæ ad proficiscendum pertinērent,[f] comparāre.

Diem deligĕrunt ad civitātem liberandam.

Prædātum exiĕrant.

---

[a] Rule 90.　[b] Rule 97.　[c] Rule 29, Rem. 4 and 5.　[d] Rule 29, Rem. 3.
[e] Rule 29, Rem. 4.　[f] Rule 100.

Ad Tissaphernem, præfectum regis Darii, se contŭlit.
Non suæ esse dignitātis statuēbat.
Milĭtum pars a barbăris circumventa periit.
Archimēdes, vir magni ingenii,[a] cæsus est.
Statuēre[b] qui sit[c] sapiens, est sapientis.[d]
Natūrâ tu illi[e] pater es.
Decemvĭri leges in duodĕcim tabŭlis scripsērunt.
Hostĭbus pugnandi potestātem fecit.
In omnĭbus rebus singulāri fuit prudentiâ.
Mirabĭle est dictu.
Ille nomĭne, non potestāte, fuit rex.

There was danger lest, by the intemperate conduct
of the soldiers, an opportunity should be given
to the enemy of overpowering our forces.
They were gone out to plunder.
He was (a person) of remarkable wisdom.
There is need of great strength.
He betook himself to Darius the king.
A part of the army perished.

LI.

Cases after Verbs.— Rules 35 to 44, and Remarks.

Antiŏchus erat rex.
Reminiscentes vetĕris famæ, ætātis miserebantur.
Is satăgit rerum suārum.
Accusātus est proditiōnis.
Intĕrest omnium rectè facĕre.
Meâ et tuâ refert.
Milĭtes tempŏris monet.
Popŭlum judicii sui pœnituit.
Reminiscĭtur pristĭni tempŏris acerbitātem.
Magni fuit ejus opĕra.
Proditiōnis damnātus est.

---

a Rule 29, Rem. 4.   b Rule 1, Rem. 5, and Rule 33, Rem. 2.   c Rule 97,
and Rules for translating, subjunctive mood, 2.   d Rule 29, Rem. 5.
e Rule 29, Rem.   f Rule 39, Rem. 3.

Alcibiădes dux delectus est.
Absurdè facis, qui angas[a] te[b] anĭmi.[b]

Postŭmus suam auctoritātem magni æstĭmat.
Recordāre tempus illud.
Admonēbat illum egestātis suæ.
Tua[c] et mea[c] maxĭme intĕrest.
Injuriārum obliviscebātur.

Domum pluris quàm fortūnam tuam æstimâsti.
Miserēre domus labentis.
Datæ fidei[d] reminiscĭtur.
Meipsum inertiæ condemno.
Res adversæ homĭnes religiōnis admŏnent.
Omnium refert vitium fugĕre.
Si vetĕris contumeliæ oblivisci, num etiam recentium
     injuriārum memoriam deponĕre possit?[e]

Numquam suscepti negotii eum pertæsum est.
Unus homo pluris quam civĭtas fuit.
Humanitātis refert.
Illum unum pluris, quàm se omnes, fiĕri vidēbant.
Cujus facti celeriùs Athenienses quàm ipsum pœni-
     tuit.
Tua et mea maxĭme intĕrest, te valēre.
Cato tribūnus milĭtum fuit, Conon fuit prætor.
Id commūne ærarium esse voluērunt.
Vidēbant, omnes præ illo parvi futūros.
Reminiscerētur pristīnæ virtūtis Helvetiōrum.

Eum sacrilegii damnârunt.
Hannĭbal factus est prætor.
Caium Verrum insimŭlat avaritiæ et audaciæ.
Egeo consĭlii.
Is pagus appellātur Tigurīnus.

Sentiēbat, se nullīus momenti apud exercĭtum futū-
rum.

Accusātus est capĭtis.

Non plura bona reminisci potuit.

Amīcus ab senātu appellātus est.

Est hoc commūne vitium, ut invidia glorĭæ comes
sit.[a]

Ejus auctorĭtas magni habebātur.

Legem tulit, ne quis antĕ actārum rerum accusarētur.[a]

Capĭtis absolūtus est.

Publius Sextius damnātus est ambĭtus.

Adolescentem suæ temeritātis implet.

Reminiscerētur[b] vetĕris incommŏdi popŭli Romāni.

Intĕrest omnium virtūtem laudāre.

Alienārum opum indigēbat.

Non tua refert.

Eos ineptiārum pœnĭtet.

We pity them.

They will remember disasters.

It concerns all to do right.

He alone was more valued than all the rest.

Conon was chosen leader.

He will repent (it will repent him) of his follies.

He was accused of treachery.

It does not concern me.

They were called friends.

LII.

Cases after Verbs Continued. — *Rules* 45, 46, 50—53.

Redditur terræ corpus.

Totum[a] se dedĭdit reipublicæ.

Datus est tibi plausus.

Sensit sibi esse pereundum.

a Rule 90. b Rule 89, 2. a Wholly.

17*

Miltiădi custodia credebātur.
Maturāvit collēgæ venīre auxilio.
Juventus plerăque Catilinæ inceptis favēbat.
Est mihi pater.
Nulli ejus fides defuit.
Nulla civĭtas illis auxilio fuit.
Pollicĭtus est sibi·eam rem curæ futūram.
Da mihi pignus amōris.
Divitiæ multis fuērunt exitio.
Deliberantĭbus Pythia respondit, ut·mœnĭbus ligneis
    se munīrent.ᵃ
Ille despērat salūti suæ.
Neque cernĭtur ulli.
Longæ regĭbus sunt manus.
Consĭlium plerisque civitatĭbus displicēbat.

Voluptatĭbus simul et virtūti nemo servīre potest.
Adhibenda est nobis diligentia.
Non ulli loco parcēbant.
Est mihi liber.
Omnĭbus maxĭmo erat usui.
Oves nobis suam lanam præbent.
Bonisᵇ nocet quisquis pepercĕritᶜ malis.
Homĭnes ampliùs ocŭlisᵈ quàm aurĭbus credunt.
Exitio est avĭdis mare nautis.
Dedit ei veniam.
Cæsar non exspectandum sibi statuit.
Imperāvit Allobrogĭbus, ut frumenti copiam facĕr-
    ent.ᵃ
Eum auxilio Cæsāri misērunt.
Sunt nobis magni honōres.
Ipse sibi perniciēi fuit.
Redeunt jam gramĭna campis.
Factiōni inimicōrum resistĕre nequīvit.
Insidias sibi fiĕri intellexit.
Licet cuivis Ephŏro, hoc facĕre regi.

a Rule 90.   *b* Rule 1, Rem. 3.   *c* Rule 89.   *d* Rule 1, Rem. 9.

His rebus commōtus statuit accuratiùs sibi agendum.

Ego autem nemĭnem nomĭno, quare irasci mihi nemo potĕrit.

Est homĭni similitūdo quædam cum Deo.

He devoted himself wholly to the state.
He perceived that he must perish,
He commanded the soldiers to spare no one.
He was a help to Cæsar.
He brought (was for) destruction upon (to) himself.
He had many honors.
They were of very great benefit to us.
The republic was entrusted to Miltiades.
We have many books.
We must use diligence.
They did not spare any place.
That counsel displeased most (persons).
Cæsar decided that he ought not to wait.

LIII.

Cases after Verbs, Continued. — *Rules* 54 *to* 57, 59.

Spargit silva frondes.[a]
Gramen carpit equus.
Pœni Hamilcărem imperatōrem fecērunt.[b]
Rex Tissaphernem hostem judicāvit.
Fortūna me, qui liber fuĕram, servum fecit.
Cato Valerium Flaccum in consulātu habuit[c] collē-
    gam.[c]
Non te celāvi sermōnem Ampii.
Spes alit agricŏlas.
Montem Vesontiōnis murus circumdătus arcem effĭcit.
Quis musĭcam docuit Epaminondam?

---

a Rule 1, Rem. 9.　　*b* Rule 55.　　*c* Rule 55, Rem.

Iram bene Ennius initium dixit insaniæ.
Ver præbet flores.
Æneas refulsit os humerosque deo simīlis.
Jurāvi verissĭmum jusjurandum.

Catilīna juventūtem mala facinŏra edocēbat.
Brutus consul collēgam sibi creāvit P. Valerium.
Epistŏlam tuam accēpi.
Interrogātus est causam.[a]
Cneus Pompeius se auctōrem[b] meæ salūtis exhibuit.[b]
Hannĭbal Philippum absens hostem reddĭdit Romā-
    nis.[c]
Posce deos veniam.
Honōres non petiit.
Labor omnia[d] vincit.
Miltiădem imperatōrem fecērunt.
Iter, quod habēbat, omnes celat.
Milĭtes nostri exaudiunt clamōrem.

Acres venābor apros.
Legāti Cæsărem pacem poposcērunt.
Omnes belli artes[a] edoctus est.
Torva leæna lupum sequĭtur.
Pugnam pugnāvit.
Vos testes habeo:
Rogātus est sententiam.
Romuŭlus creāvit centum senatōres.
Rogo te veniam.
Terrōrem ejus adventus sustŭlit.
Achæi auxilia Philippum regem orābant.
Epaminondas philosophiæ præceptōrem[b] habuit Ly-
    sim.
Ancum Marcium regem populus creāvit.
Numquam divitias deos rogāvi.

Quotidie Cæsar Æduos frumentum flagitābat.
Multi cives meum casum luctumque doluērunt.

a Rule 56, Rem. 1.   b Rule 55, Rem.   c Rule 29, Rem. 3.   d Rule 5, Rem. 4

Interrex M. Furius Camillus P. Cornelium Scipiōnem
    interrēgem prodĭdit.
Expleri mentem nequit Dido.
Amicitiam tuam, si ero adeptus, non minùs me bonum
    amīcum habēbis, quam fortem inimīcum ille ex-
    pertus est.
Cicerōnem universa civĭtas consŭlem declarāvit.
Siccius Dentātus triumphāvit triumphos novem.
Summum consilium majōres nostri appellârunt senā-
    tum.

The king esteems me as a friend.
They concealed the journey from all.
They were asked their opinion.
You should esteem me for your friend.
They made Miltiades leader.
They demanded peace from Cæsar.
They fought a battle.
Who will teach me music ?

LIV.

Cases after Verbs, Continued.— Rules 61 *to* 74.

Numĭdæ plerùmque lacte et ferīnā carne vescebantur.
Jnvĕnis, qui nitĭtur hastâ.
Atheniensĭbus licet, eōdem patre natas,[a] uxōres du-
    cĕre.
Quibus rebus indiguērunt, juvit.
Somnus nos omnĭbus sensĭbus orbat.
Naves onĕrant auro.
Contremisco tota mente.
Lætor tua dignitāte.[b]
Aquas nectăre miscuit.

Lacte atque pecŏre vivunt.

a Rule 1, Rem. 3.   *b* Rule 68, 1, (2).

Pacem fecit his conditionĭbus.*

Aves sanguĭne et prædâ assuētæ.

Julium cum his ad te litĕris misi.

Homo ex anĭmo constat et corpŏre.

Urbem omni commeātu privāvit.

Tres legāti, functi summis honorĭbus, missi sunt.

Ille pericŭlo liberātus est.

Senectus non gladio, sed consilio et ratiōne utĭtur.

Cato ortus municipio Tuscŭlo tribūnus milĭtum in Siciliâ fuit.

Naturâ loci confidēbaṇt.

Nihil honestŭm esse potest, quod*b* justitiâ vacat.

Nudāvit aciem equestri auxilio.

Terram nox obruit umbris.*c*

Nemĭnem præfĕro cónstantiâ.

Sola laurus fulmĭne non icĭtur.

Ille e concilio multis cum millĭbus ibat.

Sic præsentĭbus fruāris*d* voluptâtĭbus, ut futūris non noceas.*e*

Ignem*f* elĭci vidēmus lapĭdum conflictu.

Nihil boni*g* otio et ignaviâ parātur.

Suâ victoriâ gloriantur.

Luna interposĭtu terræ repentè defĭcit.

Fas est ab hoste*h* docēri.

Cæsar cum omnĭbus copiis Helvetios sequi cœpit.

Servōrum munĕre funguntur.

Suspiciōne carēbat.

Accĭpio excusatiōnem quâ usus es.

Equitātu ipsi abundant.

Scriptōres Græci rerum copiâ abundant.

Deus bonis omnĭbus explēvit mundum.

Totâ regiōne potītus est.

Erat inter eos regiâ dignitāte*i* quamvis carēbat nomĭne.

---

a Rule 70. *b* Rule 1, Rem. 8. *c* Rule 69. *d* Rule 89, Rem. *e* Rule 90.
f Rule 20. *g* Rules for translating, partitive genitive. *h* Rule 68, Rem.
i Rule 29, Rem. 4 and 5.

Civĭtas libertāte usus est.
Pecuniâ multātus est.
Exilio multātus est.
Corōnis aureis donātus est.
Ejus omnia arbitrio gesta sunt.
Murus defensorĭbus nudātus est.
Nostri virtūte confidēbant.
Magno pecŏrum numĕro potiuntur.
Domus amœnĭtas non ædificio, sed silvâ, constābat.
Usus est non minus prudentiâ quam fortitudĭne.
Exercĭtum, obsidiōne liberātum, reduxit incolŭmem.
Eum optĭmâ veste texit.

Licet, legĭbus eōrum, cuivis Ephŏro, hoc facĕre regi.
Nemĭnem præfĕro fide.

Dion nobĭli genĕre natus est.
Cimbri et Teutŏni a C. Mario pulsi sunt.
Aquĭla volandi[a] pernicitāte aves omnes excellit.
Subsequebātur omnĭbus copiis.[b]
Gravi opĕre perfungĭmur.
Laude aliēnâ dolet.
Summâ æquitāte[c] res constituit.
Nullo officio aut disciplīnâ assuefactus est.

Hirundĭnes luto nidos construunt, stramento robŏrant.
Corōna a popŭlo[h]data est.
Censesne te[d] ullum invenīre posse[e] homĭnem,[f] qui
  culpâ caret?
Magno metu me liberābis.
Poma ex arborĭbus, si sunt cruda, vi avelluntur, si
  matūra, decĭdunt.
A cane non magno sæpe tenētur aper.
Vacent[g] tua facta omni injustitiæ genĕre.
Dapĭbus epulāmur opīmis.
Jam pulvĕre cælum stare vident.
Cornĭbus tauri se tutantur.

---

[a] Rule 24, Rem. 2. [b] Rule 71. [c] Rule 68, 2. [d] Rule 20. [e] Rule 22, Rem.
3. [f] Rule 89, R. [g] Rule 54. [h] Rule 68, Rem.

Equis Afrĭcam locupletāvit.
Institūto suo Cæsar copias suas eduxit.
Ingressus est cum gladio.
Sine contentiōne oppĭdo potītur.
In captos clementiâ fuĕrant usi.
Prædâ onusti venērunt.
Pacem his legĭbus constituērunt.
Negat, se morę et exemplo.popŭli Romāni posse iter
    ulli per provĭnciam dare.
Ad castra Cæsăris omnĭbus copiis*a* contendērunt.
Hostes lŏco confidēbant.
Patriắm obsidiōne liberavērunt.
Virtūtum laude crevit.

He possessed the whole state.
The city was deprived of provisions.
The state was freed from all danger.
The inhabitants live on milk and flesh.
The enemy abounded in cavalry.
The soldiers were loaded with booty.
They rejoice in their liberty.
The embassadors had borne the highest honors.
He glories in a crown.
They were in want of provisions and money.
He was punished with exile.

LV.

Cases after Verbs, Continued. — Rules 47, 48, 49, 58, 60.

Cæsări diadēma imponĕre*b* voluit Antonius.
Abfuit urbe.
Pontus scopŭlos superjăcit undam.
Classi Datim præfēcit.
Maledīcit utrīque.
Nihil semper floret; ætas succēdit ætāti.
Solstitium pecŏri defendĭte

a Rule 71.   *b* Rule 22, Rem. 2.

Muros accessit.
Antefertur Themistŏcli nemo.
Transiit mare.
Multa et varia impendent hominĭbus génĕra mortis.
Cæsar Deiotăro regi tetrarchiam eripuit.

Legĭbus satisfēcit.
Non ignāra mali misĕris succurrĕre disco.
Abībant sedĭbus.
Ne addīcas*a* anĭmum*b* volŭptāti.
Flumĭna transnābant.
Magnŭs multitudĭni timor est injectŭs.
Eum amīcum sibi cupiēbant adjungi.
Tibi dii benefaciant omnes.
Sæpe ejus consiliis obstĭtit.
Cetĕris satisfacio, mihi ipsi numquam satisfacio.
Omnĭbus unus insŭlis præfuit.
Ego te manum injiciam.

Gradu depulsus est.
Nonnullos prœlio excedĕre vidit.
Accīdit huic, quod*c* cetĕris mortalĭbus, ut inconsider-
    atior in secundâ quam adversâ esset*d* fortūnâ.
Cæsar exercĭtum flumen transduxit.
Hostes loco depellunt.
Sæpe excrcitĭbus præfuit.
Suis finĭbus excessērunt.
Consilium iniit.
Ipse equo vulnerāto dejectus fortissĭmè restĭtit.
Pacem bello anteferēbant.

Ipse omnes copias castris eduxit.
Absenti magistrātum abrogavērunt.
Afflictis semper succurrit.
Omnem equitātum pontem transdūcit.
Agesilāus opulentissĭmo regno præposuit bonam exis-
    timatiōnem.

---

a Rule 89, Rem.   *b* Rule 1, Rem. 9.   *c* Rule 1, Rem. 8 (1).   *d* Rule 90.

Benefēcit reipublīcæ.
Antetŭlit iræ religiōnem.
Ipsi transīre flumen non dubitavērunt.
Conātu destitērunt.
Mihi succubuit.
Hostĭbus spes potiundi oppĭdi discessit.
Magnam se initūrum gratiam vidēbat.
Dejecti sunt loco.

He set Datis over all the islands.
They approached the city.
He was present in the battle.
Thémistocles was preferred to the others.
They were crossing the river.
I was absent from the city.
He presided over the fleet.
All opposed the plan.
He was thrown from (his) horse.
The enemy yielded to us.
He gained great favor.
All hope left our enemies.
We ceased from the attempt.

LVI.

Review Rules 35 to 74, (Cases after Verbs).

Promiscuous Examples.

Insŭlas, quæ Cyclădes nominantur, sub Athenien-
    sium redēgit potestātem.
Magni ejus opĕra existimāta est.
Miserescĭte regis.
Negotii eum pertæsum est.
Non injuriārum obliviscuntur.
Mea maxĭme intĕrest.
Duces adversariæ factiōnis capĭtis damnātos, patriā
    pepŭlit.
Milĭtes necessitātis monet.

Mĭsĕret te aliōrum, tui non misĕret.

Culpâ regem liberavērunt.

Pecŏri signum impressit.

Detrūdunt naves scopŭlo.

Equĭtes, qui toti Galliæ erant imperāti, conveniunt.

Subĭtò misericordia odio successĕrat.

Iĭdem hostes erant civitāti.

Eâ omnes stant sententiâ.

Maturandum sibi existimāvit.

Placuit ei, ut legātos mittĕret.[a]

Quæ victoria magnæ fuit Attĭcis lætĭtiæ.

Fortem se imperatōrem præbuit.[b]

Tremit artus.[c]

Auxilĭa regem orābant.

Nulla tuārum audīta mihi neque visa sorōrum.

Senectūte obiit diem suprēmum.

Mirum somniāvi somnum.

Navi egressus est.

Et natūræ et legĭbus satisfēcit.

Agesilāus Hellespontum copias trajēcit.

Cæsar prœlio supersedēre statuit.

Pari fortūnâ in terrâ usus est.

Suo honōre lætātur.

Ambæ te obsecrāmus genĭbus nixæ.

Nostros navĭbus egrĕdi prohibēbant.

Labōre assiduo et quotidiāno assuēti sunt.

Nemĭnem jacentem veste spoliāvit.

Insŭla abundat divitiis.

Non tam artis indĭgent[d] quam labōris.

Totum montem hominĭbus implēri jussit.

Consuetudĭne suâ ad pedes desiluērunt.

Nemĭnem Alçibiădi præfĕro magnitudĭne anĭmi.

Omnĭbus copiis repente ex oppĭdo eruptiōnem fecē-
    runt.

---

a Rule 90, and rules for translating, subjunctive, 4.　　b Rule 55.
c Rule 59.　　　　　　　　d Rule 40, 2.

In eo prœlio Piso, amplissĭmo genĕre natus, interfectus est.
Incŏlæ lacte et carne vivunt.

The islands are called Cyclades.
They considered his help of great value.
Let us forget injuries.
The leaders of the faction were condemned to death.
I pity soldiers.
They stripped him of his garments.
Horsemen were ordered from all Gaul.
They were enemies to the state.
We must hasten.
The victory occasioned (was for) great joy to the
soldiers.
He proved himself a very great commander.
They live on milk and flocks.
He rejoices in his own fortune.
A sally was made with all the forces.

LVII. -

Rules 75 to 84.

Scriptis[a] epistŏlis abiērunt.
Nemo, illo interfecto, se tutum putābat.
Ille, adversario admōto, bona militĭbus dispertīvit.
Ager nunc pluris est quam tunc fuit.
Vendĭdit hic[b] auro patriam.[c]
Appius cæcus multos annos fuit.
A portu stadia centum et viginti processĭmus.
Dionysius Corinthi pŭeros docēbat.
Calpurnius Romam proficiscĭtur.
Tertiâ vigiliâ eruptiōnem fecērunt.
Athēnis et Lacedæmōne nunciāta est victoria.
Dionysius Platōnem Athēnis arcessīvit.
Vixit annis viginti novem, imperāvit triennio.

---

a Rules for translating, ablative absolute. *b* Rule 1, Rem. 3. *c* Rule 1,
Rem. 9.

Biduum Laodicēæ fui.

Chersonēso tali modo constitūtâ, revertĭtur.

Barbarōrum copiis dejectis, totâ regiōne, quam petiĕ. rat, potītus est.

Eo loco omnes interiērunt.

Prædā locupletāto exercitu, maxĭmis rebus gestis ad urbem venērunt.

Me literārum exspectatio Thessalonīcæ tenet.

Hannĭbal in hiberna Capuam concessit.

Hiĕme ursi in antris dormiunt.

Magno ubique pretio virtus æstimātur.

Consulātu peracto privātus in urbe mansit.

Lis ejus æstimāta est centum talentis.

Monte occupāto, nostros exspectābat.

Conon plurĭmùm Cypri vixit.

Litĕras Athēnas publĭcè misit.

Chares Athēnis et honorātus et potens fuit.

Hoc responso dato discessit.

Darīus, exercĭtu ex Asiâ in Eurōpam trajecto, Scythis bellum inferre decrēvit.

Postĕro die Helvetii castra ex eo loco movent.

Reges pacem ingenti pecuniâ mercabantur.

Galli quondam longè ab suis sedĭbus Delphos usque profecti sunt.

Improbōrum[a] anĭmi solicitudinĭbus noctes atque dies exeduntur.

Hercŭles, Jovis et Asteriæ filius, Tyri maxĭme colĭtur.

Inde Ephĕsum pevēnit.

Athēnis natus est.

Alexander Babylōne mortuus est.

Domi se tenuit.

Domum revocātus est.

Domo[b] arcessītus est.

Domum[c] reverti noluit.

Domi[d] quiētus fuit.

Primâ luce omnem equitātum præmittit.

---

a Rule 1, Rem. 3.   b Rule 83, Rem.   c Rule 81, Rem.   d Rule 80, Rem.

1c.

Paucos dies morātus, se in fines Ubiōrum recēpit.

Eōdem loco non sunt ausi manēre.

Hac oratiōne habĭtâ, concilium dimīsit.

Multas epistŏlas Româ accēpi.

Et mari et terrâ malè res geruntur.

Dies noctesque iter faciens, Taurum transiit.

Postĕro die castra ex eo loco movent.

Galli, re cognĭtâ, obsidiōnem relinquunt.

Regnum multos annos obtinuĕrat.

Totâ nocte continenter ıērunt.

Nullam partem noctis itinĕre intermisso, in fines Lin-
gŏnum die quarto pervenērunt.

Millia passuum tria ab hostium castris castra ponit.

Parvi sunt foris arma, nisi est consilium domi.

Attĭcus annos triginta medicīnâ non indiguit.

Lælius et Scipio rus*a* ex urbe evolābant.

Isocrătes orător unam oratiōnem viginti talentis vendĭdit.

Domo profectus est.

Hac pugnâ pugnātâ, Romam profectus est, nullo
resistente.

Maxĭmis rebus gestis, Athēnas venērunt.

Ut Romæ consŭles, sic Carthagĭne quotannis annui
reges creabantur.

Ei tota respublĭca domi bellique tradĭta est.

Nemo mortalium omnĭbus horis sapit.

Philo domo profūgit, Romamque venit.

Fortè evēnit, ut ruri essēmus.*b*

Virtūte exceptâ, nihil amicitiâ præstabilius putētis.*c*

Cadmus spargit humi*d* jussos dentes.

Urbs Veii*e* decem æstātes hiemesque continuas cir-
cumsessa est.

Athenienses bello Persĭco sua*f* omnia, quæ movēri
potĕrant, partim Salamīnem, partim Trœzēnem
asportārunt.

_____

a Rule 81, Rem. b Rule 90, and Rules for translating, subjunctive, 4; also,
Rule 33, Rem. 2. c Rule 89, Rem. d Rule 80, Rem. e Rule 28. f Rule 1,
Rem. 4.

Rejectis pilis, comĭnus gladiis pugnātum est.
Reges pacem ingenti prĕtio mercabantur.
Quatuor mensĭbus diutius quam popŭlus jussĕrat, ges-
    sit imperium.
Quinto die revertĭtur.
Bellum gerĭtur et mari et terrâ.
Postĕro die hostes in collĭbus constitĕrunt.
Athēnis et Lacedæmŏne nunciāta est victoria.
Proxĭmo triennio omnes gentes subēgit.
Cumis sedem figĕre destĭnat.
Vixit Romæ.
Habĭtat Carthagĭne.
Studuit Athēnis.
Profectus est Athēnas.
Leonĭdas cum copiis delectis Thermopȳlis interiit.
Omnis humo fumat Neptunia Troja.

The letter being written, he departed from Rome.
This answer having been given, he departed to Car-
    thage.
The fifth day he went from home.
Letters were sent to Athens.
The consul being killed, no one thought himself safe
    at home.
He lived many years at Cyprus.
He sold his house for twenty talents.
Having delayed a few days, he returned home.

LVIII.

Rules 85–88.

O vir fortis atque amīcus!
O Dave, ităneᵃ contemnor abs te!
O fallācem homĭnum spem, fragilemque fortūnam, et
    inānes nostras contentiōnes!
Heu vanĭtas humāna!

_____

ᵃ ităne, i.e. ita ne.

Heu miserande puer!
Heu me infelicem!
Ecce nova turba atque rixa!
Tu, Micythe, argentum huic redde.
Heu vanitas humāna!
Desĭne, Meneclĭda, mihi exprobāre.
Heu edĕpol res turbulentas!
Hei mihi! conclāmat.
Væ victis!
O mi Furni!

LIX.

Promiscuous Examples, requiring the application of Rules of Syntax from 1 to 88.

Ingenium docĭle et bome habuit.
Cum paucis, sed viris fortĭbus, navem conscendit.
Post annum quintum in patriam[a] revocātus est.
Victi erant quinque prœliis terrestrĭbus, tribus naval-
    ĭbus.
Reipublĭcæ perītus fuit.
Quædam animalia sunt lucis timĭda.
Statuit alĭquid sibi consilii novi esse capiendum.
Civitātis regendæ perītus fuit.
Novi alĭquid inīri consilii intellexērunt.
Is locus abest circĭter millia passuum decem.
Non expers fuit perĭcŭli.
Sestertiōrum centum millia munĕri misit.
Consilia quum patriæ tum sibi inimica capiĕbat.
Obviam ei venērunt.
Postridie ejus diēi suas copias flumen transduxit.
Quo[b] quis indoctior,[b] eo impudentior.
Ita vixit ut universis Atheniensĭbus merĭtò esset[c]
    carissĭmus.
Os humerosque deo simĭlis apparuit.
Propior hostem collocātus esset.

---

a Rule 1, Rem. 9.   *b* Rule 10, Rem. 2.   *c* Rule 90.

Claudus fuit altĕro pede.

Non cessit majōrum natu auctoritāti.

Pater ejus, quòd et manu fortis et bello strenuus .et
regi fidēlis erat repertus, habuĭt provinciam partem Ciliciæ.

Illi, nullâ coactâ manu, loci præsidio freti, in silvas
paludesque confugiunt.

Quibus libris nihil potest esse dulcius iis, qui alĭquem
cupiditātem habent notitiæ clarōrum virōrum.

Non ampliùs senis millĭbus passuum interesset.

Libȳes propiùs mare Afrĭcum agitābant.

Propiùs stabŭlis armenta tenērent.

Magnis in laudĭbus*a* in Græciâ fuit victorem*b* Olym-
piæ*b* citāri.*b*

Perīre maluit, quàm armis dejectis navem relinquĕre.

Socĕrum habuĭt Hipponĭcum omnium Græcâ linguâ
loquentium ditissĭmum.

Omnium Græciæ civitātum splendidissĭma fuit Athēnæ.

Quod satis esset*c* præsidii, dedit.

Cives civĭbus parcĕre æquum*d* censēbat.

Negābat se ei vim allatūrum, qui aliquando fuisset*d*
amĭcus.

Nemo ei dicendo potuit resistĕre.

Studiōsus audiendi erat.

Argos habitātum concessit.

Pulsus, incredibĭle dictu, biduo et duābus noctĭbus
Hadrumētum pervēnit.

Consul, equo citāto subter murum hostium ad cohor-
tes advehĭtur.

Ex vitâ discēdo tamquam ex hospitio, non tamquam
ex domo.

Majōres vestri cum Antiŏcho, cum Philippo, cum
Ætōlis, cum Pœnis bella gessērunt.

---

a Rule 18.   *b* Rule 33, Rem. 2.   *c* Rule 100.
                   d Supply *esse*.

Hannĭbal, Hamilcăris filius, admŏdum adolescentŭlus
praeesse cœpit exercitui.

Apud Herodŏtum, patrem historiæ, sunt innumera-
bĭles fabŭlæ.

Saguntum, fœderātam civitātem, vi expugnāvit.

Civĭtas inter Belgas magnâ erat auctoritāte.

Reperiēbat, esse homĭnes magnæ virtūtis.

Hamilcar dixit non enim suæ esse virtūtis, arma a
patriâ accepta adversus hostes adversariis tradĕre.   ◆

Nĭhil rerum humanārum sine dęōrum numĭne geri
putābat.

Magnam partem eōrum interfecērunt.

Nihil opus pecuniâ est.

Belli judicium imperatōris esse existimavērunt.

Agesĭlāus nomĭne non potestāte fuit rex.

Hannĭbal minor quinque et viginti annis natus imperātor factus est.

Et mari et terrâ duces erant Lacedæmonii.

Vetĕris contumeliæ recordātur.

Decipĭtur labōrum.

Vidēbant, Eumĕne recevto, omnes præ illo parvi
futūros.

Magis reipublĭcæ intĕrest quàm mea.

Postquam se capĭtis damnātum audīvit, Lacedæmŏ-
nem demigrāvit.

Monet me officii.

Injuriārum oblivisĭtur.

Summæ diligentiæ imperii summam severitātem
addit.

Petunt et orant, ut sibi parcat.[a]

Sibi quemque consulĕre jussit.

Omnĭbus pericŭlis adfuit.

Inermis armātis occurrēbat.

Dixit, si Allobrogĭbus satisfaciant[b], sese cum iis
pacem esse factūrum.

Statuit alĭquid sibi consilii novi esse capiendum.

Hæc olim magnæ laudi erant.

Cæsări omnia uno tempŏre erant agenda.

In muro consistendi potestas erat nulli.

Pollicĭtus est sibi eam rem curæ futūram.

Respondit amicitiam popŭli Romāni sibi præsidio non detrimento esse oportēre.

Talem se imperatōrem præbuit, ut eo tempŏre omnĭbus apparuit, nisi ille fuisset,[a] Spartam futūram non fuisse.

Audaciùs de bello consilia inīre incipiunt.

Rhenum transīre constituit.

Cupio me[b] esse[b] clementem.[b]

Athenienses statuērunt ut[b] naves[b] conscendĕrent.[b]

Nec vero Cæsārem[c] fefellit.

Quare ejus fugæ comĭtem me adjungĕrem.[d]

Id adjūta me.[e]

Maxĭmam partem[f] lacte atque carne vivunt.

Potītus loco, duas ibi legiōnes collocāvit.

Qui pace diutīnâ volunt frui, bello exercitāti esse debent..

Hostes muro turribusque dejecti in foro ac locis patentiorĭbus constitērunt.

Istam pugnam pugnābo.

Redĭtu in patriam excludĭtur.

Urbem obsidiōne liberāvit.

Auxilio sociōrum privantur.

Petiērunt[b] ne se armis despoliāret.[g]

Campāni fuērunt superbi bonitāte[h] agrōram.

Militĭbus urbs abundat.

Exsul patriâ caruit.

Magnis munerĭbus donātus est.

Prædâ onusti Athēnas venērunt.

Datāmes matre Scythissâ natus primùm milĭtum numĕro fuit apud Artaxerxem.

a Rule 89.   *b* Rule 54, Rem. 1.   *c* Rule 54, Rem. 2.   *d* Rule 55, Rem.
e Rule 56, Rem. 2.   *f* Rule 59.   *g* Rule 90.   *h* Rule 68, 1, (1).

Nemĭnem Alcibiădi præfĕro in patriam amōre.[a]
Puĕri mulieresque ex muro passis manĭbus suo more
  pacem petiērunt.
Omnĭbus copiis[b] auxilio Nerviis venērunt.

Hamilcăre occīso, Hasdrŭbal exercitui præfuit.
Cæsar, unâ æstāte duōbus maxĭmis bellis confectis, in
  hiberna exercĭtum dednxit.
Celerĭter nostri, clamōre sublāto, pila in hostes immit-
  tunt.
Romam venit Mario consŭle.[c]
Magni æstimābat pecuniam.
Reges pacem ingenti pretio mercabantur.
Syracūsis vixit.
Spartam redīre nolēbat.
Vixit annis undetriginta.
Domi remansērunt.
Paucos dies commeātus causâ morātur.
Paucis diēbus opus efficĭtur.
Complūres dies milĭtes frumento caruērunt.
Quinque diērum iter[d] abfuit.
Exercĭtus Romānus tridui itinĕre[d] abfuit.
Conon fuit extrēmo Peloponnesio bello prætor.

Nemo Romanōrum eloquentior fuit Cicerōne.
Gallōrum omnium fortissĭmi sunt Belgæ.
Obviam hostĭbus ibant.
Postridie ejus diēi castra movērunt.
Perītus belli erat.
Habēbat equĭtum viginti millia.
Pharnabāzo id negotii dedit.
Carus suis erat.
Ætāte proxĭmus erat.
Nihil, quod ipsis esset[e] indignum, committēbant.
Hibernia dimĭdio est mĭnor quam Britannia.
Alii alios favēbant.
Gladiis in eos impĕtum fecērunt.

Libenter homĭnes id, quŏd volunt, credunt.
Docet, eum magno fore perICŭlo.
Elatiùs se gerĕre cœpit.
Exercebātur plurimùm currendo.
Agesilāum bellātum in Asiam mittunt.

Cimon, Miltiădes filius, duro admŏdum initio usus
    est adolescentiæ.
Athēnis, splendidissĭmâ cĭvitāte, natus est.
Fuit magnâ liberalitāte.
Maxĭmæ fuĭt prudentiæ..
Est hoc Gallĭcæ consuetudĭnis.
Cum parte navium in patriam venit.
Opus est consilio.
Cato ædīlis plebis factus est.
Reminiscĭtur pristīni tempŏris acerbitātem.
Princĭpes civitātis, insimulāti proditiōnis, ab Romānis
    interfecti sunt.
Ejus auctorĭtas in civitāte magni habebātur.
Admonēbat alium egestātis alium cupiditātis suæ.
Magis civitātis intĕrest quam mea.
Duces capĭtis damnāti sunt.
Reminisci vetĕris famæ.

Imperio regis non parēbat.
Argentum huic redde.
Regi satisfēcit.
Se hostĭbus obtŭlit atque interfectus est.
Sibi eam rem suscipiendam putābat.
Exĭtus fuit oratiōnis sibi nullam cum his amicitiam
    esse posse, si in Gallia remanērent.[a]
Atheniensĭbus exhaustis præter arma et naves nihil
    erat super.
Vereor ne civitātĭ sit[b] opprobrio.
Pœni Hannibălem imperatōrem fecērunt.
Cæsar Æduos frumentum flagitābat.
Flumen transīre cœpērunt.

Interrogātus est causam.
Navi egressus est.
Fungĭtur officio.
Gaude tuo bono.
Consilio et ratiōne deficĭtur.
Custodiâ liberātus est.
Naves onĕrant auro.
Obsidĭbus adductis eos in fidem recēpit.
Non satis tutum se Argis vidēbat.
Domum revertērunt.
Solis occāsu suas copias in castra reduxit.
Hìc complūres annos morātus est.
Duas fossas quindĕcim pedes latas perduxit.
O carus amīcus!
Ecce misĕrum homĭnem!
Heu virgo infēlix!
Res magnas mari gessit.

LX.

Subjunctive Mood.—Rules 89 *to* 100.

Sensit, si eo pervenisset,[a] sibi esse pereundum.
Faveat[b] fortuna.
In media[c] arma ruāmus.[b]
Pythia praecēpit ut Miltiădem sibi imperatōrem sum-
    ĕrent.
Non sum ita hebes ut istūc dicam.
Illud moneo,[d] juxta hostes castra habeas.
Utĭnam quidem istud evenisset!
Odĕrint dum metuant.[e]
Priusquam Lacedæmonii subsidio venīrent, dimicāre
    utĭle arbitrabātur.
Putābant exspectandum dum se ipsa res aperīret.
Darīus quum ex Europâ in Asiam redîsset, hortantĭ-
    bus amīcis ut Græciam redigĕret in suam potes-
    tātem, classem comparāvit.

---

a Rule 89. *b* Rule 89. R. *c* Rule 1, Rem. 7. *d* Rule 90, Rem. *e* Rule 92.

Quæ cùm ita sint, perge quò cœpisti.

Nec tamen ego sum ille ferreus, qui fratris carissĭmi
    mærōre non moveaȓ.[a]

Nihil molestum,[b] quod non desidĕres.[c]

Quod sine molestiâ tuâ fiat.[d]

Audītâ voce præcōnis majus gaudium fuit, quàm
    quod universum homĭnes capĕrent.[e]

Cæsar equitātum omnem præmittit, qui[f] videant,[g]
    quas in partes iter faciant.[h]

Erant, quibus appetentior famæ viderētur.[i]

Nulla res est, quæ perferre possit[j] continuam labō-
    rem.

O fortunāte adolescens qui tuæ virtūtis Homērum
    præcōnem invenĕris![k]

Pompeius idoneus non est, qui impĕtret.[l]

Ad te quid scribam[m] nescio.

Jussit ut, quæ venissent,[n] naves Euboeam petĕrent.

Ităque Athenienses, quod honestum non esset,[o] id ne
    utĭle quidem (esse) putavĕrunt.

Quos vicĕris[p] amīcos tibi esse cave[q] credas.

Nunc revertāmur.

Nemo dubĭtet.

Multa pollicĭtus est si se conservâsset.

Non cum quōquam arma contŭli, quin is mihi succu-
    buĕrit.

Cato priusquam honorĭbus opĕram daret, versātus[r]
    in Sabīnis.

Quum hostium devicisset exercĭtus, summâ æquitāte
    res constituit.

Epaminondas eloquentiâ[s] perfēcit, ut auxilio sociō-
    rum Lacedæmonii privarentur.

Cujus exemplum utĭnam imperatōres nostri sequi
    voluissent!

Rogat, finem orandi faciat.

a Rule 96, 1, and note.   b Supply *est*.   c Rule 96, 2.   d Rule 96, 3.   e Rule
96, 4.   f Rule 1, Rem. 8, (2).   g Rule 96, 5.   h Rule 96.   i Rule 96, 6.   j Rule
96, 7.   k Rule 96, 8.   l Rule 96, 9.   m Rule 97.   n Rule 98.   o Rule 99.
p Rule 100.   q Rule 90, Rem.   r Supply *est*.   s Rule 68.

Domi creant décem prætōres, qui exercitui præees-
sent.[a]

Aristīdes adeo excellēbat abstinentiâ, ut unus, quod
quidem nos audierĭmus,[b] cognomĭne Justus sit,
appellātus.

Pavor erat, ne castra hostis aggrederētur.

Adjūta me, quò id fiat faciliùs.

Non quicquam fecit quod fide suâ esset indignum.

Quæ latebra est, in quam non intret[c] metus mortis?

Nihil est, quin malè narrando possit depravāri.

Avertit equos, priusquam pabŭla gustâssent Trojæ.

Negat se scire, cùm tamen haud ignōret.

Zenōnem, quum Athēnis essem,[d] audiēbam frequenter.

Caninius fuit mirifĭcâ vigilantiâ,[e] qui suo toto consulātu somnum non vidĕrit.[f]

Negat jus[g] esse, qui miles non sit,[h] pugnāre[i] cum
hoste.

Mater, quid agerētur, resciit, filiumque monuit.

Se eum esse dixit, qui ad officium peccantes redīre
cogĕret, non qui urbes nobilissĭmas expugnāret
Græciæ.

Quis est, qui utilia fugiat?

Nervii incusavērunt relĭquos Belgas, qui[j] se popŭlo
Romāno dedidissent.[j]

Missi sunt delecti, qui Thermopўlas ocoupārent.

Nemo est, qui haud intellĭgat.

Legātos misērunt, qui id fieri vetārent.

An est quisquam, qui hoc ignōret?

Legātos misērunt, qui petĕrent pacem.

Domĭno navis, quæ sit,[k] aperuit.

Responsum est, obsĭdes, quo loco rogārent,[l] futūros.

Reprehendebātur, quod parum odisse malos cives
viderētur.[m]

a Rule 96, 5.   b Rule 96, 3.   c Rule 96, 7.   d Rule 95, Rem.   e Rule 29,
Rem. 4.   f Rule 96, 8.   g. Rule 22.   h Rule 99.   i Supply cum.
j Qui dedidissent, because they, etc.; Rule 96, 8.   k Rule 97.   l Rule 99.
m Rule 100.

His mandāvit, ut, quæ dicĕret*Ariovistus, cognosce-
  rent.
Qualis sit, primùm aperuit in bello.
Nemo eum responsūrum putābat, quòd, quid dicĕ-
  ret,* non habēret.*
Quærit, causæ quid sit tam repentīno consilio.
Sed illue rĕdeāmus.
Ne doleas.
Faciat quod lubet.
Miltiădes hortātus est pontis custōdes, ne occasiōnem
  liberandæ Græciæ dimittĕrent.
Si tibi vidētur, des ei filiam tuam nuptum.
Monuit, ut consulĕret sibi.
In scytălâ erat scriptum, nisi domum reverterētur,*
  se capĭtis eum damnatūros.
Quo factum est, ut Miltiădes, timens ne classis regia
  adventāret, Athenas redīret.
Erat eâ sagacitāte, ut decĭpi non posset, præsertim
  quum anĭmum attendisset ad cavendum.
Verebātur ne priùs consilium aperirētur suum, quàm
  conāta perfecisset.
Utĭnam minus vitæ cupĭdi fuissēmus!
Neque recusâvit, quo minus legis pœnam subīret.
Sic verba fecit, ut nemo tam ferus fuĕrit, quin ejus
  casum lacrimârit, proinde ac si alius populus,
  non ille ipse, qui tum flebat, eum sacrilegii dam-
  nâsset.

Dum hic venīret, locum relinquĕre noluērunt.
Cognōvit, si epistŏlam pertulisset, sibi esse pereundum.
Semper habĭti sunt fortissĭmi, qui summam imperii
  potirentur.*
Prædicābat, mirāri se, non graviorĭbus pœnis affĭci,
  qui religiōnem minuĕrint, quam qui fâna spoliā-
  rent.
Imperātor omnes cives qui arma ferre possent adesse
  jussit.

a Rule 98.   *b* Rule 100.   *c* Rule 99.   *d* Rule 96, 6.

Legātos misērunt qui eum absentem accusārent, quòd societātem cum rege Persārum fecisset.

Milĭtes ea, quæ imperarentur, libenter fecērunt.

Non venĕrat quod sciam.

Cæsar equitātum, qui sustinērent hostium impĕtum, misit.

Vidĕtur, qui aliquando impĕret, dignus esse.

Peccavisse mihi videor, qui a te discessĕrim.

Magna fuit contentio, utrum mœnĭbus se defendĕrrent, an obviam irent hostĭbus aciēque decernĕrent.

Accusātus est proditiōnis, quòd, quum Parum expugnāre possit, a rege corruptus, infectis rebus discessisset.

Misērunt Delphos consultum, quidnam facĕrent.

Legātos misērunt, qui Lysandrum accusārent, quod sacerdōtes fani corrumpĕre conātus esset.

Pontem fecit in Histro flumĭne, quà copias traducĕret.

Collēgis prædixit ut ne priùs Lacedæmoniōrum legātos dimittĕrent, quàm ipse esset remissus.

Difficĭle intellectu, utrum eum amĭci magis vererentur,ᵃ an amārent.ᵃ

Suasit, Pharnabāzo id negotii daret.

Cæsar dixit se, postquam hostes fusi essent, castra munitūrum esse.

Neque abest suspicio, quin ipse sibi mortem conscivĕrit.

Cæsar non exspectandum sibi statuit, dum in Sautŏnes Helvetii pervenīrent.

Multo graviùs, quòd sit destitūtus, querĭtur.

Ostendit, Helvetiis perfacĭle esse, quum virtūte omnĭbus præstārent, imperio potīri.

Poposcit servos, qui ad eos perfugissent.

Cæsar dixit se cum solâ decĭmâ legiōne, de quâ non
dubitāret, esse itūrum.

Qualis esset natūra montis, qui cognoscĕrent, misit.

Dicit montem, quem a Labiēno voluĕrit, ab hostĭbus
tenēri.

Querĭtur, magnam Cæsărem injuriam facĕre, quis suo
adventu vectigalia sibi deteriōra facĕret.[a]

<hr />

[a] Rule 96, 8.

VOCABULARY.

EXPLANATION OF ABBREVIATIONS.

a ....active.	*dem.* .....demonstrative	*interr* ....interrogative
abl ....ablative.	*dep* ....deponent.	*irr* ....irregular.
acc ....accusative.	*dim* ....diminutive.	*m* ....masculine.
adj ....adjective.	*disj* ....disjunctive.	*n* ....neuter.
adv ....adverb	*f* ....feminine.	*num* ....numeral.
advers ....adversative.	*fig* ....figuratively.	*part* ....participle.
c ....com. gender.	*fin* ....final.	*pass* ..... passive.
caus ......causal.	*fut* ....future.	*pl.* or *plur.* plural.
comp . ...comparative.	*gen* ......genitive.	*poss* ....possessive.
concess ...concessive.	*ger* ....gerund.	*prep* ......preposition.
condit .....conditional.	*illat* ......illative.	*pron* ....pronoun.
conj ......conjunction.	*impers* ....impersonal.	*rel* ....relative.
cop ....copulative.	*ind* ....indeclinable.	*sing* .....singular.
d ....doubt. gender.	*indef* ......indefinite.	*subst* ......substantive.
dat ....dative.	*inf* .... ..infinitive.	*sup* ....superlative.
def ....defective.	*interj* ....interjection.	*temp* .....temporal.

A.

A, Ab, or Abs, prep. with abl., *from, after; at;* with the agent of a passive verb, *by. A* is used before consonants only; *ab* before vowels and sometimes before consonants; *abs* before *q* and *t*.

Abeo, īre, iī, ĭtum, irr. n., (ab & eo), *to go away, depart.*

Abjĭcĭo, ĕre, jēci, jectum, a., (ab & jacio), *to throw away, throw.*

Abrŏgo, āre, āvi, ātum, a., (ab & rogo), *to repeal, annul; to take away, deprive of.*

Absens, tis, part. & adj., (absum), *absent; remote.*

Absolūtus, a, um, part., *from.*

Absolvo, ĕre, vi, ūtum, a., (ab & solvo), *to loose; to absolve, acquit.*

Abstinentia, æ, f., *abstinence, self-restraint, moderation, temperance;* from

Abstĭneo, ĕre, ui, tentum, a. & n., (abs and teneo), *to keep from; to abstain.*

Abstŭli, *see* Aufero.

Absum, abesse, abfui, irr. n., (ab & sum), *to be absent; to be distant* or *remote; to fail, be wanting.*

Absurde, adv., (absurdus, absurd), *absurdly, irrationally.*

Abundans, part & adj., *abounding, wealthy;* from

Abundo, āre, āvi, ātum, n. & a., (ab & undo, *to rise in waves*), *to overflow, abound.*

Ac, cop. conj., the same as atque, *and; as; than.*

Accēdo, ĕre, cessi, cessum, n., (ad & cedo), *to go,* or *come near to, to approach; to be added to.*

Accĭdo, ĕre, cĭdi, n., (ad & cado), *to fall out, happen.*

225

Accĭpio, ĕre, cēpi, ceptum, a., (ad & capio), *to take to one's self, to take, receive accept; to learn.*

Accŭrāte, adv., comp. accurātiŭs, (accurātus, *accurate*), *with care, carefully, accurately.*

Accūso, āre, āvi, ātum, a., (ad & causa), *to accuse.*

Acer, acris, acre, adj., *sharp; ardent, spirited, fierce.*

Acerbĭtas, ātis, f., (acerbus, *sour*), *sharpness, bitterness, sourness;* fig., *sorrow, trouble, affliction; harshness, severity.*

Achæi, ōrum, m. pl., *the people of Achaia, the Achæans.*

Achilles, is, m., *Achilles, a Grecian hero.*

Acies, ēi, f., *the edge; an army in battle array, an army; a battle, a fight, an action.*

Acrĭter, acrĭus, acerrĭmĕ, adv., (acer), *sharply; bravely, courageously, valiantly; fiercely.*

Ad, prep. with acc., *to: at; by, near, among, towards; even to; for, on account of, in respect of.* In composition with other words, the *d* is changed into *c, f, g, b, n, p, r, s,* and *t,* before those letters respectively.

Addĭco, ĕre, ixi, ictum, n., (ad & dico, *to adjudge*), *to give up, to devote.*

Addo, ĕre, dĭdi, dĭtum, a., (ad & do), *to add, to give: to join, to unite.*

Addūco, ĕre, xi, ctum, a., (ad & duco), *to lead to; to conduct, bring;* fig., *to persuade, induce, move.*

Adeŏ, adv., (ad & eŏ, *thither*), *so far, so much, so.*

Adeo, ire, ivi, *or* ii, ĭtum, irr n., (ad & eo), *to go to, to approach.*

Adeptus, a, um, part., (adipiscor).

Adhĭbeo, ĕre, ui, ĭtum, a., (ad & habeo), *to apply, use, employ; to admit.*

Adhuc, adv., (ad & huc), *hitherto, as yet, yet.*

Adĭmo, ĕre, ēmi, emptum, a., ad & emo, *to buy*), *to take to one's self, take away.*

Adipiscor, i, eptus sum, dep. a., (ad & apiscor, *to reach after*), *to get, obtain, acquire.*

Adjungo, ĕre, nxi, nctum, a., (ad & jungo, *to join*), *to add, join, annex, unite.*

Adjūto, āre, āvi, ātum, a., *to help, assist;* from

Adjŭvo, āre, jūvi, jūtum, a., (ad & juvo), *to assist, help, aid.*

Admĭnistro, āre, āvi, ātum, (ad & ministro *to serve*), *to administer, manage conduct, direct.*

Admīror āri, ātus, sum, dep. a., (ad & miror), *to wonder at, to admire.*

Admisceo, ĕre, scui, xtum *or* stum, a., (ad & misceo), *to mix with* pass. *to be mingled with.*

Admixtus, a, um, part., (admisceo).

Admŏdum, adv., (ad & modus), *very, very much.*

Admŏneo, ĕre, ui, ĭtum, a., (ad & moneo), *to admonish, remind.*

Adolescens, tis, part., (adolesco, *to grow up*), *growing up;* subst. c., *a youth, a young man or woman,* hence

Adolescentia, æ, f., *youth, the age succeeding* pueritia, *boyhood, which ended at the fifteenth year, and prior to* juventus, *manhood, which began at the twenty-eighth, or as some say at the thirtieth year.*

Adolescentŭlus, i, m. (adolescens), *a young man, youth stripling.*

Adŏrior, iri, ortus sum, dep, (ad & orior), *to attack; to try.*

Adsum, adesse, adfui, irr. n., (ad & sum), *to be present, at hand or near; to aid, assist, stand by.*

Advĕho, ĕre, vexi, vectum, a., (ad & veho, *to carry*), *to bear or bring to a place, to carry.*

Advento, āre, āvi, ātum, n., (advenio, *to arrive*), *to arrive at, come to.*

Adventus, ûs, m., (advenio, *to arrive*), *a coming, arrival, approach.*

Adversarius, a, um, adj., (adversus), *opposing, opposite, contrary;* subst., m., *an adversary, an enemy.*

Adversum, i, n., *misfortune, calamity, disaster, evil:* si quid adversi, *if any misfortune;* from

Adversus, a, um, adj., (adverto, *to turn to*), *opposite, fronting, hostile, unfavorable, opposing, adverse:* res adversæ, *adversity, calamities, misfortune.*

Adversus, prep., (adverto, *to turn to*), *against, towards.*

Advŏco, āre, āvi, ātum, a., (ad & voco), *to call to; to summon.*

Ædĭfĭcium, ii, n., *an edifice, building;* from

Ædĭfĭco, āre, āvi, ātum, a., (ædes, *a habitation,* & facio), *to build, construct.*

Ædīlis, is, m., (ædes, *a habitation*), *an edile, a magistrate in Rome,* who had the superintendence of public buildings and works.

Ædui, ōrum, m., the Ædui, a tribe of Celtic Gauls.

Æger, gra, grum, adj., sick, weak, feeble, infirm; sorrowful: hence

Ægritūdo, ĭnis, f., sickness.

Ægyptus, i, f., Egypt.

Æmŭlor, āri, ātus, sum, dep. a., (æmŭlus, emulous), to emulate.

Enéas, æ, m., Æneas, a Trojan hero.

Æquĭtas, ātis, f., equality: fig., equity, justice, impartiality, kindness: from

Æquus, a, ŭm, adj., plain, level; equal; favorable, advantageous: fig., just, equitable, fair, right.

Ær, is, m., the air, the atmosphere.

Ærarium, ii, n., (æs, money), the treasury.

Æstas, ātis, f., summer.

Æstĭmo, āre, āvi, ātum, a., to value; to estimate: æstimare magni, to value greatly.

Ætas, ātis, f., age, time of life, life.

Æternus, a, um, adj., eternal, everlasting.

Ætōli, ōrum, m. pl., the Ætolians, the inhabitants of Ætolia, a country of Greece

Affabĭlis, e, adj., (affor, to speak to), affable, courteous.

Affĕro, affere, attŭli, allātum, irr. a., (ad & fero), to bring or carry to a place; to assert, allege: afferre vim, to offer or do violence to.

Afficio, ĕre, fēci, fectum, a., (ad & facio), to move, affect. With an abl. it is often translated by a verb resembling the noun in sense; as, afficere poena, to punish.

Afflictus, a, um, part & adj., dashed with force against: injured, hurt: troubled, harassed; overthrown, destroyed: from

Affligo, ĕre ixi ixum, a., (ad & fligo, to strike), to dash violently against any thing; to harass, afflict, vex, trouble, distress.

Africa, æ f., Africa.

Africus, a, um, adj., African.

Ager, agri m., a field, territory, country; land.

Agesilāus, i, m., Agesilaus, a king of Sparta.

Aggrĕdior, grĕdi, gressus sum, dep. a., (ad & gradior, to go), to go to, approach; to attack, assail, assault.

Agĭto, āre, āvi, ātum, a., (ago), to move; to live, abide.

Ago, agĕre, egi, actum, a., to drive; to lead; act, do, perform, execute; to treat or discourse of.

Agricŏla, æ, m., (ager & colo), a cultivator of land, a husbandman, a farmer

Alo, ais, ait, def., to say.

Alcibiādes, is, m., Alcibiadis, an eminent Athenian, the pupil of Socrates.

Alexander, dri, m., Alexander, a king of Macedonia.

Alias, adv., (alius), in another way, at another time, otherwise.

Aliēnus, a, um, adj., (alius), belonging to another, or to others, another's, foreign.

Alĭquando, adv., at some time, once; at length, sometimes: from

Alĭquis, alĭqua, alĭquod or alĭquid, pron., (alius & quis), some, some one, something.

Alĭquot, ind. adj., (alius & quot, how many), some.

Alius, a, ud, adj., other, another: alius,—alius, one—another: alii—alii, some, —others.

Allatūrus, a, um, part., (affero).

Allŏbrox, ŏgis, m.; pl., Allobrŏges, um, the Allobroges, a people who inhabited the country near the junction of the Saone and the Rhone.

Alo, alĕre, alui, alĭtum or altum, a., to nourish, maintain, feed, support; to strengthen.

Alpes, ium, f. pl., the Alps.

Alter, ĕra, ĕrum, gen. alterius, adj., one of two, the other, the second; another: alter—alter, the one—the other, the former—the latter.

Altitūdo, ĭnis, f., height, loftiness; depth: from

Altus, a, um adj., (alo), high, lofty; deep.

Ambiāni, ōrum, m:, the Ambiani, a people of Belgic Gaul.

Ambĭtus, ūs, m., (ambio, to go around), a going round; bribery.

Ambo, æ, o, adj., pl., both, each.

Amicitĭa, æ, f., friendship: from

Amĭcus, a, um, adj., (amo), friendly, kind: subst., amĭcus, i, m., a friend.

Amitto, ĕre, īsi, issum, a., (a & mitto), to send away, let go; to lose.

Amnis, is, m., a river.

Amo, āre, āvi, ātum, a., to love.

Amoenĭtas, ātis, f., (amoenus, pleasant), pleasantness.

Amor, ōris, m., (amo) love.

Ampius, i, m., *Ampius, a Roman name.*

Amplius, adv., (comp. of amplè, *amply*), *more.*

Amplus, a, um, adj., *large, great;* fig., *illustrious, distinguished.*

An, adv. & conj., in indirect questions, *whether;* in direct questions, like other interrogative particles, it is not translated. An—an, *whether — or.* The first *an* is sometimes omitted, or its place supplied by *ne* or *utrum.*

Ancŏra, æ, f., *an anchor.*

Ancus, i, m., *Ancus. Ancus Marcus, the fourth Roman king.*

Ango, ĕre, anxi, ctum & anxum, a., *to bind; to trouble, disquiet, torment, vex*

Angustia, æ, f., *a narrow place, defile; distress:* from

Angustus, a, um, adj., (ango), *narrow, close, confined.*

Anĭma, æ, f., *the air, breath; the life; the soul.*

Animadverto, ĕre, ti, sum, a., (anĭmus & adverto, *to turn to*), *to attend to; to mark, observe, perceive.*

Anĭmal, ālis, n., (anima), *a living being, an animal.*

Anĭmus, i, m., *the soul; the mind; courage.*

Annĭbal, see Hannibal.

Annus, i, m., *a year:* hence

Annuus, a, um, adj., *annual, yearly; lasting a year.*

Ante, prep. with acc., *before;* antè, adv., *before, formerly, previously.*

Antea, adv., (ante & ea, abl. of is), *before, heretofore, formerly.*

Antecēdo, ĕre, essi, essum, n. & a., (ante & cedo), *to go before; to excel.*

Antefĕro, ferre, tŭli, lātum, irr. a., (ante & fero), *to carry before: to prefer.*

Antiŏchus, i, m., *Antiochus, a king of Syria.*

Antīquus, a, um, adj., (ante), *old, ancient*

Antonius, i, m., (Marcus), *Mark Antony, a distinguished but profligate Roman general, the friend of Cæsar.*

Antrum, i, n., *a cave, a cavern.*

Anŭlus, i, m., (anus, *a ring*), *a ring.*

Anxius, a, um, adj., (ango), *anxious, solicitous.*

Aper, apri, m., *a wild boar.*

Apĕrio, īre, erui, ertum, a., (a & pario), *to uncover; to open; to disclose.*

Apertus, a, um, part. & adj., (aperio), *opened; open, standing open:* fig. *clear, plain, manifest, evident.*

Appāreo, ēre, ui, ĭtum, n., (ad & pareo), *to appear, to be seen; to be manifest or clear.*

Apparo, āre, āvi, ātum, a., (ad & paro), *to prepare; to provide.*

Appello, āre, āvi, ātum, a., (ad & pello), *to drive to; to speak to, address, to call, name.*

Appĕtens, tis, part. & adj., *seeking after; eager for, fond of:* appetentior famæ, *too fond of fame:* from

Appĕto, ĕre, īvi, or ii, ītum, a., (ad & peto), *to strive after, try to obtain; to desire earnestly; to pursue; to desire, covet, long for; to attack, assail; to draw near, approach.*

Appius, a, um, adj., *Appian:* Appia via, *a well-known high-road, begun by Appius Claudius:* from

Appius, i. m., *Appius, a Roman prænomen, or first name.* See *Claudius.*

Apporto, āre, āvi, ātum, a., (ad & porto), *to bring, or carry.*

Aptus, a, um, adj., (apo, *to fasten*), *fit, suitable, proper.*

Apud, prep. with acc., *with; near, close by; before; at; among; in:* with the name of a person, it often signifies *in his house.*

Apulia, æ, f., *Apulia, a province of lower Italy.*

Aqua, æ, f., *water.*

Aquĭla, æ, f., *an eagle.*

Ara, æ, f., *an altar.*

Arar, ăris or Arăris, is, m., *the Saone, a river of Celtic Gaul.*

Arbitrium, i, n., (arbiter, *an umpire*), *the judgment of an arbitrator; a judgment, decision; will, pleasure.*

Arbĭtror, ări, ātus sum, dep. a., (arbiter, *an umpire*), *to believe, think, consider.*

Arbor, ŏris, f., *a tree.*

Arcadia, æ, f., *Arcadia, a mountainous country of Greece.*

Arcesso, ĕre, īvi, ĭtum, a., *to send for, summon, invite.*

Achimēdes, is, m., *Archimedes, a celebrated mathematician of Syracuse.*

Argentum, i, n., *silver; silver money, money.* m

Argos, i, ., sing. & Argi, ōrum, m.

pl., *Argos, a city in Greece, the capital of Argolis.*

Arguo, ĕre, uĭ, ūtum, a., *to show; to accuse, blame.*

Ariovistus, ĭ, m., *Ariovistus, the name of a German king.*

Aristīdes, is, m., *Aristides, an Athenian general, renowned for his integrity.*

Arma, ōrum, n. pl., *arms, weapons:* fig , *war, warfare.*

Armātus, a, um, part. & adj., (armo), *armed, equipped.* Armāti ōrum, m. pl., *armed men, men in arms, soldiers, troops.*

Armentum, ĭ, n., (aro, *to plough*), *a herd of cattle, a drove.*

Armo, āre, āvi, ātum, a., (arma), *to arm, equip.*

Ars, artis, f., *art; contrivance, skill; science; an art: profession, employment.*

Artaxerxes, is, m., *Ataxerxes, a Persian king.*

Arx, cis, f., (arceo, *to shut up*), *a castle, citadel, fortress.*

Ascendo, ĕre, ndi, nsum, a. & n., (ad & scando, *to climb*), *to ascend, mount, climb.*

Asia, æ, f., *Asia: Asia Minor.*

Asper, ĕra, ĕrum, adj., *rough:* fig., *rough, harsh: calamitous, perilous.*

Asporto, āre āvi, ātum, a., (abs & porto), *to bear or carry away.*

Assiduus, a, um, adj., (assideo, *to sit near*), *continual, incessant, constant.*

Assuefăcio, ĕre, fēci, factum, a., (assuetus & facio), *to accustom, habituate.*

Assuesco, ĕre, ēvi, ētum, n. & a., (ad & suesco, *to be wont*), *to be accustomed; to accustom one's self; to be wont or used; to accustom.*

Asteria, æ, f., *Asteria, the mother of the Tyrian Hercules.*

At, advers. conj., *but, yet.*

Athēnæ, ārum, f. pl., *Athens, the most celebrated city of Greece;* hence

Athenienses, ium, m. pl., *the Athenians, the citizens of Athens.*

Atque or ac, cop. conj., (ad & que), *and, and also, and indeed, and even: after aliter, secus, alius, &c., than; after idem, par, similis, &c., as.*

Atrox, ōcis, adj., (ater, *black*), *dark, horrible, dreadful: fig., savage, cruel, fierce.*

Attendo, ĕre, endi, entum, a., (ad & tendo), *to direct or turn toward; to attend to, consider, mind, give heed to.*

Attĭcus, ĭ, m., *Atticus, the name of a distinguished Roman.*

Attĭci, ōrum, m. pl., *the Athenians.*

Auctor, ōris, c., (augeo), *an author:* hence

Auctorĭtas, ātis, f., *authority: ability, power; influence, force, weight.*

Audacia, æ, f., (audax, *daring*), *boldness, audacity.*

Audacĭter & Audacter, audaciūs, audacissĭmē, adv., (audax, *daring*), *boldly, confidently.*

Audeo, ĕre, ausus sum, n. pass., *to dare, attempt, venture.*

Audio, īre, īvi or iĭ, ītum, a., *to hear; to obey.*

Aufĕro, auferre, abstŭli, ablātum, irr. a., (ab & fero), *to take away, carry off, withdraw, remove.*

Aufūgio, ĕre, fūgi, n., (ab & fugio), *to fly away, fly from, escape.*

Augeo, ēre, auxi, auctum, a. & n., *to increase, augment, enlarge.*

Aureus, a, um, adj., (aurum), *of gold, golden.*

Auris, is, f., *an ear.*

Aurum, ĭ, n., *gold; money.*

Ausus, a, um, part., (audeo.)

Aut, disj. conj., *or:* aut — aut, *either — or.*

Autem, advers. conj., *but, yet; moreover.*

Auxilium, ii, n., (augeo), *aid, help.*

Avaritia, æ, f., *avarice:* from

Avārus, a, um, adj., (aveo, *to long for*), *avaricious.*

Avello, ĕre, elli, or ulsi, ulsum, a., (a & vello, *to pluck*), *to pluck off.*

Averto, ĕre, ti, sum, a., (a & verto), *to turn away, avert,*

Avĭdus, a, um, adj., (aveo, *to long for*), *desirous, eager, greedy, fond of; avaricious.*

Avis, is, f., *a bird.*

B.

Babylon, ōnis, f., *Babylon, the capital of Chaldea.*

Barbărus, a, um, adj., *barbarian, barbaric, not Greek nor Roman, savage:* barbări, ōrum, m., *barbarians, savages.*

Beāte, adv., (beātus, *happy*), *happily.*

Belgæ, ārum, m. pl., *the Belgians, a warlike people in the northern part of Gaul.*

Bellicōsus, a, um, adj., (bellīcus, pertaining to war), warlike.

Bello, āre, āvi, ātum, n., to war, to wage or carry on war : from

Bellum, i, n.. war : domi bellique, in peace and in war.

Bene, adv., (bonus), comp., melius, sup., optimè, well; rightly.

Benefácio, ĕre, fēci, factum, n., (bene & facio), to do good to one, benefit, show favor : hence

Beneficium, i, n., (benefĭcus, liberal), a kindness, favor, benefit.

Benignus, a, um, adj., kind, benign.

Bibo, ĕre, bĭbi, a., to drink.

Bibrax, actis, n., Bibrax, a town in Gaul.

Biduum, ii, n., (bis, twice, & dies), two days.

Biennium, ii, n., (bis, twice, & annus), two years.

Bini, æ, a, num., adj., (bis, twice), two by two; two.

Blandus, a, um, adj., flattering; pleasant, kind, friendly.

Bonĭtas, ātis, f., (bonus), goodness, excellence.

Bonum, i, n., any good; a good thing; benefit, advantage, profit; prosperity, happiness : bona, n. pl., goods, property, effects, wealth, riches; from

Bonus, a, um, adj., comp., melior, sup., optimus, good; brave.

Brevis, e, adj., short; brief.

Britannia, æ, f., Britain, or Great Britain.

Brutus, i, m., Brutus, a Roman surname.

C.

C., an abbreviation of Caius.

Cadmus, i, m., Cadmus, a Phœnician, the inventor of alphabetic writing.

Cado, ĕre, cecĭdi, casum, n., to fall down, fall; to fall or die in battle, be slain, perish; to fail; to happen.

Cæcus, a, um, adj., blind.

Cædes, is, f., a cutting; slaughter : from

Cædo, ĕre, cecĭdi, cæsum, a., (cado), to cut; to kill, slay, slaughter.

Cælum or Cœlum, i, n. pl., cæli, ōrum, m., heaven; the sky; air.

Cæsar, ăris, m., Cæsar, a family name of the Julian gens; Julius Cæsar, the first Roman emperor.

Caius, i, m., Caius, a common Roman prænomen.

Calamĭtas, ātis, f., loss, calamity, misfortune.

Calămus. i, m., a reed.

Calendæ, ārum, f. pl., (calo, to call), the first day of the month, the calends.

Callĭdus, a, um, adj., (calleo, to know), cunning, shrewd.

Calor, ōris, m., (calleo, to be warm), warmth, heat.

Calpurnius, i, m., Calpurnius, a Roman name.

Camillus, i, m., Camillus, a Roman general.

Campus, i, m., a plain, a field.

Caninius, i, m., Caninius, a Roman, who was consul only seven hours.

Canis, is, c., a dog.

Cano, ĕre, cecĭni, cantum, n. & a., to sing; to foretell, predict : gallus canit, the cock crows : hence

Canto, āre āvi, ātum, n. & a., to sing.

Cŭpio, ĕre, cepi, captum, a., to take, seize; to capture; to take in, comprehend; to enjoy, feel; to contain: capere consilium, to form a design, adopt a plan or measures : hence

Captivus, a, um, adj., captive : captivus, i, m., a prisoner, a captive.

Captus, a, um, part., (capio), having been seized, taken.

Capua, æ, f., Capua, a city of Campania, in Italy.

Caput, ĭtis, n., the head; life : capitis damnare, to condemn to death : capitis absolvere, to declare innocent of a capital crime : capitis accusare, to accuse of a capital crime.

Cāreo, ĕre, ui, ĭtum, n., to be without, to want.

Caro, carnis, f., flesh.

Carpo, ĕre, psi, ptum, a., to crop, pick, pluck.

Carthaginiensis, e, adj., Carthaginian : subs., a Carthaginian : from

Carthāgo, ĭnis, f., Carthage, a city in the northern part of Africa.

Carus, a, um, adj., dear, precious, valued, beloved.

Casa, æ, f., a cottage, hut.

Castellum, i, n., dim., (castrum, a fort), a castle, fort, fortress, stronghold.

Castra, ōrum, n. pl., a camp.

Cassius, i. m., Cassius, the name of several Romans.

Casus, ûs, m., (cado), a falling : fig., an occurrence, event; chance, accident; a misfortune.

Catilīna, æ, m., Catiline, a Roman, who conspired against the government of his country.

Cato, ōnis, m., Cato, the name of a Roman family.

Causa, æ, f., a cause, a reason; an occasion; a lawsuit: abl., causa, for the sake of, on account of: causam dicere, to defend one's self, to plead in defence.

Căveo, ēre, cavi, cautūm, n. & a., to beware, be on one's guard, avoid: cave ut, — that not.

Cecīdi, see Cado & Cædo.

Cedo, ēre, cessi, cessum, n. & a., to move, go; to withdraw, depart: fig., to yield, give way, give place to.

Celer, ĕris, ĕre, adj., swift, speedy, fleet, quick: hence

Celerĭter celerĭŭs, celerrĭmè, adv., quickly, speedily.

Celo, āre, āvi, ātum, a., to conceal, hide.

Celtæ, ārum, m. pl., the Celts, a people of Gaul.

Censeo, ēre, ui, um, a., to weigh, value; to think, judge, suppose.

Centum, num. adj., pl. ind., a hundred: hence

Centurio, ōnis, m., (centuria, a company), a centurion; a captain of a hundred men.

Cepi, see Capio.

Cerno, ēre, crevi, cretum, a., to see, discern, perceive, comprehend, understand; to determine, decree: hence

Certus, a, um, adj., determined, fixed, certain, sure; true, faithful: certiōrem aliquem facere, to inform, acquaint, apprise: certior fio, I am informed or apprised, I receive intelligence.

Cervus, i, m., a stag, a deer.

Cetĕrus, ĕra, ĕrum, adj., other, the other: pl., the rest, the others.

Cessi, see Cedo.

Chares, ētis, m., Chares, an Athenian general.

Chersonēsus, i, f., the Chersonese, the Thracian peninsula at the west of the Hellespont.

Cicĕro, ōnis, m., Cicero, the most illustrious of the Roman orators and writers.

Cilicia, æ, f., Cilicia, a country in Asia Minor.

Cimbri, ōrum, m. pl., the Cimbrians, a people of northern Germany.

Cimon, ōnis, m., Cimon, a son of Miltiades, a distinguished Athenian general.

Circĭter, adv. & prep. with acc., (circus, a circle), about, near.

Circum, prep. with acc., (circus, a circle), around, about.

Circumdătus, a, um, part., built around: from

Circumdo, dăre, dĕdi, dătum, a., (circum, around, & do), to put around.

Circumeo or Circueo, īre, īvi or ii, circuitum, irr. n. & a., (circum & eo), to go around, to encompass.

Circumsĕdeo or Circumsĭdeo, ēre ēdi, essum, a., (circum & sedeo), to sit around, to encamp around; to besiege.

Circumvēnio, īre, vēni, ventum, a., (circum & venio), to surround.

Citātus, a, um, part. & adj., incited, stimulated, excited; hurried, swift: equo citato, at a full gallop: from

Cito, āre, āvi, ātum, a., (cieo, to put in motion), to incite, stimulate, spur; to summon, call; to mention; to proclaim, announce.

Civīlis, e, adj., of or pertaining to a citizen, civil; courteous, polite: from

Civis, is, c., a citizen: hence

Civĭtas, ātis, f., a city, a state; the citizens; citizenship.

Clam, adv. & prep. with acc. or abl., (celo), without the knowledge of, privately, secretly.

Clāmor, ōris, m., (clamo, to cry out), a loud voice, cry, shout; clamor; a noise, sound.

Clandestīnus, a, um, adj., (clam), secret, clandestine.

Clarus, a, um, adj., clear, famous, illustrious.

Classis, is, f., a fleet.

Claudius, i, m., (Appius), Claudius, a Roman consul.

Claudo, ēre, si, sum, a., to close, shut, shut up; to inclose, surround.

Claudus, a, um, adj., lame, limping.

Clemens, tis, adj., merciful: hence

Clementia, æ, f., kindness, clemency, mercy.

Cnæus, or Cneus, i, m., Cneus, a Roman prænomen.

Coactus, a, um, part., (cogo), collected; assembled; compelled.

Codrus, i, m., Codrus, the last king of the Athenians.

Cœpi, isse, a def., I begin, or I began.

Cogĭto, āre, āvi, ātum, a., (con & agĭto), *to think, consider, reflect; to think or reflect upon, ponder; to intend.*

Cognōmen, ĭnis, n., (con & nomen), *a surname.*

Cognosco, ĕre, gnōvi, gnĭtum, a., (con & nosco, *to know*), *to know; to hear, learn, find out, discover, ascertain.*

Cogo, ĕre, coēgi, coactum, a., (con & ago), *to drive together, collect; fig., to compel, constrain, force.*

Cohors, rtis, f., *the tenth part of a legion, a cohort.*

Cohortor, āri, ātus sum, dep., (con & hortor), *to exhort, encourage.*

Collēga, æ, m., (con & lego), *a partner in office, a colleague.*

Collīgo, ĕre, ēgi, ectum, a., (con & lego), *to collect.*

Collis, is, m., *a hill.*

Collŏco, āre, āvi, ātum, a., (con & loco), *to place together, post, station; to dispose arrange; to put, set, place:* collocare, or nuptum collocare, *to give in marriage.*

Colloquium, ĭi, n., *a conversation, discourse; a conference:* from

Collŏquor, i, cūtus sum, dep., (con & loquor), *to speak together, converse.*

Colo, ĕre, ui, cultum, a., *to cultivate, till: fig., to cherish; to respect; to reverence, worship:* hence

Colōnus, i, m., *a colonist, husbandman.*

Com, (cum), an inseparabl preposition. Its final *m* is sometimes changed to *n, l,* or *r,* and is sometimes dropped, thus making *con, col, cor,* or *co.*

Combūro, ĕre, ussi, ustum, a., (con & uro, *to burn*), *to burn up, consume.*

Comes, ĭtis, c., (cum & eo), *a companion, comrade.*

Comĭnus, adv., (con & manus), *hand to hand, in close combat.*

Comis, e, adj *kind, obliging, friendly, courteous, affable.*

Commeātus, ūs, m., (commeo, *to go and come*), *a passage; a convoy; provisions, supplies.*

Commemŏro, āre, āvi, ātum, a., (con & memoro), *to mention, recount, relate.*

Committo, ĕre, mīsi, missum, a., (con & mitto), *to join together, unite; to do, act, perform:* committere pugnam, *to join battle.*

Commōtus, a, um, part., *moved; affected:* from

Commŏveo, ēre, mōvi, mōtum, a., (con & moveo), *to move together; to more; to excite: fig., to affect, disquiet, trouble, alarm.*

Commūnio, ire, ivi or ii, ītum, a., (con & munio), *to fortify all around; fortify.*

Commūnis, e, adj., (con & munus), *common, general, joint; courteous, condescending, affable.*

Compăro, āre, avi, ātum, a., (con & paro), *to procure, get, furnish, prepare.*

Compello, ĕre, pŭli, pulsum, a., (con & pello), *to drive together; to drive, force, compel.*

Compĕrio, īre, pĕri, pertum, a., (con & pario), *to ascertain, find out.*

Compleo, ĕre, ētum, a., (con & pleo, *to fill*), *fill up, fill; to complete, finish.*

Complūres, ūra, gen., urium, adj., (con & plus), *many, a good many; several; very many.*

Compōno, ĕre, posui, posĭtum, a., (con & pono), *to put together; to place in order; to finish.*

Comprehendo, ĕre, di, sum, a., (con & prehendo, *to seize*), *to comprehend: to seize.*

Compròbo, āre, āvi, ātum, a., (con & probo), *to approve; to prove.*

Con, see Com.

Conātum, i, n., (conor), *an endeavor, effort, undertaking.*

Conātus, ūs, m., (conor), *an attempt, endeavor, effort, undertaking.*

Concēdo, ĕre, cessi, cessum, a. & n., (con & cedo), *to go; to depart, retire; to yield.*

Concĭdo, ĕre, ĭdi, n., (con & cado), *to fall down, to fall to the ground, fall.*

Concĭdo, ĕre, cĭdi, cisum. a., (con & cædo), *to cut, cut in pieces; to kill, slay, destroy.*

Concĭlio, āre, āvi, ātum, a., *to unite: fig., to make friendly, conciliate, gain, win; to bring about, obtain, procure, make:* from

Concilium, ii, n., (concieo, *to call together*), *an assembly, meeting, council.*

Conclāmo, āre, āvi, ātum, n. & a., (con & clamo, *to cry*), *to cry together, cry aloud; to shout, exclaim.*

Concurro, ĕre, curri, cursum, n., (con & curro), *to run together, flock together; to fight:* hence

Concursus, ûs, m., *a running together; an assembly; a conflict, charge, engagement, onset.*

Condemno, āre, āvī, ātum, a., (con & damno), *to condemn.*

Conditio, ōnis, f., *a condition; terms: from*

Condo, ĕre, dĭdi, dĭtum, a. (con & do), *to put together, build, found; to conceal, hide.*

Confectus, a, um, part. (conficio), *made; finished, ended.*

Confĕro, conferre, contŭli, collātum, a. irr. (con & fero), *to bring together, collect; to bring or join together in a hostile manner; to confer; to give: conferre se, to betake or turn one's self, to go.*

Conficio, ĕre fēci, fectum, a. (con & facio), *to make, prepare; to execute, perform; to finish, complete, settle; to weaken, wear out, destroy.*

Confido, ĕre, ısus sum, n. pass. (con & fido, to trust), *to trust, confide in.*

Confirmo, āre, āvī, ātum, a. (con & firmo, to make firm), *to strengthen, establish, confirm; to encourage; to affirm, assert.*

Confĭtor, ēri, fessus sum, a. dep. (con & fateor, to confess), *to confess, own.*

Conflictus, ûs, m., *a striking together, collision: from*

Confligo, ĕre, xi, a. (con & fligo, to dash against), *to contend, fight.*

Confŭgio, ĕre, fūgi, n. (con & fugio), *to fly to; to flee.*

Congrĕdior, i, gressus sum, dep. (con & gradior, to go), *to meet; to join battle.*

Conjectus, a, um, part.: from

Conjĭcio, ĕre, jēci, jectum, a (con & jacio), *to throw together; to throw, cast, hurl; to conclude, infer, conjecture: conjicere in vincula, to put in chains, to imprison.*

Conjuratio, ōnis, f. (conjūro, to swear together), *a conspiracy, plot.*

Conjux, ŭgis, c. (conjungo, to bind together), *a spouse; a husband; a wife.*

Conon, ōnis, m. *Conon, a renowned general of the Athenians.*

Conor, āri, ātus sum, a. dep., *to try, strive, attempt, endeavor.*

Conscendo, ĕre, di, sum, n. & a. (con & scando, to climb), *to climb or go up, mount, ascend: conscendere navem or in navem, to go on board ship, take ship, embark.*

20 *

Conscisco, ĕre, scivi scītum, a. (con & scisco, to ordain), *to vote together, resolve, decree; to execute: consciscere sibi mortem, to lay violent hands on one's self, kill one's self, commit suicide.*

Conscrībo, ĕre, psi, ptum, a. (con & scribo), *to write together: conscribere milites, to enroll, enlist.*

Consector, āri, ātus sum, dep. (con & sector, to pursue), *to follow after eagerly, pursue; to overtake.*

Consecūtus, a, um, part.: from

Consĕquor, i, cūtus sum, dep. con & sequor, *to follow, pursue; to attain to, obtain.*

Consĕro, ĕre, sertum, a. (con & sero, to interweave), *to join.*

Conservo, āre, āvī, ātum, a. (con & servo), *to preserve, take care of, defend; to observe.*

Consido, ĕre, sēdi, sessum, n. (con & sido, to sit down), *to sit down together; to sit down, seat one's self; to light, settle, take up one's abode, pitch, pitch a camp.*

Considĕro, āre, āvī, ātum, a., *to inspect: fig., to consider, contemplate.*

Considius, i, m., *Considius, one of Cæsar's officers in the Gallic war.*

Consĭlium, ii, n., *deliberation, a plan, course, design, intent, purpose, counsel, advice; prudence, wisdom, discretion; a council.*

Consimĭlis, e, adj. (con & simĭlis), *wholly similar, like.*

Consisto, ĕre, stĭti, stĭtum, n. & a. (con & sisto, to place), *to stand still, halt, stop; to draw up, post one's self; to stand, make a stand.*

Conspectus, ûs, m. (conspicio), *a view, sight, presence.*

Conspectus, a, um, part.: from

Conspĭcio, ĕre, spexi, spectum, a. (con & specio, to see), *to see, perceive, behold: hence*

Conspĭcor, āri, ātus sum, dep. *to see, behold, descry.*

Constantia, æ, f. (constans, firm), *firmness, constancy.*

Constat, impers., *see Consto.*

Constĭti, see Consisto & Consto.

Constĭtuo, ĕre, ui, ūtum, a. (con & statuo), *to set, place, erect, make, build, found, establish; to regulate, manage; to fix, appoint; to determine, resolve, decide.*

Consto, āre, stĭti, stătum, n., (con & sto), *to stand still; to consist or be composed of; to stand at, to cost.*

Constat, impers., *it is evident, clear, plain, certain; it is agreed, it appears.*

Construo, ĕre, uxi, uctum, a., (con & struo, *to pile up*), *to heap up; to build, construct.*

Consuesco, ĕre, suĕvi, suētum, a. & n., (con & suesco, *to be accustomed*), *to accustom one's self, to be accustomed:* hence

Consuetūdo, ĭnis, f., *custom, use.*

Consul, ŭlis, m., *a consul, one of the chief magistrates annually elected at Rome:* hence

Consulātus, ûs, m., *the office of consul, consulship.*

Consŭlo, ĕre, lui, ltum, n. & a. *to consult, deliberate; to provide for, take care of, look to.*

Consūmo, ĕre, sumpsi, sumptum. a. (con & sumo, *to consume, devour, waste, destroy, kill; to spend, employ, pass.*

Contemno, ĕre, tempsi, temptum. a. (con & temno, *to slight*), *to contemn, despise.*

Contendo, ĕre, di, tum, a. & n., (con & tendo), *to stretch out; to stretch, strain, exert; to seek to arrive at, hasten, go to; to strive, contend against, vie with:* hence

Contentio, ōnis, f., *a straining; an effort, exertion; a contention, controversy, contest.*

Contentus, a, um, adj., (contineo, *to contain*), *content, satisfied.*

Contĭgi, *see* Contingo.

Continenter, ado. (contĭnens, *holding*), *continually.*

Contingo, ĕre, tĭgi, tactum, a. & n., (con & tango), *to touch; to reach, arrive at; to fall out, happen, fall to.*

Continuus, a, um, adj., (contineo, *to contain*), *continued, incessant, perpetual, continual.*

Contrăho, ĕre, xi, ctum, a., (con & traho, *to draw*), *to draw together, assemble.*

Contremisco, ĕre, mui, n., (con & tremisco, *to shake*), *to tremble all over, shake; to tremble from fear, be agitated.*

Contŭli, *see* Confĕro.

Contumelia, æ, f., *an insult, reproach; injury.*

Convĕnio, īre, vēni. ventum, n. & a., (con & venio), *to come together, meet, flock, assemble, collect; to agree:* convenire aliquem, *to meet, or have an interview with.*

Converto, ĕre, ti, sum, a. & n., (con & verto), *to turn; to change.*

Convŏco, āre, āvi, ātum, a., (con & voco), *to call together, assemble, summon.*

Copia, æ, f., (con & ops), *abundance, plenty, copiousness; a supply, store; troops, forces:* facere copiam, *to supply or furnish.*

Coram, prep. with abl., *before, in presence of.*

Corinthus, i, f., *Corinth, a city of Greece.*

Cornelius, i, m., *Cornelius, a Roman name.*

Cornu, ûs, n., *a horn.*

Corōna, æ, f., *a crown, a garland.*

Corpus, ŏris, n., *a body, the person.*

Corrumpo, ĕre. rūpi, ruptum, a., (con & rumpo, *to burst*), *to waste, impair; to spoil; to corrupt, bribe.*

Crassus, i, m., *Crassus, a Roman family name.*

Credo, ĕre dĭdi, dĭtum, a. & n., *to trust, believe; to confide, intrust.*

Creo, āre, āvi, ātum, a., *to create, appoint, choose, elect:* hence

Cresco, ĕre, crevi, crctum, n., *to grow, increase; to be promoted, advanced, rise, thrive; to become greater.*

Critias, æ, m., *Critias, a tyrant of Athens.*

Crudēlis, e, adj., (crudus), *cruel:* hence

Crudelĭter, adv., *cruelly.*

Crudus, a, um, adj., (cruor, *blood*), *bloody; raw: unripe.*

Culpa, æ, f., *a crime, fault.*

Cum, prep. with abl., *with, along with, together with.* It is annexed to the ablative of personal, and sometimes of relative pronouns, as mecum, vobiscum, &c.

Cům or **Quum**, caus. conj., *when, since; although.*

Cumae, ārum, f. pl., *Cumae, a city of Italy.*

Cunctus, a, um, adj., (conjunctus), *all, the whole.*

Cupĭde, adv., (cupidus), *fondly, eagerly.*

Cupidĭtas, ātis, f., *desire, eagerness; avarice, covetousness:* from

Cupĭdus, a, um, adj., *desirous, eager, fond; avaricious, covetous:* from

Cŭpio, ĕre, ĭvi, or ĭi. ĭtum, a., *to desire, wish.*

Cur, adv., (quare), *why? wherefore?*

Cura, æ, f., (quaero), *care, concern:*

est mihi curæ, *I have a care, I take care of, attend to :* hence

Curo, āre, āvi, ātum, a., (cura), *to take care of, see to, look to, regard.* With a fut. pass. part., *to order, cause.*

Curro, ĕre. cucurri, cursum, n., *to run, hasten :* hence

Cursus, ûs, m., *a course, a running.*

Custodia, æ, f., (custos), *charge, custody ; a prison.*

Custōdio, īre, īvi, or ii, ītum, a., *to watch, protect, defend, guard, preserve :* from

Custos, ōdis, c., *a keeper, guard, watch.*

Cyolădes, um, f. pl., *the Cyclades islands in the Ægæan sea.*

Cyprus, i, f., *Cyprus, an island in the Mediterranean Sea, on the coast of Asia Minor.*

Cyrus, i, m., *Cyrus, a king of Persia.*

D.

Damnātus, a, um, part., *condemned :* from

Damno, āre, āvi, ātum, a. (damnum, *a fine*), *to condemn, sentence.*

Daps, dapis, f., *a feast, a meal.*

Darius, i, m., *Darius, a king of Persia.*

Datāmes, is, m., *Datames, a Persian general.*

Datis, is, m., *Datis, a general under Darius.*

Datus, a, um, part., (do), *given.*

Davus, i, m., *Davus, the name of a slave.*

De, prep. with abl., *of, in respect of, about, concerning, touching, in regard to ; from, out of.*

Dēbeo, ēre, ui, ītum, a., (dē & habeo), *to owe :* pass., *to be due or owing, to become due.* With the infinitive it denotes duty, *it is proper, it is indispensable, one ought.*

Debilīto, āre, āvi, ātum. a., (debĭlis, *weak*), *to weaken.*

Decem, num. adj. ind., *ten.*

Decemvĭri, ōrum, m. pl., (decem & vir), *the Decemviris, Roman magistrates.*

Decerno, ĕre, crēvi, crētum, a. & n., de & cerno), *to decree, determine, resolve ; to fight, combat, contend, engage.*

Decĭdo, ĕre, ĭdi, n., (de & cado), *to fall off, fall.*

Decĭmus, a, um, num. adj., (decem), *the tenth.*

Decĭpio, ĕre, cēpi ceptum, a., (de & capio), *to deceive, beguile.*

Declāro, āre, āvi, ātum, (de & claro, *to make clear*), *to make clear ; to announce, proclaim.*

Decrēvi, see Decerno.

Decurro, ĕre, cucurri & curri, cursum, n., (de & curro), *to run down or along ; to run, hasten.*

Dedo, ĕre dĭdi, dĭtum, a., (de & do), *to give or deliver up ; to submit, surrender ; to devote one's self.*

Dedūco, ĕre, xi, ctum, a., (de & duco), *to bring down ; to draw off, withdraw ; to lead forth, lead, conduct.*

Defendo, ĕre, di, sum, a., *to fend or ward off, avert, keep off ; to defend :* hence

Defensor, ōris, m., *a defender.*

Defĕro, ferre, tŭli, lātum, irr. a., (de & fero), *to carry down, to bring, carry, convey ; to tell.*

Deficio, ĕre, fēci, fectum, a. & n. (de & facio), *to fail, be wanting, deficient ;* of the sun and moon, *to be eclipsed ; to leave, desert ; to rebel, revolt.*

Defui, see Desum.

Dego, ĕre, degi, a. & n., (de & ago), *to spend, pass ; to live.*

Deinde, & Dein, adv., (de & inde), *then, afterward.*

Deiotărus, i, m., *Deiotarus, a king of Galatia.*

Dejectus, a, um, part. & adj., *thrown down :* dejectus equo, *dismounted, thrown from — :* from

Dejĭcio, ĕre jēci jectum, a., (de & jacio), *to throw or cast down ; to overthrow, kill, slay ; to drive out.*

Delecto, āre, āvi, ātum, a. (delicio, *to entice*), *to delight, please.*

Delectus, a, um, part. & adj., (deligo), *chosen, selected.*

Deleo, ēre, levi, letum, a., *to destroy.*

Delibĕro, āre, āvi, ātum, a., (de & libra, *a balance*), *to deliberate, consult, consider.*

Delictum, i, n., (delinquo, *to offend*), *a fault, crime.*

Delĭgo, ĕre, lēgi, lectum, a., (de & lego), *to choose out : to select.*

Delos, i, f., *the island Delos, one of the Cyclades.*

Delphi, ōrum, m. pl., *Delphi, a town of Phocis, in Greece.*

Dementia, æ, f., (demens, *mad*), *madness, folly.*

Demetrius, i, m., *Demetrius, a king of Macedonia.* This was the name also of several other distinguished Greeks.

Demigro, āre, āvi, ātum, a., (de & migro, *to remove*), *to remove, migrate.*

Democritus, i, m., *Democritus, a Grecian philosopher.*

Dens, dentis, m., *a tooth*: hence

Dentātus, i, m., *Dentatus, a Roman name.*

Depello, ēre, pŭli, pulsum, a., (de & pello), *to drive, put* or *thrust down*: *to drive away, expel, remove.*

Depōno, ēre, posui, posĭtum, a., (de & pono), *to lay* or *put down; to leave, leave off, give up.* Deponere memoriam alicujus, *to forget.*

Deprāvo, āre, āvi, ātum, a., (de & pravus, *crooked*), *to pervert, distort.*

Depressus, a, um, part., *sunk*: from

Deprīmo, ēre, pressi, pressum, a., (de & premo), *to press down, depress; to sink.*

Desēro, ēre, rui, rtum, a., (de & sero, *to interweave*), *to sever; to desert.*

Desĭlio, ire, ilui, ultum, n., (de & salio, *to leap*), *to leap down, alight.*

Desĭno, ēre, ivi or ii, ĭtum, n. & a., (de & sino, *to permit*), *to cease, leave off, give over, desist, end.*

Desisto, ēre, stĭti, stĭtum, n. & a., (de & sisto, *to stand*), *to stand still; to cease, desist from.*

Despēro, āre, āvi, ātum, n. & a. (de & spero), *to despair of, despond.*

Despólio, āre, āvi, ātum, a., (de & spolio), *to spoil, plunder, ravage, strip, rob, deprive of.*

Destĭno, āre, āvi, ātum, a., *to make fast; establish, determine.*

Desum, esse, fui, n, irr. (de & sum), *to fail, be wanting* or *lacking.*

Detĕrior, adj., *worse, poorer, meaner*: facere deterius, *to make worse, injure, impair.*

Detrăho, ēre, xi, ctum, a, (de & traho, *to draw*), *to draw off, take away.*

Detrimentum, i, n. (detĕro, *to wear*), *detriment, disadvantage, damage, loss, harm.*

Detrūdo, ēre, si, sum, a. (de & trudo, *to push*), *to thrust* or *push down.*

Deus, i, m., *God; a god, deity.*

Devictus, a, um, part. : from

Devinco, ēre, ici, ictum, a. (de &

vinco), *to conquer, vanquish, subdue, overcome.*

Dexter, tĕra & tra, tĕrum & trum, adj., *on the right hand, right.*

Diadēma, ătis, n., *a diadem.*

Dico, ēre, xi, ctum. a., *to speak, say, tell; to call.*

Dictātor, ōris, m. (dicto, *to dictate*), *a dictator.*

Dido, ûs or ōnis, f., *Dido, a queen of Carthage.*

Dies, ēi, m. or f. in sing., m. in pl., *a day.*

Diffĕro, ferre, distŭli, dilātum, irr. a. & n. (dis & fero), *to carry different ways, scatter, disperse; to defer, put off, delay; to differ, be different.*

Diffĭcĭle, adv., *difficultly, with difficulty*: from

Diffĭcĭlis, e, adj. comp. difficĭlior, sup. difficillĭmus, (dis & facĭlis, *easy*), *hard, difficult; troublesome; hard to manage* or *to please, morose, surly, obstinate.*

Digĭtus, i, m., *a finger.*

Dignĭtas, ātis, f., *merit, desert; dignity, rank, greatness; honor*: from

Dignus, a, um, adj. *worthy, deserving.*

Dil, *see* Dens.

Dilĭgens, tis, part. & adj. (diligo), *careful, attentive, diligent, accurate*: *fond of*: hence

Dilĭgentia, æ, f., *diligence, carefulness, attention.*

Dilĭgo, ĕre, lexi, lectum, a. (dis & lego), *to love, esteem.*

Dimidius, a, um, adj. (dis & medius), *halved*: *half.*

Dimĭco, āre, āvi, ātum, n. (dis & mico, *to move quickly*), *to fight, contend.*

Dimitto, ēre, mīsi missum, a. (dis & mitto), *to send different ways; to dismiss, discharge, let go; to omit; to lose, let slip, let pass.*

Dion, ōnis, m., *Dion, a general of Syracuse.*

Dionysius i, m., *Dionysius, the name of two tyrants of Syracuse.*

Direxi, *see* Dirigo.

Dirĭgo, ēre, rexi, rectum, a. (dis & rego), *to direct.*

Diruo, ēre, rui, rŭtum, a. (dis & ruo, *to rush down*), *to destroy, overthrow, raze.*

Dirus, a, um, adj., *direful, dreadful, horrible.*

Dis, m. & f. dite, n gen. ditis, adj. ditior, ditissĭmus, (dives), *rich, wealthy, opulent.*

Dis, an inseparable preposition signifying *asunder*. It sometimes becomes *di*, rarely *dif*.

Discēdo, ĕre, cessi, cessum, n. (dis & cedo), *to separate; to depart, go away, leave*.

Disciplina, æ, f. (discipulus, *a learner*), *discipline, instruction*.

Disco, ĕre, didĭci, a., *to learn*.

Disertus, a, um, adj. (dissero, *to discuss*), *fluent; eloquent*.

Disjĭcio, ĕre, jēci, jectum, a. (dis & jacio), *to disperse, scatter, rout*.

Dispergo, ĕre, si, sum, a. (dis & spargo), *to spread, scatter about, disperse*.

Dispertio, ire, īvi *or* ii, ītum, a. (dis & partio, *to part*), *to distribute, divide*.

Displĭceo, ĕre, ui, ĭtum, a. (dis & placeo), *to displease*.

Dispono, ĕre, posui, posĭtum, a. (dis & pono), *to place here and there, set in order, dispose, arrange*.

Disto, āre, n. (dis & sto), *to be distant*.

Distringo, ĕre, nxi, ctum, a. (dis & stringo, *to draw tight*), *to bind fast*.

Ditissimus, a, um, adj. sup. of dis.

Diu, adv., diutius, diutissime, (dies), *long, a long time*: hence

Diutĭnus, a, um, adj., *long, durable, lasting*.

Diutius, adv. comp. of diu, *longer*.

Dives, ĭtis, adj., *rich, wealthy*.

Divĭdo, ĕre, visi, vīsum, a., *to divide; to distribute*.

Divīnus, a. um, adj. (divus, *divine*), *divine*.

Divitĭacus, i, m., *Divitiacus, a chief of the Ædui, in Gaul*.

Divitiæ, ārum, f. pl. (dives), *riches*.

Do, dare, dedi, datum, a., *to give, bestow, grant, commit, confer; to concede, allow; to yield, surrender*.

Dŏceo, ĕre, cui, ctum, a., *to show, point out; to teach, instruct*: hence

Docĭlis, e, adj., *easily taught, docile*.

Dŏleo, ĕre, ui, ĭtum, n. & a., *to grieve, sorrow; to be sorry for; to sympathize in*: hence

Dolor, ōris, m., *grief, pain, sorrow*.

Dolus, i, m., *a device, crafty purpose, stratagem; artifice, fraud*.

Domesticus, a, um, adj. (domus), *domestic*.

Domicilium, i, n, (domus), *a house, abode, residence*.

Dominatio, ōnis, f. (dominor, *to rule*), *authority, power, sovereignty*.

Domĭnus, i, m., *a master of a house, owner, master, lord*: from

Domus, ūs & i, f., *a house, home; a family, household*: domi, *at home*; domum, *home*; domo *or* ex domo, *from home*.

Donec, temp. conj., *until; as long as*.

Dono, āre, āvi, ātum, a., *to give, present, bestow*: from

Donum, i, n., (do), *a gift, present*.

Dormio, ire, īvi, *or* ii. ītum, n., *to sleep*.

Dubĭto, āre, āvi, ātum, n. & a., *to doubt, be in doubt, be uncertain, hesitate*.

Dubius, a, um, adj. *doubtful, dubious, uncertain*.

Ducenti, æ, a, núm. adj. (duo & centum), *two hundred*.

Duco, ĕre, xi, ctum, a., *to draw, lead, conduct, take along; to command; to esteem, hold, think, consider, reckon, account;* ducere uxorem, *to take a wife, to marry*.

Dulcis, e, adj., *sweet; pleasant*.

Dum, temp. conj., *while, whilst, until; provided that*.

Dumnŏrix, ĭgis, m., *Dumnorix, a leader of the Ædui*.

Duo, æ, o, num. adj., *two*.

Duodĕcim, ind. num. adj. (duo & decem), *twelve*.

Duplex, ĭcis, adj. (duo & plico, *to fold*), *twofold, double*.

Durus, a, um, adj., *hard, solid; toilsome, laborious, difficult; hardy*.

Dux, ducis, m. & f. (duco), *a leader, guide, conductor; a general, commander*.

Duxi, see Duco.

E.

E, *or* Ex, prep. with abl. *from, out of, of; after; on account of; according to*.

Ecce, interj., *lo! behold!*

Edepol, a lengthened vocative of *Pollux*, used adverbially, *by Pollux! indeed! truly!*

Edŏceo, ĕre, cui, ctum, a. (e & doceo), *to teach thoroughly, instruct, inform; to tell, show*.

Edūco, ĕre, xi, ctum, a. (e & duco), *to draw or lead forth, draw out, draw, bring; to bring up, maintain*.

Efficio, ĕre, ēci, ectum, a. (ex & facio), *to bring to pass, do, effect, accomplish, complete, finish, execute, make.*

Efflo, āre, āvi, ātum, a. & n. (e & flo, *to blow*), *to breathe out :* efflare animam. *to breath one's last, to expire, to die.*

Effugio, ĕre, ūgi, n. & a. (ex & fugio), *to flee from, flee away, flee, escape.*

Egestas, ātis, f. (egeo, *to need*), *indigence, extreme poverty, necessity, want.*

Egi, *see* Ago.

Ego, mei, subst. pro., *I.*

Egrĕdior, i, gressus sum, dep. n & a. (e & gradior, *to go*), *to go out, depart, depart from.*

Egregius, a, um, adj. (e & grex, *a herd*), *excellent, remarkable, eminent.*

Ejectus, a, um, part., *cast* or *thrown out :* from

Ejicio, ĕre, jēci, jectum, a. (e & jacio), *to cast* or *throw out, eject, expel ; to banish.*

Elātè, adv. (elātus, *raised*), *loftily, proudly, haughtily.*

Elatiùs, adv. comp. of elatè.

Elĕgans, tis, adj. (eligo, *to select*), *refined, polished, elegant.*

Elephantus, i, m., *an elephant.*

Elicio, ĕre, licui & lexi, licĭtum, a. (e & lacio, *to allure*), *to draw forth, to elicit.*

Elŏquens, tis, adj. (elŏquor, *to speak out*), *eloquent.*

Eloquentia, æ, f. (elŏquor, *to speak out*), *eloquence.*

Elūceo, ĕre, uxi, n. (e & luceo, *to shine*), *to shine forth ; to be apparent, manifest.*

Emax, ācis, adj. (emo, *to buy*), *eager to buy, fond of buying.*

Emico, āre, ui, n. (e & mico, *to quiver*), *to break forth, appear quickly, shine forth.*

Emitto, ĕre, mīsi, missum, a. (e & mitto), *to send forth.*

Enim, caus. conj., *for ; indeed.*

Ennius, i, m., *Ennius, an early Roman poet.*

Enumĕro, āre, āvi, ātum, a. (e & numĕro, *to number*), *to reckon up ; to recount, relate.*

Enuncio, āre, āvi, ātum, a. (e & nuncio), *to spread abroad, divulge, disclose, reveal, report, tell ; to declare.*

Eo, ire, ivi, *or* ii, itum, n. irr, *to go, walk.*

Eò, adv. (is), *thither, to that place.*

Eo, *see* Is.

Epaminondas, æ, m, *Epaminondas, a Theban general.*

Ephĕsus, i, f. *Ephesus, a city of Ionia.*

Ephŏrus, i, m., *a member of the Ephori, a body of Spartan magistrates.*

Epistŏla, æ, f., *a letter, epistle.*

Epŭlor, āri, ātus sum, dep. n. & a. (epŭlum, *a feast*), *to feast, feast upon, eat.*

Eques, itis, m. (equus), *a horseman ; a trooper ; a knight.* Equites, *Knights*, a title of rank among the Romans. The Knights constituted an order of citizens between the patricians & plebeians.

Equester, tris, tre, adj. (eques), *equestrian.*

Equitātus, ûs, m. (equito, *to ride on horseback*), *cavalry.*

Equus, i, m., *a horse, steed.*

Erga, prep. with acc., *towards.*

Ergo, illat. conj., *then, therefore.*

Eripio, ĕre, ipui, eptum, a. (e & rapio, *to snatch*), *to snatch away, take away.*

Erro, āre, āvi, ātum, n. & a., *to wander about ;* fig. *to err.*

Erūdio, īre, ivi, *or* ii, ītum, a. (e & rudis, *rough*), *to polish, educate, instruct.*

Eruptio, ōnis, f. (erumpo, *to break forth*), *a sally, violent assault.*

Et, cop. conj., *and, also ; even :* et — et, *both — and.*

Etiam, cop. conj. (et & jam), *also, even.*

Eubœa, æ, f., *Eubœa, a large island in the Ægean sea.*

Eumĕnes, is, m., *Eumenes, a famous general under Alexander the Great.*

Eurōpa, æ, f., *Europe.*

Evĕnio, īre, vēni, ventum, n. (e & venio), *to come out :* fig. *to fall out, happen :* impers., evēnit, *it happens.*

Everto, ĕre, ti, sum, a. (e & verto), *to overturn, overthrow.*

Evĭto, āre, āvi, ātum, a. (e & vito), *to shun, avoid.*

Evŏlo, āre, āvi, ātum, a. (e & volo, āre), *to fly forth, fly from.*

Ex, prep. *see* E.

Exagĭto, āre, āvi, ātum, a. (ex & agĭto), *to drive out of its place ; to harass, vex, agitate.*

Exaudio, īre, īvi, *or* ii, ītum, a. (ex & audio), *to hear ; to hearken.*

Excēdo, ĕre, cessi, cessum, n. & a. (ex & cedo), *to go forth* or *out, depart :* fig., *to exceed, surpass.*

Excellens, tis, adj., *distinguished, superior, excellent :* from

Excello, ĕre, llui, lsum, a. & n., *to raise up ; to rise, be eminent, excel, surpass.*

Excĭpio, ĕre, cēpi, ceptum, a. (ex & capio), *to take out ; to except ; to receive, take ; to follow, succeed.*

Excĭto, āre, āvi, ātum, a. (excio, *to call out*), *to call out ; to raise, excite.*

Exclūdo, ĕre, si, sum, a. (ex & claudo), *to shut out, exclude ; to hinder, prevent, prohibit, debar.*

Excusatio, ōnis, f. (excūso, *to excuse*), *an excuse.*

Exēdo, ĕre, ēdi, ēsum, a. (ex & edo, *to eat*), *to eat up, consume.*

Exemplum, i, n. (eximo, *to take out*), *an example, instance.*

Exeo, īre, īvi, *or* ii, ĭtum, n. & a. irr. (ex & eo), *to go out or forth.*

Exerceo, ēre, ui, ĭtum, a. (ex & arceō, *to drive away*), *to practice, train, exercise.*

Exercĭtātus, a, um, part, & adj. *exercised, versed, trained, practiced, accustomed :* from

Exercĭto, āre, āvi, ātum, a. (exerceo), *to exercise, practice.*

Exercĭtus, ūs, m.(exerceo), *an army.*

Exhaurio, īre, hausi, haustum, a. (ex & haurio, *to draw*), *to draw out ; to exhaust.*

Exhĭbeo, ēre, ui, ĭtum, a. (ex & habeo), *to hold forth ; to show, exhibit.*

Exiguus, a, um, adj., *small, little, slender, scanty, slight ; few.*

Exilium, *see* Exsilium.

Eximius, a, um, adj. (eximo, *to take out*), *remarkable, extraordinary.*

Existimatio, ōnis, f., *an opinion, judgment :* from

Existĭmo, āre, āvi, ātum, a. (ex & æstimo), *to judge, consider, think, esteem, suppose, imagine.*

Exitiōsus, a, um, adj. *destructive, pernicious:* from

Exĭtium, ii, n. (exeo), *a going out; destruction.*

Exĭtus, ūs, m. (exeo), *a going forth; an end, close, termination, result, amount, sum, purport.*

Expĕrior, īri, ertus sum, dep. a., *to try, prove ; to find out by experience, find out.*

Expers, tis, adj. (ex & pars), *having no part in, without, destitute of.*

Expleo, ēre, ēvi, ētum, a., *to fill :* fig. *to satisfy.*

Explĭco, āre, āvi & ui, ātum & ĭtum, a. (ex & plico, *to fold*), *to unfold :* fig., *to unfold, explain.*

Explorātor, ōris, m., *an explorer ; a spy, scout :* from

Explōro, āre, āvi, ātum, a. (ex & ploro, *to cry out*), *to search out, explore.*

Exprŏbro, āre, āvi, ātum, a. (ex & probrum, *a shameful act*), *to reproach.*

Expugno, āre, āvi, ātum, a. (ex & pugno), *to take or carry by storm, or assault ; to conquer, subdue, overcome.*

Exsilium, ii, n. (exsul), *banishment, exile.*

Exspectatio, ōnis, f., *expectation :* from

Exspecto, āre, āvi, ātum, a. (ex & specto), *to look or wait for, expect ; to long, hope or wish for, desire ; to wait, delay ; to fear, apprehend.*

Exsul, ŭlis, c. (ex & solum, *the ground*), *an exile.*

Extorqueo, ēre, si, tum, a. (ex & torqueo, *to twist*), *to twist ; to wrest.*

Extrēmus, a, um, adj. (sup. of extĕrus, *outward*), *outermost ; extreme, last, final.*

F.

Fabius, i, m., *Fabius, the name of an illustrious Roman family.*

Fabŭla, æ, f. (fari, *to speak*), *a story ; a fable.*

Facĭlè, facĭliùs, facillĭmè, adv. (facilis, *easy*), *easily, readily.*

Facĭnus, ŏris, n., *a deed, an action, an exploit ; a bad action, a crime :* from

Făcio, ĕre, feci, factum, a. & n., *to make, form, effect : to do ; to act :* facere aliquem certiorem, *to inform, apprise.* Pass. fio.

Factio, ōnis, f. (facio), *a making ; a company of persons acting together, a party, faction.*

Factum, i, n. (facio), *a deed, act, action.*

Factus, a, um, part. (facio), *made, done :* quid facto opus sit, *what must be done.*

Facultas, ātis, f. (facĭlis, *easy*), *power, faculty, opportunity*.

Fallax, ācis, adj., *fallacious, deceitful:* from

Fallo, ĕre, fefelli, falsum, a. & n. *to deceive, cheat, mislead.*

Fama, æ, f., *fame, report, rumor, news; reputation, character, · renown.*

Fames, is, f., *hunger; famine.*

Familiāris, e, adj. (familia, *a family*), *familiar, intimate.*

Fanum, i, u. (fari, *to speak*), *a temple.*

Fas, n. ind. (fari, *to speak*), *divine law; right:* fas est, *it is well, fit or proper.*

Fatum, i, n. (fari, *to speak*), *an oracle; destiny, fate.*

Făveo, ēre, fari, fautum, n., *to favor.*

Feci, *see* Facio.

Fefelli, *see* Fallo.

Felicĭtas, ātis, f., *felicity, happiness, good fortune, success:* from

Felix, īcis, adj., *fruitful, fertile; happy, fortunate.*

Ferax, ācis, adj. (fero), *fruitful, fertile.*

Ferīnus, a, um, adj. (ferus), *of a wild beast.*

Fero, ferre, tuli, latum, irr. a. & n., *to bear, carry, bring; to produce; to bear, suffer, endure, submit to, sustain, withstand, stand.* Pass., *to be borne* or *carried,* & hence, *to move, go, ride, fly, sail, run, hasten:* ferre legem, *to propose a law.*

Ferox, ōcis, adj., *wild, bold, courageous, warlike; savage, untamable.*

Ferreus, a, um, adj., *of iron:* fig. *hard, cruel, unfeeling:* from

Ferrum, i, n., *iron; the sword.*

Ferus, a, um, adj., *wild, rude; fierce, savage.*

Fessus, a, um, adj. (fatiscor, *to grow weak*), *wearied, tired, fatigued; worn-out, weak, feeble.*

Festino, āre, āvi, ātum, a. & n. (fero), *to hasten, make haste.*

Fidēlis, e, adj. (fides), *trusty, faithful:* hence

Fidelĭter, adv., *faithfully.*

Fides, ei, f. (fido, *to trust*), *faith, truth, honor; fidelity; a promise, assurance; protection:* dare fidem, *to pledge one's faith:* recipere in fidem, *to receive into favor,* or *under one's protection.*

Figo, ĕre, xi, xum, a., *to fix, fasten.*

Filia, æ, f., *a daughter:* from

Filius, i, m., *a son.*

Fingo, ĕre, finxi, fictum, a., *to form, fashion, make; to suppose, feign.*

Finis, is, d., *a boundary, limit, border: an end* in the pl., *borders, territory, country:* hence

Finitĭmus, a, um. adj., *neighboring, bordering upon.*

Fio, fiĕri, factus sum, irr. pass. of facio, *to be made; to be done* or *executed; to become; to be; to occur, happen, fall out, come to pass; to be valued, esteemed.*

Fīrmus, a, um, adj., *firm, stable:* fig., *steadfast, resolute.*

Flagitium, ii, n., *a shameful act; a crime:* from

Flagĭto, āre, āvi, ātum, a., *to demand.*

Flagro, āre, āvi, ātum, n., *to burn:* fig., *to be inflamed with passion.*

Flamma, æ, f., *a flame, blaze.*

Flavus, a, um, adj., *yellow.*

Fleo, ēre, flēvi, flētum, n. & a. *to weep.*

Flōreo, ēre, ui, n. (flos, *a flower*), *to bloom:* fig., *to flourish; to be eminent, be distinguished.*

Flumen, ĭnis. u. (fluo, *to flow*), *a river.*

Fœderātus, a, um, adj., *leagued together, confederated, allied:* from

Fœdus, ĕris, n., *a league, treaty.*

Forem, es, et, &c. def. n., *I might be,* &c.: inf., fore, the same in sense as futurus esse, *to be about to be:* with a subject acc. *will* or *would be, occur* or *happen.*

Foris, adv., *abroad, without.*

Forma, æ, f., *form, shape; beauty:* hence

Formōsus, a, um, adj., *beautiful.*

Fors, tis, f. (fero), *chance, fortune:* hence

Forte, adv., *by chance, accidentally; perhaps.*

Fortis, e. adj. (fero), *strong, powerful; brave, valiant, gallant, courageous:* hence

Fortĭter, fortiŭs, fortissĭmè, adv., *strongly; bravely, gallantly, courageously.*

Fortitūdo, ĭnis, f., (fortis), *fortitude, bravery, courage.*

Fortuĭto, adv. (fortuĭtus, *accidental*), *by chance, casually.*

Fortūna, æ, f. (fors), *fortune, chance; good fortune; bad fortune, misfortune; the goddess Fortune.*

Fortunātus, a, um, adj. (fortūno, *to prosper*), *happy, fortunate.*

Forum, i, n., *a market place, market; the Forum,* a public place in Rome where assemblies of the people were held, justice was administered, and other public business was transacted.

Fossa, æ, f. (fodio, *to dig*), *a ditch*

Fragĭlis, e, adj. (frango, *to break*), *brittle, fragile:* fig., *frail, inconstant.*

Frater, tris, m., *a brother.*

Fremĭtus, ûs, m. (fremo, *to murmur*), *a dull murmuring, roaring; a noise, clamor.*

Frequenter, adv. (frequens, *frequent*), *frequently.*

Fretus, a, um, adj., *trusting to, relying on.*

Frigĭdus, a, um, adj. (frigeo, *to be cold*), *cold, chilly.*

Frons, dis, f., *foliage, leaves.*

Frons, tis, f., *the front* or *forepart of the head, the forehead, brow.*

Frugis, see Frux.

Frumentum, i, n. (frux), *corn, grain,* particularly *wheat* and *barley.*

Fruor, i, fruitus or fructus sum, dep. n., *to enjoy, reap the fruits of.*

Frustra, adv., *in vain.*

Frux, frugis, (fruor), f. *corn;* pl. fruges, *fruits, produce of the fields.*

Fuga, æ, f., *a fleeing, flight.*

Fūgio, ĕre, fugi, fugĭtum, n. & a., *to flee* or *fly; to flee away, run away, escape; to avoid, shun:* hence

Fŭgo, āre, āvi, ātum, a., *to cause to flee, put to flight, rout.*

Fui, &c., see Sum.

Fulgeo, ĕre, fulsi, n., *to shine:* fig., *to be conspicuous:* hence

Fulmen, ĭnis, n., *lightning.*

Fumo, āre, n., (fumus, *smoke*), *to emit smoke, to smoke.*

Fundo, ĕre, fudi, fusum, a., *to pour, pour out;* fig., *to overthrow, overcome, beat, vanquish, rout.*

Fungor, fungi, functus sum, dep. n., *to perform, execute, discharge, administer.*

Furius, i, m.. *Furius, a Roman family name.*

Furnius, i, m., *Furnius, the name of a Roman gens.* C. Furnius, Caius *Furnius, a friend of Cicero.*

Furor, ōris, m. (furo, *to rage*), *rage, madness, fury.*

Fusus, a, um, part. (fundo).

Futūrus, a, um. part. (sum), *about to be, future, to come.*

G.

Gallia, æ, f., *Gaul.* This country included France and the northern part of Italy. It was divided into two parts, *Transalpine* and *Cisalpine Gaul,* the former on the west and the latter on the east of the Alps.

Gallus, i, m., *a Gaul, an inhabitant of Gaul.*

Gallus, i, m., *a cock, dunghill cock.*

Gallĭcus, a, um, adj. (Gallia), *belonging to Gaul, Gallic.*

Gaudeo, ēre, gavīsus sum, n. pass., *to rejoice, be glad:* hence

Gaudium, i, n., *joy, gladness.*

Gelĭdus, a, um, adj. (gelu, *cold*), *icy cold, cold.*

Genēva, æ, f., *Geneva, a town of the Allobroges, at the western extremity of the lake of Geneva.*

Gens, gentis, f., (geno, from gigno, *to beget*), *a clan,* among the Romans containing many families descended from a common ancestor; *a race, people, nation, tribe.*

Genu, us, n., *the knee.*

Genus, ĕris, n., *a race, people, nation, tribe.*

Gero, ĕre, gessi, gestum, a., *to bear, carry; to manage: to conduct; to do, perform, execute, carry on, accomplish:* gerere bellum, *to wage* or *carry on war:* gerere se, *to bear, deport, behave* or *conduct one's self.*

Germāni, ōrum, m., *Germans, the Germans.*

Gessi, see Gero.

Gestus, a, um, part. (gero), *borne; performed:* res gestæ, *see* Res.

Gladius, i, m., *a sword.*

Gloria, æ, f., *glory, fame, renown:* hence

Glōrior, āri, ātus, sum, dep. a. & n., *to glory, boast.*

Glorĭōsus, a, um, adj. (gloria), *glorious.*

Gradus, ûs, m. (gradior, *to step*), *a step, pace; a condition, grade, rank.*

Græcia, æ, f., *Greece:* hence

Græcus, a, um, adj., *of Greece, Grecian, Greek.*

Gramen, ĭnis, n., *grass.*

Gratia, æ, f. (gratus), *favor, thanks:* gratia, abl. *for the sake.*

Gratŭlor, āri, ātus sum, dep. n. & a., *to congratulate, wish one joy:* from

Gratus, a, um, adj., *pleasing, grateful, agreeable.*

Gravis, e, adj, *heavy, weighty, ponderous; burdensome, oppressive troublesome grievous, painful hard, harsh, severe, sore, disagreeable, unpleasant; of weight or authority eminent, venerable great:* hence

Gravĭter, graviùs gravissĭmè, adv, *weightily heavily vehemently, strongly, violently severely, bitterly, harshly, unpleasantly.*

Gusto, ări, ăvi, ătum, a. (gustus, *a tasting*), *to taste.*

H.

Hăbeo, ēre, uì, ĭtum, a. & n., *to have, hold, keep, possess, cherish, entertain; to reckon, judge, think, consider:* habere orationem, *to utter, deliver—:* habere iter, *to travel, journey:* magni habere, *to esteem highly, think highly of:* non habeo quid dicam, *I know not what to say:* hence

Habĭto, āre, ăvi, ătum, a. & n., *to have, hold; to dwell, live in, inhabit.*

Hac, Hæc &c., see Hic.

Hadrumētum, ĭ, n., *Hadrumetum, a city of Africa.*

Hamilcar, ăris, m., *Hamilcar, a Carthaginian general, father of Hannibal.*

Hannĭbal, ălis, m., *Hannibal, a very celebrated Carthaginian general, son of Hamilcar.*

Hasdrŭbal, ălis, m., *Hasdrubal, a Carthaginian general, brother of Hannibal.*

Haud, adv., *not.*

Hebes, ĕtis, adj. (hebeo, *to be blunt*), *blunt, dull:* fig., *dull, stupid.*

Hei, interj., *ah! woe!* hei mihi, *ah me! woe is me!*

Helĕna, æ, f., *Helen, a beautiful Grecian queen.*

Helvetĭi, ōrum, m. pl., *the Helvetians or Swiss.*

Hellespontus, ĭ, m., *the Hellespont, a strait between Thrace & Asia Minor, now called the Dardanelles.*

Hercŭles, is, m., *Hercules, a famous Grecian hero.*

Heredĭtas, ătis, f. (heres, *an heir*), *inheritance.*

Herodótus, i, m., *Herodotus, the earliest Greek historian.*

Heu, interj., *ah! alas!*

Hiberna, ōrum, n. pl. (hibernus, *wintry*), *winter quarters.*

Hibernia, æ, f., *Ireland.*

Hic, haec, hoc, dem. pron., *this, the latter, he, she, it:* hence

Hic, adv., *here.*

Hiĕmo, āre, āvi, ātum, n. & a., *to winter, pass the winter:* from

Hiems, ĕmis, f., *winter.*

Hippŏnĭcus, i, m., *Hipponicus, an Athenian, father-in-law of Alcibiades.*

Hirundo, ĭnis, f., *a swallow.*

Hispania, æ, f., *Spain.*

Hister, see Ister.

Historia. æ, f., *history.*

Hodĭe, adv. (hoc & die), *to-day.*

Homērus, i, m., *Homer, the most ancient and illustrious of the Greek poets.*

Homo, ĭnis, c., *a man or woman; a person.*

Honestus,, a, um, adj., *honorable, noble. respectable:* from

Honor or os, ōris, m., *honor, respect, esteem, reverence, regard; a public office, magistracy, preferment, post, dignity, office:* hence

Honorātus, a, um, part. & adj., *honored, respected; honorable, respectable, distinguished:* from

Honōro, āre, āvi, ātum, a (honor), *to honor, respect.*

Hora, æ, f., *an hour, the twelfth part of a day or night; a space of time, period.*

Hortor, āri, ātus sum, dep. (horior, *to urge*), *to exhort, encourage.*

Hospĭtium, ii, n. (hospes, *a guest*), *an inn.*

Hostia, æ, f. (hostio, *to strike*), *a victim, sacrifice.*

Hostis, is, c., *a stranger; an enemy.*

Huc, adv. (hic), *to this place, hither.*

Humanĭtas, ătis, f., *humanity, gentleness, kindness:* from

Humānus, a, um, adj. (homo), *human; humane, kind, gentle, courteous.*

Humĕrus, i, m., *the shoulder.*

Humĭlis, e, adj., *low; fig., low, mean, humble:* from

Humus, i, f., *the ground;* humi, *on or in the ground.*

Hyperborei, ōrum, m., *the Hyperboreans, a northern nation.*

I.

Ibam, Ibo, &c., see Eo.

Ibi, adv., (is), *in that place, there.*

Ibīdem, adv. (ibi & the suffix dem), *in the same place.*

Ico, ĕre, ĭci, ictum, a., *to strike.*

Idcirco *illat.* conj. (id & circa, *around*), *on that account, there-fore.*

Idem, eădem, ĭdem, dem. pron. (is & the suffix dem), *thè same :* idem qui, et ac &c., *the same as.*

Idoneus, a um adj. *fit, meet, suita-ble, proper.*

Ignārus, a, um, adj., (2. in & gnarus, *knowing*), *ignorant, inexperienced.*

Ignavia, æ, f., *inactivity, sloth, idle-ness :* from

Ignāvus, a, um, adj. (2. in & gnavus, *active*), *inactive, indolent, idle, lazy.*

Ignis, is, m., *fire.*

Ignōro, āre, āvi, ātum, n. & a. (igna-rus), *to be ignorant of.*

Ignōtus, a, um, part. & adj. (2. in & gnotus, *known*), *not known, un-known.*

Ille, illa, illud, dem. pron., *that ; he, she, it.*

Illuc, adv. (ille), *thither.*

Illustris, e. adj. (in & lustro, *to puri-fy*), *clear, bright ; illustrious, fa-mous :* hence

Illustro, āre, āvi, ātum, a., *to enlight-en ; to illustrate ; to render famous.*

Immitto, ĕre, īsi, issum, a. (in & mitto), *to send or let into ; to cast, throw, hurl to throw into :* immit-tere se, *to rush.*

Immodestia, æ, f. (immodestus, *un-restrained*), *intemperate conduct, immodesty, violence in behavior, licentiousness.*

Immŏlo, āre, āvi, ātum, a. (in & mola, *coarse meal*), *to sacrifice immo-late.*

Immortālis, e, adj. (2. in & mortalis), *undying, immortal.*

mpēdio, īre, īvi, *or* ii, ītum, a, (in & pes), *to entangle* fig., *to hinder.*

mpendeo, ĕre, n. (in & pendeo, *to hang over*), *to overhang, hang over ;* fig., *to threaten, impend, be near.*

Imperātor, ōris, m. (impero), *a com-mander, leader, general the com-mander in chief of an army ; an emperor.*

Imperitus, a, um, adj. (2. in & perit-us), *inexperienced in, not knowing,*
unacquainted with, unskilled, ig-norant.

Imperium, ii, n., *a command ; power, authority ; empire, dominion, sov-ereignty, supreme power ; a domin-ion, realm: the chief command:* from

Impĕro, āre, āvi, ātum, n. & a. (in & paro, *to prepare*), *to command, or-der ; to govern, rule.*

Impĕtro, āre, āvi, ātum, a. (in & pa-tro, *to perform*), *to obtain, get ; to accomplish, effect.*

Impĕtus, ûs, m. (impĕto, *to assail*), *an attack, assault.*

Impius, a, um. adj. (2. in & pius, *pi-ous*), *undutiful, impious, wicked.*

Impleo, ĕre, ēvi, ētum, a., *to fill.*

Implōro, āre, āvi, ātum, a. (in & ploro, *to wail*), *to implore entreat.*

Impōno, ĕre, sui, sĭtum, a. (in & pono), *to place or put upon , to lay upon, impose.*

Imprimis, adv., *chiefly, especially, in the first place,* see Primus.

Imprimo, ĕre, pressi, pressum, a. (in & premo), *to impress, imprint.*

Imprŏbus, a, um, adj. (2. in & pro-bus), *bad, wicked.*

Imprūdens, tis, adj. (2. in & pru-dens), *not knowing ; imprudent ; unawares.*

Impūdens, tis, adj. (2. in & pudens, *modest*), *shameless, impudent.*

In, prep with acc. & abl. With acc., *into ; to, unto ; towards ; upon, on , through ; over ; among ; until ; for ; against.* With abl., *in ; in time of ; upon ; on ; among ; amidst over ; at ; in the case of, concerning re-specting, in regard to.*

2. In, an inseparable particle, equiva-lent to *un, im,* or *not,* in English.

Incendium, ii, n., *a fire, conflagra-tion :* from

Incendo, ĕre, di, sum, a. (in & can-deo, *to glow*), *to kindle, set fire to, burn.*

Inceptum, i, n. (incipio), *a beginning; an undertaking ; a design.*

Incertus, a, um, adj. (2. in & certus), *uncertain.*

Incĭdo, ĕre, cĭdi, cāsum, n. (in & cado), *to fall into or upon ; to fall out, happen, occur.*

Incĭpio, ĕre, cēpi, ceptum, a, (in & capio), *to begin, commence.*

Incĭto, āre āvi, ātum, a. (in & cito), *to hasten, urge forward, incite, spur on.*

Incŏla, æ, c. (in & colo), *an inhab-itant.*

Incŏlo, ĕre, colui, cultum, a (in & colo) to inhabit, dwell.

Incolŭmis e adj. (in & columis, safe), safe uninjured, whole.

Incommŏdum , n, (2. in & commodum advantage disadvantage, damage, loss, harm, disaster.

Inconsiderātus, a, um, adj (2. in & consideratus, considerate), inconsiderate, heedless, thoughtless.

Incredibĭlis e. adj. (2. in & credibilis, credible), incredible.

Incūso, āri, āvi, ātum, a. (in & causa), to accuse, complain of, blame.

Inde, adv , thence.

Indĭco, āre, āvi, ātum, a. (in & dico), to show, discover.

Indĭgeo, ĕre ui, n. (indu for in & egeo, to need), to want, need.

Indignus, a, um, adj. (2. in & dignus), unworthy.

Indoctus, a, um, adj. (2. in & doctus, learned), unlearned, illiterate ignorant.

Indūco, ĕre, xi. ctum, a. (in & duco), to bring in introduce; fig., to persuade.

Industria, æ, f., industry, diligence.

Ineo, īre, īvi or ii, ĭtum, n. & a. irr. (in & eo), to go into, enter; to commence, begin; inire consilium, to form a design or plan, enter into a plot; also, to deliberate, consult.

Ineptiæ, ārum, f. pl. (ineptus, unsuitable), absurdities, silly behavior, folly.

Inermis, e, & inermus, a, um, adj. (2. in & arma), without arms, unarmed.

Inertia. æ, f. (2. in & ars), unskilfulness inactivity, idleness, laziness.

Infectus, a, um, adj. (2. in & factus), not done, undone, unfinished. imperfect, unaccomplished; infectâ re, without accomplishing one's designs or business, without success.

Infēlix, īcis, adj. (2. in & felix). unfruitful; unfortunate, unhappy, wretched.

Infĕro, ferre, intŭli, illātum, a, irr. (in & fero), to bring into to bring upon: inferre bellum to make war upon, wage war, carry on war.

Infĕrus, a, um, adj., below, beneath, low: comp. inferior, lower, inferior; sup inf ĭmus or imus, lowest, last meanest.

Inficĭo, ĕre, fēci, fectum, a. (in & facio), to put into; to dye, stain; to infect.

Infĭmus, see Inferus.

Inflīgo, ĕre, ixi, ictum, a. (in & fligo, to strike), to strike one thing on or against another; to inflict, impose.

Influo, ĕre xi.. xum, n. (in & fluo, to flow , to flow or run into, discharge, empty.

Ingenĭum, ii, n. (in & geno from gigno to beget), the disposition; genius talents, character.

Ingens, tis, adj. (2. in & gens), great, vast, immense, enormous.

Ingenuus, a, um, adj. (ingeno, to implant), native, innate; ingenuous noble.

Ingratus, a, um, adj. (2. in & gratus), unpleasant; ungrateful, unthankful.

Ingrĕdior i, grēssus, sum, dep. a. (in & gradior, to go), to go in, enter

Inimīcus, a, um, adj. (2. in & amicus) unfriendly, hostile.

Inĭquus, a, um, adj. (2. in & æquus), unequal; unfavorable; unjust.

Initĭum, ii, n. (ineo), a beginning.

Injĭcio, ĕre, jēci, jectum, a. (in & jacio), to throw or put in or upon; to lay on; to cause or occasion.

Injuria, æ, f. (injurius, injurious), injury, wrong.

Injustitĭa, æ, f. (injustus, unjust), injustice.

Innoxĭus, a, um, adj. (2. in & noxius, hurtful), harmless, innocent.

Innumerabĭlis, e, adj. (2. in & numerabilis, that can be numbered), innumerable.

Inopia, æ, f. (inops, helpless), want, poverty.

Inquam or Inquio, def. I say.

Insania, æ, f. (insānus, mad) madness.

Insidĭæ, ārum, f. (insideo, to sit upon), an ambush, ambuscade, snares insidias facere alicui, to lay an ambush for one.

Insimŭlo, āre, āvi, ātum a. (in & simulo, to feign), to charge, accuse.

Instans, tis, part. & adj. (insto), present; pressing, urgent, important.

Instĭtuo, ĕre, ui, ūtum, (in & statuo), to appoint, institute: to begin, commence; to undertake; to adopt: hence

Institūtum, i, n., a custom, institution a practice: instituto suo, abl., *according to his design* or *custom.*

Insto, āre, stĭti, n. (in & sto), *to stand in* or *upon; to be near* or *at hand, draw nigh, approach:*

Instruo, ĕre, struxi, structum, a. (in & struo, *to build*), *to construct, erect, build; to set in order, dispose, arrange, marshal, draw up in battle array; to prepare, furnish.*

Insŭla, æ, f., *an island, isle.*

Integrĭtas, ātis, f. (intĭger, *entire*), *completeness;* fig., *honesty, probity, integrity.*

Intellĭgo, ĕre, exi, ectum, a. (inter & lego), *to understand, know, perceive, see.*

Inter, prep. with acc., *between, among, amongst, amid; during.*

Interemptus, a, um, part. (interimo).

Intĕreo, īre, ii, ĭtum, n, irr. (inter & eo), *to perish, be lost, die.*

Intĕrest, impers. (intersum), *it concerns, interests.*

Interfĭcio, ĕre, ēci, ectum, a. (inter & facio), *to kill, slay, put to death, destroy.*

Interĭmo, ĕre, ēmi, emptum *or* emtum, a. (inter & emo, *to buy*), *to take away; to destroy, slay, kill.*

Interĭtus, ūs, m. (intereo), *destruction, death.*

Intermissus, a, um, part., *broken off, interrupted, intermitted: from*

Intermitto ĕre, īsi, issum, a. & n. (inter & mitto), *to leave off; to cease; to neglect.*

Interposĭtus, ūs, m. (interpōno, *to put between*); *a putting between, an interposition.*

Interrex, ēgis, m, (inter & rex), *a regent, an interrex.*

Interrŏgo, āre, āvi, ātum. a. (inter & rogo), *to question, ask, interrogate.*

Intersum, essi, fui, irr, n. (inter & sum), *to be in the midst, to come or lie between; to be present, take part in; to be distant; to differ.*

Intĭmus, a, um, adj. (sup. of interior, *inner*), *the inmost, innermost, most intimate;* subst. intĭmus, *a most intimate friend.*

Intra, prep. with acc. (intera, scil. parte), *within, in.*

Intro, āre, āvi, ātum, a., *to go into, enter.*

Invĕnio, īre, ēni, entum, a. (in & venio), *to meet with, find out, find.*

Invidia, æ, f., *envy, jealousy, ill-will, hatred, dislike: from*

Invĭdus, a, um, adj. (invideo, *to envy*), *envious.*

Invītus, a, um, adj., *unwilling.*

Invŏco, āre, āvi, ātum, a. (in & voco) *to call upon; to invoke.*

Ipse, ipsa, ipsum, intensive pron., *self, himself, herself, itself; he, she, it:* when *ego, tu, ille* &c. *are understood, I myself,* &c.

Ira, æ, f. *anger, wrath, ire:* hence

Irascor, i, dep. n., *to be angry.*

Ire, see Eo.

Is, ea, id, dem. pron., *that* or *this; he, she, it; the same, such:* eo, with comparatives, *by so much* or *the.*

Isocrătes, is, m., *Isocrates, an Athenian orator.*

Iste, ista, istud, dem. pron., *that* or *this; that of yours; thy, your; he she, it.*

Ister, or Hister, tri, m., *the Ister* or *Hister, the name of the Danube after it enters Illyricum.*

Istic, istaec, istoc & istuc, dem. pron. (iste & hic), *this same; this, that.*

Ita, adv., *so, thus.*

Ităque, illat, conj. (ita & que), *and so; therefore.*

Iter, itinĕris, n. (eo, ire), *a going, walk, way: a journey, course, passage:* iter facere, *to go, pass, advance, march, travel.*

J.

Jacens, tis, part. & adj., *lying, extended, prostrate:* jacentes, *the fallen, the slain: from*

Jăceo, ēre, cui, cĭtum, n., *to lie; to be situated; to lie dead, be fallen* or *slain.*

Jăcio, ĕre, jeci, jactum, a., *to throw, cast, fling, hurl.*

Jam, adv., *now; already.*

Jocus, i, m., *a joke, jest.*

Jovis, see Jupiter.

Jŭbeo, ĕre, jussi, jussum, a., *to order bid, command.*

Jucundus, a, um, adj. (jocus, *a jest*), *agreeable, pleasant, delightful.*

Judicium, ii, n. (judex, *a judge*), *a judgment, trial, sentence, decision; opinion, belief.*

Judĭco, āre, āvi, ātum, a. (jus & dico), *to judge, give judgment, determine; to judge, think, deem, suppose, be-*

lieve; to declare, pronounce; to conclude.

Julius, i, m., *Julius, a Roman name,*

Juno, ōnis, f., *Juno, the wife of Jupiter.*

Jupiter, Jovis, m., *Jupiter,* according to the Grecian and Roman mythology, *the king of gods and men.*

Juro, āre, āvi, ātum, a. & n., *to swear:* from

Jus, juris, n., *right, justice, law.*

Jusjurandum, jurisjurandi, n. (jus & jurandum, *an oath*), *an oath.*

Jussus, a, um, part. (jubeo).

Jussus, ûs, m., used only in the abl. sing. (jubeo), *an order, command.*

Justitia, æ, f., *justice:* from

Justus, a, um, adj. (jus), *right; just, proper.*

Juvěnis, is, c., *a young man or woman, a youth.*

Juventus, ūtis, f. (juvenis, *young*), *the age of youth,* (from the 20th to the 40th year), *youth.*

Juvo, āre, juvi, jutum, a. & n., *to aid, help, assist.*

Juxta, prep. with acc., *near to, hard by, nigh.*

K.

Kalendæ, *see* Calendæ.

L.

L., *an abbreviation of* Lucius.

Labiēnus, i, m., *Labienus, one of Cæsar's lieutenants in the Gallic war.*

Labor, ōris, m., *labor, toil, fatigue; trouble, distress.*

Labor, labi, lapsus sum, dep. n. *to glide down, descend, fall.*

Laboriōsus, a, um, adj. (labor, ōris), *laborious.*

Lac, tis, n., *milk.*

Lacedæmon, ōnis, f., *Lacedæmon or Sparta, a celebrated city of Greece:* hence

Lacedæmonius, a, um, adj, *Lacedæmonian or Spartan:* subst., *a Lacedæmonian, a Spartan.*

Lacrĭmo, āre, avi, ātum, n. (lacrĭma, *a tear*), *to weep: to lament.*

Lacus, ûs, m., *a lake.*

Lælius, i, m, *Lælius, the name of a Roman gens.*

Lætitia, æ, f. (lætus), *joy, gladness.*

Lætor, āri, ātus, sum, dep. n., *to rejoice, be glad.*

Lætus, a, um, adj., *glad, joyful; fertile, fruitful.*

Lana, æ, f., *wool.*

Laodicēa, æ, f., *Laodicea, a city of Asia.*

Lapis, ĭdis, m., *a stone.*

Largitio, ōnis, f. (largior, *to bestow*), *a giving liberally; bribery, corruption.*

Latĕbra, æ, f.. *a lurking-place, hiding place, shelter, retreat:* from

Lateo, ēre, ui, n., *to lurk, lie hid, be concealed, live retired,*

Latro, ōnis, m., *a highwayman, robber.*

Latus, a, um, adj., *broad, wide.*

Laudo, āre, āvi, ātum, a. (laus), *to praise, extol.*

Laurus, i, & us, f., *the laurel.*

Laus, laudis, f., *praise: glory, honor, fame, renown, esteem; estimation, value.*

Leæna, æ, f., *a lioness.*

Legatio, ōnis, f. (lego, āre, *to send as embassador*), *an embassy, legation.*

Legātus, i, m. (lego, āre, *to send as embassador*), *an embassador, legate; a lieutenant-general, deputy.*

Legio, ōnis, f., *a legion, a body of soldiers consisting of ten cohorts:* from

Lego, ĕre, legi, lectum, a., *to collect, gather; to read.*

Leonĭdas, æ, m., *Leonidas, a king of the Lacedæmonians.*

Lepus, ŏris, m., *a hare.*

Levis, e, adj, *light, small: fig., trifling, trivial.*

Lex, legis, f., (lego), *a law; a condition.*

Libenter, adv. (libens, *willing*), *willingly.*

Liber, bri, m., *the inner bark of a tree; a book.*

Liber, ĕra, ĕrum, adj. (libet), *free:* hence

Liberālis, e, adj., *generous, liberal.*

Liberalĭtas, ātis, f. (liber, ĕra), *liberality.*

Liberalĭter, adv. (liberalis), *liberally, kindly.*

Libĕre, adv., (liber), *freely:* liberius, *too freely.*

Libĕro, āre, āvi, ātum, a. (liber), *to set at liberty, free, make free; to deliver, release.*

Libertas, ātis, f. (liber), *liberty, freedom.*

Libet, lĭbuĭt or lĭbĭtum est. impers., *it pleases.*

Libys, yos, m., *a Libyan.*

Licet, lĭcuĭt & lĭcĭtum est, impers., *it is permitted, it is lawful; one may or can.*

Ligneus, a, um, adj. (lignum, *wood*), *wooden.*

Lilium, ĭi, n., *a lily.*

Lingŏnes, um, m., *the Lingones, a people of Gaul.*

Lingua, æ, f., *the tongue; language; speech.*

Lis, lĭtis, f., *a strife, controversy; a lawsuit; the matter in dispute; a fine.*

Lĭtĕra or Littĕra, æ, f. (lino, *to smear*), *a letter, (of the alphabet); a letter, epistle; literature, letters, learning.*

Loco, āre, āvĭ, ātum, a. (locus), *to place, put, lay.*

Locŭples, ĕtis, adj. (locus & plenus), *rich in lands: rich, wealthy: hence*

Locuplēto, āre, āvĭ, ātum. a., *to make rich, enrich.*

Locus, i, m., (pl. loci, m. & loca, n.,) *a place.*

Longè, adv., *far, far off; at a distance; much, very much: from*

Longus, a, um, adj., *long; remote.*

Loquor, i, cūtus sum, dep. n. & a., *to speak, talk, say, tell.*

Lubet, see Libet.

Lucius, i, m., *Lucius, a Roman præ-nomen.*

Luctus, ûs, m. (lugeo, *to mourn*), *grief.*

Lucus, i, m., *a sacred grove: a wood.*

Ludo, ĕre, sĭ, sum, a. & n., *to play, sport: hence*

Ludus, i, m., *a game, play.*

Lumen, ĭnis, n. (luceo, *to be light*), *light; the light of the eye, the eye.*

Luna, æ, f. (luceo, *to be light*), *the moon.*

Lupus, i, m., *a wolf.*

Lutum, i, n., *mud, mire, clay.*

Lux, lucis, f. (luceo, *to be light*), *light, day-light, day.*

Luxuria, æ, f. (luxus, *excess*), *luxury.*

Lycomēdes, is, m., *Lycomedes, a king of the island of Scyros.*

Lysander, dri, m., *Lysander, a celebrated Lacedæmonian general.*

Lysis, is, m., *Lysis, a Pythagorean of Tarantum, instructor of Epaminondus.*

M.

M., an abbreviation of Marcus.

Macŭlo, āre, āvĭ, ātum, a. (macŭla, *a spot*), *to stain; fig., to defile, dishonor, disgrace.*

Mæror, ōris, m. (mæreo, *to be sad*), *sadness, grief.*

Magis, adv. (magnus), maxĭmè, *more, rather.*

Magister, tri, m., *a master; a teacher: hence*

Magistrātus, ûs, m., *a magistracy; a magistrate.*

Magnitūdo, ĭnis, f., *greatness, size: from*

Magnus, a, um, adj., major, maxĭmus, *great, large: powerful, mighty, excellent: æstimare magni, to value highly.*

Majestas, ātis, f. (majus, *great*), *greatness, grandeur, dignity, majesty.*

Major, us, ōris, adj. (comp. of magnus), *greater, larger, more excellent: hence*

Majōres, um, m. pl. (magnus), *ancestors, forefathers.*

Malè, adv. (malus), *badly, ill, wrongly, amiss.*

Maledīco, ĕre, xi, ctum, a. (male & dico), *to speak ill of, abuse, revile, slander, asperse.*

Malo, malle, malui, irr. n. & a. (magis & volo), *to choose rather, prefer.*

Malus, a, um, adj., *bad, evil, wicked: subst., malum, i, n., an evil: a misfortune, calamity.*

Manlius, i, m., *Manlius, a Roman name.*

Mando, āre, āvĭ, ātum, a. (manus & do), *to commit to one's charge, bid, enjoin, order, command; to commit, confide, entrust: mandare se fugæ, to betake one's self to flight, to flee.*

Maneo, ĕre, mansi, mansum, n. & a., *to remain, stay, wait.*

Mansi, see Maneo.

Manus, ûs, f., *a hand; the armed hand, personal valor: an armed force, corps, band, army.*

Marcellus, i, m., *Marcellus, the name of a Roman general.*

Marcius, i, m., *Marcius, a Roman name.*

Marcus, i, m., *Marcus, a Roman prænomen.*

Mare, is, n., *the sea: hence*

Maritĭmus, a, um, adj., *of the sea,* *lying near the sea, maritime.*

Marius, i, m., *Marius, a Roman general.*

Massiliensis, is, m. (Massilia, *Marseilles***),** *an inhabitant of Marseilles.*

Mater, tris, f., *a mother :* hence

Matrimonium, ii, n., *wedlock, marriage :* dare in matrimonium, *to give in marriage.*

Matūro, āre, āvi, ātum, a. & n., *to ripen, mature ;* fig., *to hasten :* with inf., *to make haste, hasten :* from

Matūrus, a, um, adj., *ripe, mature.*

Mauri, ōrum, m., *the Moors, Mauritanians.*

Maxĭmè, adv. (sup. of magis), *very greatly, most, most of all, very much.*

Maxĭmus, a, um, adj. (sup. of magnus), *greatest, very great.*

Medicīna, æ, f. (medĭcus, *a physician***),** *medicine.*

Medĭus, a, um, adj., *middle in the* *middle or midst.*

Meĭpsum, *myself ;* acc. of ego & ipse.

Melĭor, adj. (comp. of bonus), *better.*

Membrum, i, n., *a member, limb.*

Memĭni, def. n., *I remember :* hence

Memor, ŏris, adj., *mindful :* hence

Memorĭa, æ, f., *memory, recollection, remembrance :* memoriæ prodere, *to hand down to posterity, to record, relate.*

Memŏro, āre, āvi, ātum, a. (memor), *to bring to remembrance ; to relate, say.*

Meneclīdes, is, m., *Meneclides, a Theban, a traducer of Epaminondas.*

Mens, mentis, f., *the mind.*

Mensis, is, m., *a month.*

Mentĭor, iri, ĭtus sum, dep. n. & a., *to lie ; to deceive.*

Mercor, āri, ātus sum, dep. a. (merx, *goods***),** *to trade ; to buy, purchase.*

Mergo, ĕre, si, sum, a., *to sink, dip, plunge ; to dive.*

Merĭtò, adv. (merĭtus, *deserving***),** *deservedly, justly.*

Mersus, a, um, part. (mergo).

Metuo, ĕre, ui, ūtum, a. & n., *to fear :* from

Metus, ûs, m., *fear, dread.*

Meus, a, um, poss. pron. (me), *my, mine.*

Micythus, i, m., *Micythus, the name of a young man who was a party to an attempt to bribe Epaminondas.*

Miles, ĭtis, c. (mille), *a soldier :* hence

Milĭtāris, e, adj., *military, warlike :* res militaris, *the art of war, military affairs, war.*

Mille, num. adj. ind., *a thousand ;* also, a subst. n. indeclinable in the sing., in pl. millia, ium, &c.

Miltĭādes, is, m., *Miltiades, an Athenian general, victor in the battle of Marathon.*

Minĭmè, adv. (sup. of parum), *least, least of all, very little ;* in negation, *by no means.*

Minor, us, gen. ōris, adj. (comp. of parvus), *less, smaller ; younger.*

Minuo, ĕre, ui, ūtum, a. (minus, *less***),** *to lessen, diminish, abate, impair.*

Minùs, adv. (comp. of parum), *less ; not.*

Mirabĭlis, e, adj. (miror), *wonderful, astonishing :* hence

Mirabĭlĭter, adv., *wonderfully.*

Mirifĭcus, a, um, adj. (mirus & facio), *wonderful, marvellous, astonishing.*

Miror, āri, ātus sum, dep. a. & n., *to wonder, admire, be astonished.*

Mirus, a, um, adj., *wonderful, strange, marvellous, extraordinary.*

Misceo, ēre, miscui, mistum, or mixtum, a., *to mingle, mix.*

Miser, ĕra, ĕrum, adj., *miserable, wretched, unfortunate.*

Miserandus, a, um, part. & adj. (misĕror, *to pity***),** *to be pitied ; pitiable, lamentable, deplorable.*

Misĕreor, ēri, erĭtus or ertus sum, dep. n. (miser), *to deplore : to pity.*

Miseresco, ĕre, n. (miserĕo, *to pity***),** *to pity.*

Misĕret, miseruit, miserĭtum est, impers. (miser), *it pitieth :* me miseret, *I pity.*

Misericordĭa, æ, f. (misericors, *tender-hearted***),** *compassion, pity.*

Misi, see Mitto.

Missus, a, um, part. (mitto), *sent.*

Mithridātes, is, m., *Mithridates, a king of Pontus.*

Mitto, ĕre, misi, missum, a. (meo, *to go***),** *to send.*

Mobĭlis, e, adj. (moveo), *easy to be moved, moveable ; inconstant, fickle ; changeable.*

Modestus, a, um, adj., *moderate ; kind, gentle ; modest :* from

Modus, i, m., *a measure ; a manner, method.*

Mœnĭa, um, n., *the walls of a city ; a city inclosed by walls.*

Molestĭa, æ, f., *trouble, annoyance ;*

sine molestiâ tuâ, *without trouble to yourself :* from

Molestus, a, um, adj. (moles, *a load*), *troublesome.*

Momentum, i, n. (moveo), *a motion; movement; a moment* or *minute; value, weight, influence, consequence, importance.*

Móneo, ēre, ui, ĭtum, a., *to remind, admonish, teach, advise.*

Mons, tis, m., *a mountain.*

Mora, æ, f., *a delay.*

Morbus, i, m., *a disease, disorder, sickness.*

Mŏrior, i & īri, mortuus sum, dep. n., *to die, expire.*

Moror, āri, ātus sum, dep. n. & a. (mora), *to delay, tarry, stay, remain : to hinder.*

Mors, tis, f. (morior), *death :* hence

Mortālis, e, adj., *mortal.*

Mos, moris, m., *a manner, custom, way, practice; conduct, behavior;* pl. mores, *manners, morals, character :* more or ex more, *according to custom, after the manner, according to the usage* or *practice.*

Moveo, ēre, movi, motum, a. & n., *to move, stir; to remove :* fig., *to excite, occasion; to affect.*

Mulier, ĕris, f., *a woman, a female.*

Multimŏdis, adv. (multis & modis), *in many ways, variously.*

Multitŭdo, ĭnis, f. (multus), *a multitude.*

Multo or Mulcto, āre, āvi, ātum, a. (multa, *a penalty), to punish :* aliquem pecuniâ, *to fine in a sum of money.*

Multò, adv. (multus), *much; by far.*

Multùm, adv. (comp. plùs, sup. plurimùm), *much, very much, greatly, very :* from

Multus, a, um, adj. (comp. plus, sup. plurimus), *many, much.* Multo, n. abl., joined often with comparatives, superlatives, &c., *much, by much, far, by far, a great deal.*

Mundus, i, m., *the world.*

Municipium, ii, n. (municeps, *a citizen of a* municipium), *a free town.*

Munio, ire, ivi, *or* ii, ītum, n. & a. (mœnia), *to fortify :* hence

Munitio, ōnis, f., *a fortification, defense.*

Munitus, a, um, part. & adj. (munio), *fortified; guarded, defended.*

Munus, ĕris, n., *an office; a present, gift, reward.*

Murus, i, m., *a wall of a city, wall.*

Musa, æ, f., *a muse.*

Musica, æ, & Musĭce, es, f., *music.*

Muto, āre, āvi, ātum, a., *to change.*

N.

Nactus, a, um, part. (nanciscor).

Nam, & Namque, caus. conj., *for.*

Nanciscor, i, nactus sum, dep. a., *to meet with, find; to get, obtain.*

Narro, āre, āvi, ātum, a., *to tell, relate, narrate.*

Nascor, i, natus sum, dep. n., *to be born.*

Natu, m. abl. (nascor), *by birth, in age :* major natu, *older :* majores natu, *men advanced in years, old men, elders.*

Natūra, æ, f. (nascor), *nature, constitution : disposition.*

Natus, a, um, part. & adj. (nascor), *born.*

Nauta, æ, m. (navis), *a sailor, seaman.*

Navālis, e, adj. (navis), *naval.*

Navīgo, āre, avi, ātum, a. & n. (navis & ago), *to sail; to navigate.*

Navis, is, f., *a ship.*

Nè, adv. & fin. conj., *not :* after verbs of avoiding, *that not, lest;* after verbs of fearing, *that, lest.*

Nĕ, enclitic interr. conj., in *indirect* questions, *whether :* in *direct* questions it is not translated.

Nec, or Neque, cop. conj. (nē & que), *and not, but not, not, nor :* nec — nec, *neither — nor.*

Necesse, adj. ind., *necessary :* hence

Necessĭtas, ātis, f., *necessity.*

Nectar, ăris, n., *nectar, the drink of the gods; wine.*

Neglĭgo, ĕre, exi, ectum, a. (nec & lego), *to slight, neglect.*

Nego, āre, āvi, ātum, n. & a. (nē & aio), *to say no, to deny, refuse.*

Negotium, ii, n. (nec & otium), *business.*

Nemo, ĭnis, c. (nē & homo), *no man, no one.*

Neoptolēmus, i, m., *Neoptolemus, the son of Achilles.*

Neptunius, a, um, adj., *of* or *belonging to Neptune, Neptunian :* from

Neptūnus, i, m., *Neptune, the brother of Jupiter, and god of the sea.*

Nequam, adj. ind., *worthless, good for nothing, wretched, vile.*

Neque, *see* Nec.

Nĕqueo, ire, ivi *or* ii, ĭtum, irr. n.

(nĕ & queo, *I can*), *not to be able;
I cannot.*

Nervii, ōrum, m., *the Nervii, a people of Gaul.*

Nescio, ire, īvi & ii, itum, a. (nĕ & scio), *to be ignorant, not to know.*

Nex, uecis, f., *violent death, murder :* vitæ necisque potestas, *power of life and death, absolute* or *unlimited power.*

Nidus, i, m., *a nest.*

Nihil, & Nil, ind. n. (nĕ & hilum, *a trifle*), *nothing, nought.*

Nil, *see* Nihil.

Nimius, a, um, adj. (nimis, *too*), *too much, excessive.*

Nisi, condit. conj. (ni, *not,* & si), *if not, unless, except.*

Nisus, i, m., *Nisus, a king of Megara.*

Nitor, i, nisus, & nixus, sum, dep. n., *to strive, labor, attempt; to lean upon, rest upon :* genibus nixæ, *kneeling.*

Nix, nivis, f., *snow.*

Nixus, a, um, part. (nitor).

No, nare, navi, n., *to swim.*

Nobilis, e, adj. (nosco, *to know*), *known : famous, illustrious; celebrated, renowned, noble :* hence

Nobilitas, ātis, f., *fame; nobility.*

Nobilito, āre, avi, ātum, a. (nobilis), *to render famous, ennoble.*

Nŏceo, ēre, cui, citum, n., *to hurt, injure.*

Nolo, nolle, nolui, irr. n. (nĕ & volo), *to be unwilling :* the imperative of nolo, with an infinitive, is translated by *not,* and the infinitive by an imperative; as, esse noli, *be not.*

Nomen, inis, n. (nosco, *to know*), *a name ; reputation ; a pretext, pretence, color :* hence

Nomino, āre, avi, ātum, a., *to call, name ; to n minate, elect.*

Non, alv., *not, no.*

Nonnullus, a, um, adj. (non & nullus), *some.*

Nos, nom. & acc. pl. of ego, *we, us.*

Noster, tra, trum, poss. pron. (nos), *our :* nostri, pl., *our friends, our soldiers, our troops.*

Notitia, æ, f. (notus, *known*), *knowledge.*

Novem, num, adj., ind., *nine.*

Novus, a, um, adj., *new, fresh.*

Nox, noctis, f., *night.*

Nubes, is, f., *a cloud.*

Nubo, ēre, nupsi & nupta sum, nuptum, a. & n., *to cover, veil ;* hence,

to marry, be married, spoken of the bride only: nuptum dare, *to give in marriage.*

Nudo, āre, āvi, ātum, a., *to strip, bare ; to spoil, plunder :* from

Nudus, a, um, adj., *naked, bare.*

Nullus, a, um, adj. (nĕ & ullus), *not any, none, no, nobody, no one.*

Num, interr. conj., in *indirect* questions, *whether ;* in *direct* questions it is not translated.

Numen, inis, n. (nuo *to nod*), *a nod : the will ; the divine will ; influence, power, authority ; a deity, a god.*

Numĕrus, i. m., *a number ; rank, place ; estimation.*

Numidæ, ārum, m.pl., *the Numidians, a people of Northern Africa.*

Numquam *or* Nunquam, adv. (nĕ & umquam), *never.*

Nunc, adv., *now.*

Nuncio, or Nuntio, āre, āvi, ātum, a., *to announce, report, make known :* from

Nuncius, or Nuntius, ii, m., *a messenger ; news, tidings : a message.*

Nuptus, *see* Nubeo.

O.

O, interj., *O! Oh!*

Ob, prep. with acc., *for, on account of.*

Obdūco, ēre, xi, ctum, a. (ob & duco), *to lead* or *conduct against ; to draw over.*

Obeo, īre, īvi, or ii, itum, n. & a. irr. (ob & eo), *to go to ; to go down, set ; to perish, die :* obire diem supremum, *to die :* hence

Obitus, ûs, m., *death, decease.*

Obliviscor, i, oblitus sum, dep. a. (oblivio, *oblivion*), *to forget.*

Obruo, ēre, ui. ūtum, a. (ob & ruo), *to cover over, cover, bury, overwhelm ; to conceal ; to obscure.*

Obsĕcro, āre, āvi, ātum, a. (ob & sacro, *to consecrate*), *to entreat.*

Obses, idis, m. & f. (ob & sedeo), *a hostage ; a surety.*

Obsidio, ōnis, f. (obsideo, *to besiege*), *a siege, blockade.*

Obsto, āre, stiti, ātum, n. (ob & sto), *to stand before, stand against, oppose.*

Obsum, esse, fui, irr. n. (ob & sum), *to be against ; to hinder, hurt, injure.*

Obtŭli, *see* Offero.

Obtĕro, ĕre, trivi, tritum, a. (ob & tero, *to rub*), *to bruise, crush; to disparage, contemn.*

Obtĭneo, ĕre, tĭnui, tentum, a. & n. (ob & teneo), *to hold, to have, possess; to keep, retain, preserve; to gain, obtain, acquire.*

Obtrectatĭo, ōnis, f. (obtrecto, *to disparage*), *a disparaging; detraction, disparagement.*

Obvĭam, adv. (ob & vĭam), *in the way, toward, against, so as to meet:* obviam venire, *to come to meet, advance to meet or attack.*

Occasĭo, ōnis, f. (occido, *to fall*), *an occasion, opportunity.*

Occāsus, ûs, m. (occido, *to fall*), *fall; the going down or setting of the heavenly bodies:* solis occasus, *the setting of the sun, sunset, the west.*

Occido, ĕre, cīdi, cīsum, a. (ob & cædo), *to kill, slay.*

Occulto, āre, āvi, ātum, a. (occŭlo, *to cover*), *to conceal, hide.*

Occŭpo, āre, āvi, ātum, a.(ob & capio), *to occupy; seize, take possession of.*

Occurro, ĕre, curri, & cucurri, cursum, n (ob & curro), *to go or come to meet, meet; to encounter; to oppose, resist.*

Oceănus, i, m., *the ocean:* mare oceanum, *the ocean,* in which expression oceanum appears to be an adjective.

Ocŭlus, i, m., *an eye.*

Odi, *or* osus sum, def. n., *I hate:* hence

Odium, ii, n., *hatred.*

Offĕro, ĕre, obtŭli, oblātum, a, irr. (ob & fero), *to bring or put before; to offer, present; to expose.*

Officium, ii, n. (ob & facio), *duty, office.*

Oleum, i, n., *oil, olive oil.*

Olim, adv. (ille), *once, formerly; hereafter.*

Olympia, æ, f., *Olympia, a sacred region in the Peloponnesus, with an olive wood, where the Olympian game were held.*

Omitto, ĕre, īsi, issum, a. (ob & mitto), *to omit; to neglect.*

Omnis, e, adj., *all, every, the whole of.*

Onĕro, āre, avi, ātum, a., *to load, lade:* from

Onus, ĕris, n., *a load, burden;* hence

Onustus, a, um, adj., *loaded, laden; filled.*

Opĕra, æ, f. (opus), *pains, exertion,* *work, labor; help, assistance, aid; care, attention:* operam dare, *to bestow care* or *pains on, to give attention to, manage, effect.*

Opīmus, a, um, adj. (ops), *rich; dainty.*

Opinio, ōnis, f. (opinor, *to be of opinion*), *an opinion, belief, expectation.*

Oportet, ĕre, uit, impers., (opus, need), *it behooves; it is fit or proper; it ought.*

Oppĭdum, i, n. (ops & do), *a town.*

Opprimo, ĕre, essi, essum, (ob & premo), *to press against; to fall on suddenly; take by surprise, surprise; to overpower, subdue, rout; to subdue, oppress.*

Opprobrium, ii, n. (op & probrum, *a shameful act,*) *a reproach, scandal, disgrace, dishonor.*

Oppugno, āre, āvi, ātum, a. (ob & pugno), *to fight against, assail, attack, assault, storm, besiege.*

Ops, opis, f. (nom. not in use), *power, strength, riches, wealth, treasure; resources, authority, might; help.*

Optĭmè, adv. (sup. of bene), *best of all, best, very well.*

Optĭmus, a, um, adj. (sup. of bonus), *best, very good.*

Opŭlens, tis, & Opulentus, a, um, adj. (ops), *rich, wealthy.*

Opus, ĕris, n., *work, toil, labor; a a work; a military work, either a defensive work, fortification, or a work of besiegers, a siege-engine.*

Opus, ind. subst. and adj., *need, necessity; necessary, needful.*

Oraculum, i. n. (oro), *an oracle.*

Oratio, ōnis, f. (oro), *a speech, oration.*

Orātor, ōris, m. (oro), *an orator.*

Orbo, āre, āvi, ātum, a. (orbus, bereaved), *to bereave, deprive.*

Orgetŏrix, ĭgis, m., *Orgetorix, a Helvetian of noble birth and of great wealth.*

Orior, iri, ortus sum, dep, n., *to rise, arise; to spring, originate.*

Ornātus, a, um, part. and adj. (orno, *to fit out*), *fitted out, furnished, equipped, splendidly furnished; adorned.*

Oro, āre, āvi, ātum a. (os), *to speak; to beg, ask, entreat.*

Ortus, a, um, part. (orior), *sprung, descended, born.*

Os, oris, n., *the mouth; the face, countenance.*

Ostendo, ĕre, di, sum and tum, a. (ob & tendo), *to stretch before; to show, disclose; to declare.*

Otium, ii, n., *leisure, inactivity; repose, quiet, peace.*

Ovis, is, f., *a sheep.*

P.

P., an abbreviation of Publius.

Pabŭlum, i, n, (pasco, *to feed), food; pasture, fodder.*

Pagus, i, m., *a district, canton, province.*

Palliŏlum, i, n. dim. (pallium, *a covering), a small cloak or mantle.*

Palus, ūdis, f., *a marsh, morass, swamp.*

Pan, Panis, m., *Pan, the god of shepherds.*

Pando, ĕre, pandi, pansum and passum, a., *to spread out; to open.*

Par, paris, adj., *equal.*

Parătus, a um, part. & adj. (paro), *prepared, ready, provided, fitted, equipped.*

Parco, ĕre, peperci & parsi, parsitum & parsum, a. (parcus, *sparing), to spare.*

Pāreo, ĕre, ui, ĭtum, n., *to appear; to obey.*

Pario, ĕre, pepĕri, parĭtum & partum, a., *to bear or bring forth; to produce, create, bring about, procure.*

Paro, āre, āvi, ātum, a., *to make ready, prepare; to procure, obtain.*

Paros, or Parus, i. f., *Paros, one of the Cyclades, famous for its white marble.*

Pars, tis, f., *a part, portion, share; a region, quarter, place:* aliam in partem, *into another quarter, in another direction:* maximam partem, *for the most part, chiefly, principally:* hence

Partim, adv., *partly.*

Parum, adv. (comp. minus, sup. minime), *a little, but a little, too little.*

Parus, see Paros

Parvus, a, um, adj. (comp. minor, sup. minimus), *little, small; mean:* parvi sunt arma, *are of little value.*

Passus, a, um, part. (pando), *spread out, stretched out, extended.*

Passus, ûs, m. (pando), *a step, pace; a pace, as a measure of length,*

consisting of 5 Roman feet: mille passus, *a mile.*

Patefăcio, ĕre, ēci, āctum, a. (pateo & focio), *to open, throw open; to disclose:* hence

Patefio, ĕri, factus, sum, irr, pass., *to be opened, thrown open; to be disclosed or discovered.*

Patens, tis, part. & adj., *open, lying open, extended, wide:* from

Patĕo, ĕre, ui, n., *to be open; to stretch out, extend; to be clear, plain, manifest.*

Pater, tris, m., *a father.*

Patiens, part. & adj. (patior, *to bear), patient.*

Patria, æ, f., (patrius, *of a father), one's native land, or country; native place.*

Pauci, æ, a adj., *few, a few:* pauci, *a few men:* pauca, *a few things.*

Pausanias, æ, m., *Pausanias, a Spartan general.*

Pavor, ōris, m. (paveo, *to tremble with fear,) fear, alarm.*

Pax. pacis, f., *peace.*

Pecco, āre, āvi. ātum, n. & a., *to do amiss, err, commit a fault, sin.*

Pectus, ōris, n., *the breast;* fig., *the heart, the mind.*

Pecunia, æ, f., *property, wealth, riches; money:* from

Pecus, ōris, n., *cattle; a herd, a flock.*

Pedes, ĭtis, m. (pes), *on foot; a foot-soldier; infantry.*

Pejor, us, adj, (comp. of malus), *worse.*

Pejŭs, adv. (comp. of malè), *worse.*

Pello, ĕre, pepŭli, pulsum, a., *to drive out; to drive back, discomfit, rout; to beat, conquer, overcome.*

Peloponnesius, a, um, adj. (Peloponnesus, *the Peloponnesus), Peloponnesian.*

Peperci, see Parco.

Pepŭli, see Pello.

Per, prep. with acc., *through; by, by means of; during; for:* per se, *by itself, alone.*

Perăgo, ĕre, ēgi, actum, a. (per & ago), *to thrust through; to go through with, finish, execute.*

Percello, ĕre, cŭli, culsum, a. (per & cello, *to impel), to beat down, throw down; to overthrow.*

Percŭli, see Percello.

Perdo, ĕre, dĭdi, dĭtum, a. (per & do) *to destroy, ruin; to lose, squander.*

Perdūco, ĕre, xi, ctum, a. (per & duco) *to lead through; to lead, bring, conduct; to draw out, extend; to bring over, persuade:* perducere fossam, *to extend, make.*—

Pĕreo, īre, īvi *or* ii, ĭtum, n. (per & eo), *to go through: to perish, be lost* or *ruined; to die.*

Perfacĭlis, e, adj. (per & facĭlis, *easy*), *very easy.*

Perfĕro, ferre, tŭli, lātum, a. irr. (per & fero), *to carry through; to carry, bring, convey; to bear, endure.*

Perfĭcio, ĕre. fēci, fectum, a. (per & facio), *to finish, complete, perform; to effect, cause.*

Perfrĭngo, ĕre, frēgi, fractum, a. (per & frango, *to break*), *to break through, burst through, force one's way through.*

Perfŭgio, ĕre, fūgi, n. (per & fugio), *to flee to a place for refuge.*

Perfungor, i, nctus, dep. n. (per & fungor), *to fulfill, perform, discharge; to go through, undergo.*

Pergo, ĕre, perrexi, perrectum, a. & n. (per & rego), *to go on, proceed, go forward, advance.*

Pericŭlōsus, a, um, adj., *dangerous: from*

Pericŭlum, i, n., *a trial, experiment; danger, risk.*

Perindulgens, tis, adj., (per & indulgens, *indulgent*), *very kind* or *indulgent.*

Perĭtus, a, um, adj., *skilled in, skillful, expert.*

Permitto, ĕre, mīsi, missum, a. (per & mitto), *to let go, give up, leave, surrender; commit; to allow, permit.*

Permōtus, a, um, part., *moved: from*

Permŏveo, ēre, ōvi, ōtum, a. (per & moveo), *to move deeply; to stir up, excite; to persuade; to terrify.*

Pernicies, ēi, f. (pernĕco, *to kill outright*), *destruction, ruin.*

Pernicĭtas, ātis, f. (pernix, *nimble*), *swiftness.*

Perpetuus, a, um, adj. (per & peto), *perpetual.*

Persæ, ārum, m., pl., *the Persians.*

Persĕquor, i, cūtus & quutus sum, dep. a. & n. (per & sequor), *to follow after, pursue; to seek to obtain, strive after; to prosecute; to revenge, avenge; to execute, perform, accomplish.*

Persĭcus, a, um, adj. (Persæ), *Persian.*

Persolvo, ĕre, solvi, solūtum, (per & solvo), *to release; to pay:* persolvere poenam, *to suffer punishment.*

Perspĭcio, ĕre, exi, ectum, a. (per & specio, *to look*), *to look through; to examine; to perceive:* hence

Perspicuus, a, um, adj., *plain, transparent: fig., evident.*

Pertaedet, taesum, est. impers. (per & taedet, *it disgusts*), *to be disgusted* or *wearied* with anything.

Perterreo, ēre, ui ĭtum, a. (per & terreo), *to frighten greatly, terrify.*

Pertĭneo, ēre, ui, n. (per & teneo), *to extend to; to reach, stretch; to belong, relate* or *pertain to; to concern; to be of use* or *service.*

Perturbo, āre, āvi, ātum, a. (per & turbo, *to disturb*), *to throw into confusion, confuse, disturb, trouble, disquiet, embroil.*

Pervĕnio, īre, vēni, ventum, n. (per & venio), *to come to, arrive at, reach; to come, arrive.*

Pes, pedis, m., *a foot;* also, the measure, *a foot:* ad pedes, *on foot:* referre pedem, *to draw back, retire, retreat, recede.*

Peto, ĕre, īvi & ii, ĭtum, a., *to fall upon; to rush at, attack; to go to, travel to; to seek after, covet, desire; to ask, request, beg, entreat, desire, beseech.*

Phalanx, angis, f., *a band of soldiers drawn up in close order; a phalanx, a squadron, battalion.*

Pharnabazus, i, m., *Pharnabazus, a Persian satrap.*

Phĭlippus, i. m., *Philip, a king of Macedonia.*

Philo, ōnis, m., *Philo, a Grecian philosopher.*

Philosophia, æ, f., *philosophy.*

Philosŏphus, i, m., *a philosopher.*

Piĕtas, ātis, f. (pius, *dutiful*), *dutiful conduct; piety; duty; affection.*

Pignus, ōris, n., *a pledge, security: fig., a proof.*

Pilum, i, n., *a javelin* or *dart.*

Piso, ōnis, m., *Piso, a Roman surname.*

Plăceo, ēre, cui & cĭtus sum., cĭtum, n., *to please.*

Plato, ōnis, m., *Plato, a Grecian philosopher.*

Plausus, ûs, m. (plaudo, *to clap*), *a clapping; applause.*

Plebs, plebis & plebes, ēi, f., *the common people, the commons* or *commonalty, the plebeians,* opposed to the patricians, senators, and knights.

Plecto, ĕre, xi & xui, xum, a., *to plait, braid.*

Plecto, ĕre, a., *to punish.*

Plenus, a, um, adj. (pleo, obsolete, *to fill), full, filled; replete; abundant.*

Plerŭmque, adv., *mostly, for the most part;* from

Plerusque, rǎque, rumque, adj. (plerus, *very many), very many, the most, most, the greatest part;* it occurs more commonly in the plural.

Plurĭmùm, adv. (sup. of multùm), *most of all, most, especially, very much.*

Plurĭmus, a um, adj. (sup. of multus), *very many, very much, most.*

Plus, plurĭs, adj. (comp of multus), pl. plures, plura, *more, several, many; of a higher price; of more value; higher, dearer.*

Poena, æ, f., *satisfaction; punishment.*

Poeni, ōrum, m. pl., *the Carthaginians.*

Poenĭteo, ĕre, ui, a. & impers. (poenio, i.e. punio), *to make repent;* impers. poenitet me, *it repents me,* i.e., *I repent.*

Poëta, æ, m., *a poet.*

Pollĭceor, ēri ĭtus sum, dep. a. (pote, able & liceor, to bid), *to offer, promise.*

Pompeius, i. m., *Pompey, a distinguished Roman general.*

Pomum, i, n., *fruit; an apple.*

Ponè, prep. with acc., *behind.*

Pono, ĕre, posui, posĭtum, a., *to put, place, set; to set up, erect;* ponere castra, *to pitch a camp.*

Pons, pontis, m., *a bridge.*

Pontus, i. m., *the sea.*

Poposci, see Posco.

Popŭlor, āri, ātus sum, dep. a., *to lay waste, ravage, plunder; to depopulate;* from

Popŭlus, i. m., *a people.*

Porta, æ, f. *a city gate, a gate.*

Porto, āre, āvi, ātum, a., *to carry, bear, bring.*

Portus, ûs. m., *a port; a harbor.*

Posco, ĕre, poposci, a., *to ask, demand.*

Possum, posse, potui, irr. n. (potis, able & sum), *to be able, have power; I can.*

Post, prep, with acc. & adv., *behind, in the rear of; after, afterwards;* hence

Postĕrus, a, um, adj., *coming after, following, next.*

Postquam, temp. conj. (post & quàm), *after that, after; since; when, as soon as.*

Postridie, adv. (posterus & dies), *the day after.*

Postŭlo, āre, āvi, ātum, a. (posco), *to ask, demand, request.*

Postŭmus, i. m., *Postumus, a Roman name.*

Potens, tis, adj. (possum), *able; powerful;* hence

Potentia, æ, f., *power.*

Potestas, ātis, f. (possum), *power; authority; possibility, opportunity.* pugnandi potestatem facere, *to offer battle.*

Potĭor, īri, ītus sum, dep. n. (potis, able), *to be or become master of; acquire, get, obtain, gain possession of, capture, take.*

Præ, prep. with abl., *before; in comparison with; for, on account of.*

Præbeo, ĕre, ui, ĭtum, a. (præ & habeo), *to hold forth, proffer, exhibit, show, present; to afford, give, furnish, supply.*

Præcēdo, ĕre, cessi, cessum, a. & n. (præ & cedo), *to go before, precede; to surpass, excel.*

Præceptor, ōris, m., *one who seizes beforehand; a teacher, instructor, preceptor;* from

Præcĭpio, ĕre, cēpi, ceptum, a. (præ & capio), *to take or seize before; to advise, instruct, teach.*

Præcĭpĭto, āre, āvi, ātum, a. (præceps, head-foremost), *to throw down headlong, precipitate; to hasten, hurry, to urge, impel.*

Præcĭpuus, a, um, adj. (præcipio), *peculiar, especial; chief, principal, distinguished.*

Præco, ōnis, m., *a crier, herald; a publisher.*

Præcordia, ōrum, n. pl. (præ & cor, the heart), *the midriff or diaphragm, the muscle which separates the heart and lungs from the abdomen.*

Præda, æ, f., *booty, spoil, plunder.*

Prædĭco, āre, āvi, ātum, a. (præ & dico, āre, to proclaim), *to publish, proclaim; to declare.*

Prædīco, ĕre, xi, ctum, a. (præ & dico), *to predict, foretell.*

Prædo, ōnis, m. (præda), *a robber;* hence

Prædor, āri, ātus sum, dep. n. & a., to rob, plunder, pillage.

Præfectus, i. m. (præficio), an overseer, president; a general, commander.

Præfĕro, ferre, tŭli, lătum, a. (præ & fero), to bear before; to prefer, give the preference to.

Praeficio, ĕre, fēci, fectum, a. (præ & facio), to set over: appoint over, appoint to the command of.

Præmitto, ĕre, īsi, issum, a (præ & mitto), to send before, send forward.

Præmium, ii, n., a reward.

Præoccŭpo, āre āvi, ātum, a. (præ & occupo), to seize upon beforehand, preoccupy.

Præpōno, ĕre, sui, sĭtum, a. (præ & pono), to put or set before, place first; to prefer; to set over.

Præsens, tis, adj. (præsum), present.

Præsertim, adv., especially.

Præsidium, ii, n. (præses, a protector), a protection, defense; a guard, garrison, escort.

Præstabĭlis, e, adj., excellent: from

Præsto, āre, ĭti, ĭtum & ātum, a. & n. (præ & sto), to stand before; to surpass, excel; to perform, execute.

Præsum, esse, fŭi, n. irr. (præ & sum), to be before; to be set over, preside over, have the charge or command of.

Præter, prep. with acc., past, beyond; before; over; besides, except; contrary to; near.

Prætĕreo, ire, īvi, & ii, ĭtum, n. & a. (præter & eo), to pass by; to omit; to excel: hence

Prætĕrĭtus, a. um, part. & adj., past, gone by.

Prætor, ōris, m. (for præitor from præeo, to go before), a prætor, chief: hence

Prætūra, æ, f., the office of a prætor, the prætorship. [depraved.

Pravus, a, um, adj., crooked; vicious.

Premo, ĕre, essi, essum, a., to press; to press upon, harass; to oppress.

Pretium, ii. n., worth, value, price; a reward. [day before.

Pridie, adv. (for priori die), on the

Primùm, adv., first, first of all, in the first place: from

Primus, a, um, adj. (sup. of prior), first, the first: in primis or imprimis, above all, especially, particularly, first: a prima ætate, from one's earliest years.

Princeps, ĭpis, adj., m. & f, (primus & capio), first, foremost, chief, most distinguished, the first: subst., a chief, head, leader; a prince, ruler: hence

Principātus, ûs, m., the first place pre-eminence; dominion, sovereignty.

Principium ii, n. (princeps), a beginning, commencement.

Prior, us, ōris, adj., former, prior, first; the elder.

Pristinus, a, um, adj., former, early.

Prius, adv. (prior) first, at first, before, sooner: prius-quam, before that, before, rather.

Priusquam, adv. & temp. conj. (prius & quam), before that, before.

Privātus, a, um, adj., private: subst., a private person, one not in a public office: from

Privo, āre, āvi, ātum, a. (privus, single), to deprive.

Pro, prep. with abl., before; for; on account of; according to.

Probo, āre, āvi, ātum, a., to try, test; to approve of; to show, prove: from

Probus, a, um, adj., good, honest, upright.

Procēdo, ĕre, essi, essum, n. (pro & cedo), to go forth, proceed; to advance.

Procul, adv., (procello, to drive away), far, far off.

Proditio, ōnis, f. (prodo), treason, treachery.

Proditor, ōris m., a traitor: from

Prodo, ĕre, dĭdi, dĭtum, a., to give forth, make known, disclose: to appoint, elect; to betray; to hand down, transmit.

Proelium, ii, n., a battle, combat.

Profectio, ōnis, f. (proficiscor), a setting out, departure: a journey, march.

Profectus, a, um, part. (proficiscor).

Profĕro, ferre, tŭli, lătum, a. irr. (pro & fero), to bring forth, produce; to bring forward, quote, cite, mention.

Proficiscor, i. fectus sum, dep. n. (pro & facio), to set out, depart, go.

Profiteor, ēri, fessus, sum, dep. a. (pro & fateor, to confess), to declare, profess.

Profligo, āre, āvi, ātum. a. (pro & fligo, to strike), to strike to the ground; to rout, put to flight.

Profūgio, ĕre, ūgi, a. & n. (pro & fugio), *to flee, escape.*

Prŏhĭbeo, ĕre, ui, ĭtum, a. (pro & habeo), *to keep or ward off; to hinder; to forbid, prohibit.*

Proinde, adv. (pro & inde), *just so, in the same manner, in like manner, equally, just, even; therefore.*

Projĭcio, ĕre, jĕci, jectum, a. (pro & jacio), *to throw before; to throw, cast, fling:* projicere se, *to cast one's self, prostrate one's self.*

Propāgo, āre, āvi, ātum, a., *to propagate; to extend, enlarge, increase.*

Prope, adv., comp, propiùs, sup. proxĭmè, *near, almost.*

Prop'nquĭtas, ātis, f. (propinquus.' *near, nearness; relationship.*

Propiùs, adv. (comp. of propè), *nearer.*

Propōno, ĕre, sui, sĭtum, a. (pro & pono), *to put forth; to offer, propose, to promise.*

Propter, prep. with acc. (prope, *near;* fig., *for, on account of.*

Prosterno, ĕre, strāvi, strātum, a. (pro & sterno), *to throw down, overthrow, prostrate.*

Prosum, ˋdesse, fui. irr. n. (pro & sum), *to do good, benefit, profit.*

Provĭdeo, ĕre, vīdi, visum, n. & a. (pro & video), *to foresee; to provide.*

Provincia, æ, f. (pro & vinco), *a province.*

Proxĭmè, adv. (sup. of prope), *next, very near.*

Proxĭmus, a, um, adj. (sup. of propior), *very near, neighboring, nearest, next, last.*

Prudens, entis, adj. (contracted from providens), *foreseeing; skilled, experienced, versed; wise, discreet, prudent:* hence

Prudentia, æ, f., *acquaintance with, knowledge of, skill in; sagacity, good sense, prudence.*

Publĭcè, adv. (publicus, *of the people), publicly.*

Publius, i. m., *Publius, a Roman prænomen.*

Pudor, ōris, m. (pudeo, *to be ashamed), shame, modesty.*

Puella, æ, f. (puellus, *a little boy), a girl, maiden, lass.*

Puer, ĕri, m., *a child, a boy.*

Pugna, æ, f., *a battle, fight, engagement, combat:* from

Pugno, āre, āvi, ātum, n., *to fight* pugnātur, pass. imp. *the battle is fought, they fight.*

Pulcher, chra, chrum, adj. (ior, errĭmus), *beautiful, fair, handsome; noble, honorable.*

Pulsus, a, um, part, (pello), *struck; beaten, routed.*

Pulvis, ĕris, m. & f., *dust.*

Punio, īre, īvi, *or* ii, ĭtum, a., *to punish.*

Puto, āre, āvi, ātum, a., *to trim, prune; to account, think, judge, reckon; to suppose; to esteem.*

Pythia, æ, f., *the priestess of Apollo at Delphi, the Pythoness.*

Q.

Quà, adv. (abl. fem. of qui, sc. viâ *or* parte), *where; in what way.*

Quæro, ĕre, sivi *or* sii sĭtum, a., *to seek; to ask, inquire.*

Qualis, e, adj., (quis), *of what kind or sort, what:* after talis, *as.*

Quàm, adv. & comp. conj., *how, how much, as much:* quam — tam, so — as: with comparatives and words implying comparison, *as, than:* with superlatives or possum, *as possible.*

Quamquam, concess. conj (quàm & quàm), *although.*

Quamvis, adv. & concess. conj. (quàm & vis, from volo), *as you will; however much, although.*

Quantùm, adv., *as much, how much:* from

Quantus, a, um, adj. (quàm), *how great, how much:* tantus — quantus, *as great — as.*

Quare, adv. (quis & res), *by which means; for which reason, whence, wherefore.*

Quartus, a, um, num. adj., *the fourth:* from

Quatuor, ind. num. adj., *four.*

Que, enclitic cop. conj., *and.*

Queror, i, questus sum. dep. a. & n., *to lament, bewail, bemoan, complain, complain of.*

Qui, quæ, quod, rel. pron., *who, which, what:* quo, abl. n. with comparatives, *by that, by how much, the.*

Quid, see Quis.

Quidam, quædam, quoddam & quiddam, indef. pron., *a certain, a certain one, somebody:* pl. *some.*

Quidem, adv., *indeed, truly* ne quidem, *not even.*

Quies, ētis, f., *rest, quiet, repose, ease; neutrality.*

Quiētus, a, um. adj. (quiesco, *to rest), quiet.*

Quin, iin. conj. (qui & ne), *that not, but that, so as not, that, so but that, from,* with the English gerundive of the verb following it: as, temperare sibi quin exiret, *to restrain one's self from going out,* i.e., *to refrain from ——:* retinere quin conjicerent, *to restrain from throwing.*

Quindĕcim, ind. num. adj. (quinque & decem), *fifteen.*

Quingenti, æ, a, num. adj. (quinque & centum), *five hundred.*

Quinquaginta, ind. num. adj., *fifty.*

Quinque, ind. num. adj., *five:* hence

Quintus, a um, adj., *the fifth.*

Quis, quæ, quid, interr. pronoun., *who? which? what?* as an indef. pron., *each, every, every one, any one, anything:* ne quis, *that no one, lest any one.*

Quisnam, quænam, quidnam, interr. pron, (quis & nam), *who? which? what?*

Quisquam, quæquam, quidquam, *or* quicquam, indef. pron. (quis & quam), *any, any one, anybody, anything.*

Quisque, quæque, quodque & quicque, *or* quidque, indef. pron. (quis & que), *every man,* &c., *each, all every, any one, any.*

Quisquis, quæque, quodquod & quicquid *or* quidquid, indef. pron. (quis & quis), *whoever, whatever.*

Quivis, quævis, quodvis & quidvis, indef. pron. (qui & vis, from volo), *any one you please, whosoever, whoever, whatever, any one, any, every.*

Quo, adv. & fin. conj. (qui), *whither; to the end that, so that, that:* quò minùs, after clauses denoting hindrance, *that not, from, for not,* with the English gerundive of the verb following it.

Quod, caus. conj. (qui), *that; because; though.*

Quod, (neut. of qui), *what, that which:* for propter quod, *as far as.*

Quominus, conj., *that not, from:* see quo.

Quondam, adv., *once, formerly.*

Quotannis, *see* Quot.

Quot, ind. num. adj., *how many, as many as, every:* quot annis, or

quotannis, *every year, yearly, annually.*

Quotidiānus, a. um, adj., *daily:* from

Quotidie, adv., (quot & diés), *daily.*

Quum, or Cùm, caus. conj., *when, since, as:* quum — tum, *not only — but also, as — so also, as well — as also, both — and.*

R.

Rapĭdus, a, um, adj. (rapio, *to seize & carry off), rapid, swift.*

Ratio, ōnis, f. (reor, *to reckon), a reckoning; a mode, manner, method, way; reason.*

Re *or* Red, an inseparable particle, signifying *again, back.*

Recens, tis, adj., *recent. late.*

Recipio, ĕre, cēpi, ceptum, a (re & capio), *to take again, get back, recover; to receive:* recipere *or* recipire se, *to make a retreat, retreat, withdraw; to retire, return, come back:* also, *to recover, recover one's strength.*

Recordor, āri, ātus sum, dep. a. & n. (re & cor, *the heart, mind), to call to mind, remember, recollect.*

Rectè, adv. (rectus, *right), rightly, well.*

Recūso, āre, āvi, ātum, a. (re & causa), *to refuse, deny:* with quin & quo minus, *to refuse to, be unwilling to.*

Reddo, ĕre, dĭdi, dĭtum, a. (red & do), *to give back, return, restore; to render, make; to give, deliver; to pay, requite, recompense.*

Redeo, ire, ii, ĭtum, irr. n. (red & eo), *to go or come back, return.*

Redigo, ĕre, ēgi, actum, a. (red & ago), *to drive or bring back; to reduce.*

Redintĕgro, āre, āvi, ātum, a. (red & integro, *to renew), to renew.*

Reditus, ûs, m. (redeo), *a return.*

Redūco, ĕre, xi, ctum, a (re & duco), *to lead or bring back; to draw off, withdraw.*

Refĕro, ferre, tŭli, lātum, irr. a. (re & fero), *to bring back; to report.*

Refert, retŭlit, impers., *it concerns, is for one's interest.*

Refertus, a um, part. & adj. (refercio, *to fill up), filled; full.*

Reflcio, ĕre, fēci, fectum, a. (re &

facio) *to make again; to repair, rebuild; to refresh; to recruit.*

Refulgeo, ēre, fulsi, n. (re & fulgeo), *to shine, glitter.*

Refulsi, *see* Refulgeo.

Regio, ōnis, f. (rego), *a line; a boundary; a region, territory, district.*

Regius, a, um, adj. (rex), *regal, royal.*

Regno, āre, āvi, ātum, n. & a., *to reign, rule:* from

Regnum, i, n. (rex), *a kingdom.*

Rego, ēre, xi, ctum, a., *to keep straight; to guide, conduct, direct; to rule, govern.*

Rejicio, ēre, jēci, jectum, a (re & jacio), *to cast back; to repel; to refuse, reject.*

Religio, ōnis, f , *religion, piety, reverence. the fear of God.*

Relinquo, ēre, liqui, lictum, a. (re & linquo, *to leave ;) to leave behind; to leave, relinquish, abandon:* hence

Reliquus, a, um, adj., *that is left or remains, remaining; the other, the rest.*

Remāneo, ēre, mansi, n. (re & maneo), *to remain, continue.*

Reminiscor, i, dep, n. & a. *to remember.*

Remitto, ēre, misi, missum, a, & n. (re & mitto), *to send back; to slacken, relax ; to abate, remit.*

Removeo, ēre, mōvi, mōtum, a. (re & moveo), *to remove.*

Renovo, āre, āvi, ātum, a. (re & novo, *to make new), to renew.*

Renuncio, āre, āvi, ātum, a. (re & nuncio), *to bring back word, report, give notice, declare ; to proclaim, announce.*

Repello, ēre, repūli, repulsum, a. (re & pello), *to drive back; to reject, repulse, repel.*

Repentè, adv. (repens, *sudden), suddenly.*

Repentinus, a, um, adj. (repens, *sudden), sudden, unexpected.*

Reperio, īre, pēri, pertum, a. (re & pario), *to find again; to find out, discover, ascertain.*

Repertus, a, um, part. (reperio).

Repōno, ēre, posui, positum, a (re & pono), *to replace.*

Reprehendo, ēre, di, sum, a. (re & prehendo, *to seize), to seize ; to check ; to reprove, blame.*

Reprimo, ēre, pressi, pressum. a.

(re & premo), *to press back, to check, restrain, repress, confine.*

Repulsus, a, um, part, (repello).

Requiro, ēre, sīvi or sii, sītum, a. (re & quæro), *to seek again ; to seek to know, to ask or inquire after; to ask for, need, want, require.*

Res, rei, f., *a thing : a matter, affair ; an event, circumstance : a material ; a state, empire, government, republic; res gestæ, actions, exploits.*

Rescindo, ēre, scidi, scissum. a. (re & scindo, *to cut), to cut off, cut or break down ; to rescind, repeal.*

Rescisco, ēre, īvi or ii, ītum, n. (re & scisco, *to inquire), to learn, find out, ascertain.*

Resisto, ēre, stīti, n. (re & sisto, *to set or place). to stand still; to withstand, oppose, resist.*

Respondeo, ēre, di, sum, a. (re & spondeo, *to promise), to promise in return ; to answer, reply:* hence.

Responsum i., n., *an answer, reply, response.*

Respublica, gen. & dat. reipublicæ, acc., rempublicam, &c., f. (res. & publicus, *public), the commonwealth, state, republic, government; politics, public affairs or business.*

Restituo, ēre, ui, ūtum, a. (re & statuo), *to restore; to give back, return.*

Restiti, *see* Resisto.

Retineo, ēre, ui, tentum, a. (re & teneo), *to hold back, detain, retain ; to restrain ; to hold fast, keep, preserve, maintain.*

Reverto, ēre, ti, sum, a. & more commonly, revertor i, sus sum, dep. n. (re & verto), *to turn back; to return.*

Revoco, āre, āvi, ātum, a. (re & voco), *to call back, recall.*

Rex, regis, m. (rego), *a king.*

Rhenus, i, m., *the river Rhine.*

Rhipæus, a, um, adj., *of or belonging to the Rhipæan mountains, (Rhipæi), in Scythia.*

Rhodānus. i, m., *the river Rhone.*

Rixa, æ, f., *a quarrel, brawl, dispute, strife.*

Roboro, āre, āvi, ātum, a., (robur, *strength), to strengthen.*

Rogo, āre, āvi, ātum, a., *to ask, request.*

Roma, æ, f., *Rome, the chief city of Italy.*

Romānus, a, um, adj. (Roma), *Ro-*

man: Romāni, ōrum, m., *the Romans.*

Romŭlus, i, m., *Romulus, the founder and first king of Rome.*

Rosa, æ, f., *a rose.*

Rubīgo, ĭnis, f., *rust.*

Ruo, ĕre, i, rutum, n. & a., *to rush down; to run headlong, rush.*

Rus, ruris, n., *the country:* abl. sing. rure *or* ruri.

S.

Sabīni, ōrum, m., *the Sabines, a people of Italy.*

Sacerdos, ōtis, c. (sacer, *sacred*), *a priest; a priestess.*

Sacrilegium, ii, n. (sacrilĕgus, *that steals sacred things*), *sacrilege.*

Sæpe, adv. (saepis, *often*), *often, oft, frequently.*

Sagacĭtas, ātis, f. (sagax, *sagacious*), *sagacity; shrewdness.*

Sagĭtta, æ, f., *an arrow.*

Saguntum, i, n. & Saguntus, i. f., *a town of Spain.*

Salămis, is, f., (Greek acc. Salamĭna) *Salamis, an island and city of Greece.*

Salus, ūtis, f. (salvus, *safe*), *safety, health.*

Sanguis, ĭnis, m., *blood.*

Santōnes, um, & Santōni, ōrum m. pl. *the Santones, a people of Gaul.*

Sapiens, tis, adj., *wise:* subst., *a wise man:* from

Sapientia, æ, f., *wisdom.* [*wise.*

Săpio, ĕre, ivi *or* ii, n. & a., *to be*

Satăgo, ĕre, ēgi, n. & a. (satis & ago), *to be busily occupied with, have one's hands full.*

Satis, adj. & adv., *enough, sufficient; sufficiently.*

Satisfăcio, ĕre, fēci, factum, a. (satis & facio), *to satisfy.*

Scelus, ĕris, n., *a crime, a sin.*

Scio, ire, ivi, *or* ii. itum, a., *to know, understand, perceive.*

Scipio, ōnis, m., *Scipio, the name of several distinguished Romans.*

Scopŭlus, i, m., *a rock, cliff.*

Scribo, ĕre, psi, ptum, a., *to write:* hence

Scriptor, ōris, m., *a writer.*

Scriptus, a, um, part. (scribo).

Scutŭla, æ, f., *a wooden roller or cylinder; a secret writing, secret letter among the Lacedæmonians,*

(it being written on a slip of papyrus wrapped round a staff.)

Scythes, æ, m., *an inhabitant of Scythia, a Scythian.*

Scythissa, æ, f. Scythae, *the Scythians*), *a Scythian woman.*

Secrēto, adv. (secrētus, *separate*), *separately, secretly.*

Secŭlum, i. n. (secus, *a sex*), *a race; a generation, an age, the times.*

Secum, *for* Cum se: see Sui.

Secundus, a, um, adj. (sequor), *second; favorable, prosperous.*

Secūrus, a, um, adj. (se, *without* & cura), *free from care, untroubled, fearless; serene, cheerful.*

Sed, advers. conj., *but, yet.*

Sĕdeo, ĕre, sēdi, sessum, n., *to sit; to remain encamped, keep the field:* hence

Sedes, is, f., *a seat; a residence, habitation.*

Semirămis, ĭdis, f., *Semiramis, a queen of Assyria.*

Semper, adv., *ever, always.*

Senātor, ōris, m. (senex, *old*), *a senator.*

Senātus, ūs, m. (senex, *old*), *a council of elders, a senate.*

Senectus, ūtis, f. (senex, *old*), *old age.*

Seni, æ, a, num. adj. (sex), *six each, six.*

Sensus, ūs, m. (sentio), *sense, perception, feeling.*

Sententia, æ, f., *an opinion; a sentence:* from

Sentio, īre, si, sum, a., *to discern, understand, perceive; to think, deem.*

Sepĕlio, īre, pelivi, or ii, pultum, a., *to bury, inter:* hence

Sepulcrum, i, n., *a grave, tomb, sepulchre.*

Sepultus, a, um. part. (sepelio).

Sequor, sequi, secūtus sum, dep. a., *to follow, attend; to pursue, strive for, aim at.*

Sermo, ōnis, m., *talk, discourse, speech, conversation.*

Sero, ĕre, sevi, satum, a., *to sow; to plant.*

Servio, īre, ivi, or ii. ītum, n. (servus), *to be a servant; to serve.*

Servĭtus, ūtis f. (servus), *slavery, servitude, bondage.*

Servo, āre, āvi, ātum, a., *to save, deliver, preserve, protect; to keep, lay up; to watch, observe.*

Servus, i, m., *a slave, servant.*

Sese, *see* Sui.

Sestertius, i, m. (semis. *a half,* & tertius), *two and a half; a sesterce, a small silver coin, of the value of about four cents.*

Sevērĭtas, ātis, f. (sevērus, *severe*), *severity, rigor.*

Sex, ind. num. adj. *six.*

Sextĭlis, e, adj. (sextus, *the sixth*), *the sixth.* Calendæ Sextiles, *the calends of the sixth month, or the first day of August, March, in the Roman calendar, being the first month.*

Sextius, i, m., *Sextius, a Roman name.*

Sī, condit. conj., *if; since.*

Sīc, adv., *so, thus.*

Siccius, i, m., *Siccius, (Dentatus); a brave Roman soldier.*

Sicilia, æ, f., *the Island of Sicily.*

Sidus, ĕris) n., *a constellation; a star.*

Signum, i. n., *a mark, sign, token; a military standard, ensign; a signal.*

Silva, æ, f., *a wood, forest.*

Sĭmĭlis, e, adj., *like, similar;* hence

Sĭmĭlĭtūdo, ĭnis, f., *likeness, resemblance.*

Simul, adv., *together; at the same time.*

Sine, prep. with abl. *without.*

Singŭlārĭs, e, adj. (singuli, *one by one*), *single; singular, remarkable, extraordinary.*

Socer, ĕri, m, *a father-in-law.*

Socĭĕtas, ātis, f. *society; alliance:* from

Socius, i, m., *a companion; an ally, confederate.*

Socrătes, is, m., *Socrates, an illustrious Athenian philosopher.*

Sol, solis, m., *the sun.*

Sollĭcĭtūdo, or Solicĭtūdo, ĭnis, f. (sollicitus, *anxious*), *anxiety, solicitude, care.*

Solstĭtium, ii, n. (sol & sisto, *to stop*), *the summer solstice, the longest day of the year; summer-time, the heat of summer.*

Sōlùm, adv., *only, alone:* from

Solus, a, um, adj., *alone, only, sole.*

Solvo, ĕre, solvi, solūtum, a., *to loose, untie, unbind;* solvere navem, or simply solvere, *to loose a ship, put to sea, set sail.*

Somnio, āre, āvi, ātum, n. (somnium, *a dream*), *to dream.*

Somnus, i, m., *sleep; a dream.*

Sordĭdus, a, um, adj., (sordeo, *to be filthy*), *filthy, squalid; base, mean.*

Sŏror, ōris, f., *a sister.*

Spargo, ĕre, sparsi, sparsum, a., *to strew, scatter.*

Sparta, æ, f., *Sparta* or *Lacedæmon, the capital of Laconia.*

Spatium, ii, n., *space, room; time.*

Specto, āre, āvi, ātum, a. (specio, *to behold*), *to look at; to see, behold; to look to* or *towards, have regard to.*

Spero, āre, āvi, ātum, a., *to hope, expect.*

Spes, ei, f. (spero), *hope.*

Splendĭdus, a, um, adj. (splendeo, *to shine*), *bright; splendid.*

Splendor, ōris, m. (splendeo, *to shine*), *splendor; magnificence, sumptuousness; lustre, honor, dignity, excellence.*

Spolio, āre, āvi, ātum, a. (spolium, *spoil*), *to strip, rob, plunder, pillage, spoil: to deprive of.*

Stabŭlum, i. n. (sto), *a standing place; a stable, stall.*

Stadium, ii, n., *a stadium; a measure of 125 paces.*

Statim, adv. (sto), *immediately.*

Statua, æ, f., *an image, statue:* from

Statuo, ĕre, ui, ūtum, a. (sto) *to set, place; to raise, erect; to decide, conclude, determine, resolve.*

Stella, æ, f., *a star.*

Sterno, ĕre, stravi, stratum, a., *to spread out, stretch out; to throw to the ground, overthrow, prostrate.*

Stipendium, ii, n. (stips, *a contribution* and pendo, *to pay*), *pay: stipend; tribute.*

Sto, are, steti, statum, n., *to stand, stand firm; to remain, abide, be: to make a stand, hold out; agree to, abide by, stand to; to be filled* or *covered with; to persevere in, stick to.*

Stoĭcus, a, um, adj., *Stoic:* Stoĭci, subst. m. pl., *the Stoics, a sect of Grecian philosophers.*

Stramentum, i, n. (sterno), *straw, litter.*

Stratus, a, um. part. (sterno).

Strenuus, a, um, adj., *active, energetic.*

Studeo, ĕre, ui, n. & a., *to study; to desire, aim, wish.*

Studĭōsus, a, um, adj., *eager, zealous, fond or studious of:* from

Studium, ii, n. (studeo), *eagerness, zeal; care, attention, diligence; study.*

Suadeo, ĕre, si, sum, n. & a., *to advise, persuade.*

Sub, prep. with acc. & abl., *under, beneath ; at, near.*

Subdūco, ĕre, xi, ctum, a. (sub & duco), *to draw up; to withdraw, remove.*

Subeo, īre, ii, ĭtum, irr. n. & a. (sub & eo), *to go under, to come up to; to undergo.*

Subĭgo, ĕre, ēgi, actum, a, (sub & ago), *to bring under; to conquer, subjugate, subdue.*

Subĭtò, adv. (subĭtus, *sudden*), *suddenly.*

Sublātus, a, um, part. (tollo).

Subruo, ĕre, ui, ŭtum, a (sub & ruo), *to dig under, undermine; to overthrow.*

Subsĕquor, i, cūtus sum, dep. n. & a. (sub & sequor), *to follow soon after, come after, follow.*

Subsidium, ii. n, (subsideo, *to sit down*), *troops stationed in reserve; aid, succor, help, assistance, relief.*

Subter, prep. with acc. and abl., *under, beneath.*

Succēdo, ĕre, cessi, cessŭm, n. & a. (sub & cedo), *to go toward, approach; to follow, succeed.*

Succumbo, ĕre, cubui, cubĭtum, a. (sub & cumbo, obsolete, *to lie down*), *to yield.*

Succurro, ĕre, curri, cursum, n. (sub & curro), *to run under: to run to one's assistance; to aid, help, relieve.*

Suevi, ōrum m., *the Suevi, a nation of Germany.*

Sui, pron., *of himself, of herself, of itself; of themselves.* In the acc. & abl., it is often doubled, *sese.* The prep. *cum* when used with se is annexed to it; as, *secum.*

Sum, esse, fui, irr. n., *to be, to exist;* with a dat. of the person, *to belong to;* with two datives, *to be, serve, afford.*

Summa, æ, f. (sc. res, from summus), *the sum* or *aggregate; summa* or summa imperii, *the highest* or *supreme power, supreme command, command in chief.*

Summus, a, um, adj., sup. of superus), *highest; greatest; last.*

Sumo, ĕre, sumpsi, sumptum, a., *to take, take up, assume.*

Super, prep. with acc. & abl., *above, over; on, upon; remaining over, left.*

Superbè, adv., *proudly, haughtily: from*

Superbus, a, um, adj., (super), *proud.*

Superior, us, adj. (comp. of superus), *higher; superior; past, former, previous.*

Superjăcio, ĕre, jēci, jectum, a. (super & jacio), *to throw over.*

Supĕro, āre, āvi, ātum, n. & a. (super), *to go over; overcome; to be superior, surpass, excel; to conquer, vanquish, subdue.*

Supersĕdeo, ēre, sēdi, sessum, n. & a. (super & sedeo), *to sit upon; to omit, forbear, leave off, give over, cease, desist:* proelio supersedere, *to abstain from* or *decline battle.*

Supersum, esse, fui, n. irr. (super & sum), *to be over and above, to remain, be left behind; to survive.*

Supĕrus, a, um, adj. (super) *above, upper, on high, higher:* hence

Supra, adv. & prep. with acc., *above; over; upon; before, formerly, previously; beyond, more.*

Suprēmus, a, um, adj. (sup of superus), *highest; greatest; last.*

Suscĭpio, ĕre, cēpi, ceptum, a (sub & capio), *to take up, undertake, enter upon; to support.*

Suspĭcax, ācis, adj. (suspĭcor, *to suspect*), *suspicious, distrustful.*

Suspicio, ōnis, f. (suspĭcor, *to suspect*), *suspicion, distrust.*

Sustĭneo, ēre, tinui, tentum, a. (sub & teneo), *to hold up, sustain; to withstand, hold out against.*

Sustŭli, see Tollo.

Suus, a, um, poss. reflexive pron. (sui), *his own, her own, its own; their own; his, hers, its, their:* sui, pl., *one's party, people, countrymen, soldiers, &c.:* sua, n. pl., *one's property, effects, possessions.*

Syracūsæ, ārum, f., pl., *Syracuse, a celebrated city of Sicily.*

T.

T., an abbreviation of Titus.

Tabŭla, æ, f. *a board; a table, tablet.*

Talentum, i, n., *a talent, a sum of money.* The Attic talent, which is usually meant, was about $1083. Also, *a weight,* usually about half a hundred.

Talis, e, adj., *such, such like.*

Tam, adv., *so, so much.*

Tamen, advers. conj., *yet, nevertheless.*

Tamquam *or* Tanquan, comp. conj. & adv. (tam & quàm), *just as, as if, as, as it were.*

Tango, ĕre, tetĭgi, tactum, a., *to touch.*

Tantopĕre, adv. (tantus & opus) *so much, s› greatly.*

Tautus, a, um, adj., *so great, so much.*

Tardo, āre, āvi, ātum, a. & n., *to hinder, detain, impede :* from

Tardus, a, um. adj., *slow.*

Taurus, i, m., *Taurus, a high mountain range in Asia.*

Taurus, i, m., *a bull.*

Tego, ĕre, texi, tectum, a., *to cover : to hide, conceal; to protect, defend.*

Telum, i, n., *a missile weapon, missile, dart, spear, javelin.*

Temerĭtas, ātis, f., (temĕre, *by chance*), *chance ; rashness, temerity.*

Tempestas, ātis, f., *a time, season : a storm, tempest :* from

Tempus, ŏris, n., *time ; opportunity, occasion.*

Tendo, ĕre, tetendi, tentum & tensum, a. & n., *to stretch out, extend : to go, advance, direct one's course.*

Teneo, ĕre, tenui, tentum, a. & n., *to hold, keep ; to possess, occupy ; to detain.*

Tento, āre, āvi, ātum, a. (tendo), *to try, attempt.*

Tenus, adv. with gen., *or* prep. with abl., *up to, as far as.*

Tergum, i. n., *the back ; the rear.*

Terra, æ, f., *the earth : the ground, soil ; a country ; a land.*

Terreo, ĕre, ui, ĭtum a., *to terrify.*

Terrestris (& terrester), tre, adj. (terra), *of the earth or land, terrestrial, land :—*

Terror, ŏris, m, (terreo) *terror, alarm.*

Tertius, a, um, num. adj. (ter, *three times*), *third.*

Testis, is, c., *a witness :* hence

Testor, āri, ātus, sum, a., *to bear witness, to testify ; to declare ; to invoke.*

Tetrarchia, æ, f., *the dominions of a tetrarch, a tetrarchy.*

Teutŏni, ōrum, m. pl., *the Teutons, a people of Germany.*

Theātrum, i, n., *a theatre.*

Themistŏcles, is, m., *Themistocles, a celebrated Athenian commander.*

Theophrastus, i, m., *Theophrastus, a Grecian philosopher.*

Thermopyæ, ārum, f. pl., *Thermopylœ, a narrow passage in Thessaly, between mount Octa and the sea.*

Thessalonica, æ, f., *Thessalonica, a city of Macedonia.*

Thrasybŭlus, i, m., *Thrasybulus, an Athenian general, celebrated for freeing his country from the thirty tyrants.*

Thrax, ācis, m., *a Thracian :* Thraces, pl., *the Thracians.*

Thyus, i, m., *Thyus, a ruler of Paphlagonia.*

Tibĕris, is, m., *the Tiber, a river of Italy.*

Tigurinus, a. um, adj., *of Zurich,* Tigurinus pagus, *the canton of Zurich, in Helvetia.*

Timeo, ĕre, ui, a. & n., *to fear, dread:* hence

Timĭdus, a. um, adj., *timorous, fearful.*

Timor, ōris, m., (timeo), *fear, dread, apprehension.*

Timotheus, i, m., (a trisyllable), *Timotheus, a Grecian general.*

Tissaphernes, is, m., *Tissaphernes, a Persian satrap.*

Titus, i, m., *Titus, a Roman prænomen.*

Tollo, ĕre, sustŭli, sublātum, a., *to raise, exalt; to extol; to take away.*

Torrĭdus, a, um, adj. (torreo, *to parch*), *dry, parched, sultry, hot.*

Torvus, a, um, adj., *grim, savage.*

Totus, a, um, adj., *all, all the, the whole of.*

Tractus, ūs, m. (traho, *to draw*), *a drawing or dragging ; a tract, region.*

Trado, ĕre, dĭdi, dĭtum, a, (trans & do), *to hand over, deliver, give up ; to surrender ; to transmit.*

Tradūco, ĕre, xi, ctum, a, (trans & duco), *to bring or carry over or across, lead or convey over or through, transport, transfer; to lead, carry.*

Trajĭcio, ĕre, jēci, jectum, a. & n. (trans & jacio), *to throw over ; to transport, carry over.*

Trans, prep. with acc., *across, over, beyond.*

Transduco, *see* Traduco.

Transeo, ire, ii, ĭtum, irr, n. & a. (trans & eo), *to go over, pass over, pass, cross.*

Transno *(or* Trano) āre, āvi, ātum, a. (trans & no), *to swim over.*

Trebia, æ, f., *Trebia, a river in Upper Italy.*

Trecenti, æ. a. num, adj. (tres & centum), *three hundred.*

Tres, tria, num, adj., *three.*

Tribūnus, -i, m. (tribus, *a tribe*), *a tribune.*

Tribuo, ĕre, ui, ūtum, a., *to give, grant, assign; to show, pay, render; to ascribe.*

Triduum, i, n, (tres & dies) *the space of three days, three days.*

Triennium, ii, n. (tres & annus), *the space of three years, three years.*

Triginta, num, adj. ind., *thirty.*

Tristis, e, adj ¬sad, *sorrowful.*

Triumpho, āre, āvi, ātum, n., *to triumph:* triumphare triumphum, *to celebrate a triumph:* from

Triumphus, i, m., *a triumphal procession, a triumph.*

Trœzen, ēnis, f., *Trœzen, a town of the Peloponnesus.*

Troja, æ, f., *Troy, a famous city of Asia Minor:* hence

Trojānus, a, um, adj., *Trojan.*

Tu, tui, subst. pron., *thou, you.*

Tueor, ēri, tuītus & tutus sum. dep. a., *to see; to see to, defend, guard, protect.*

Tuli, *see* Fero.

Tum, adv., *then, thereupon.*

Tumultus, ûs, m. (tumeo, *to swell*), *an uproar, disturbance, tumult.*

Tunc, adv., *then.*

Turba, æ, f., *a disorder, tumult, commotion, disturbance; a crowd, multitude:* hence

Turbulentus, a, um, adj., *confused, disturbed, stormy, tempestuous.*

Turpis, e, adj., *ugly, deformed, shameful, base, dishonorable, disgraceful.*

Turranius, i, m, *Turranius, a Roman.*

Turris, is, f., *a tower.*

Tusculus, a, um, adj., *of or belonging to Tusculum* (a city of Latium).

Tutus, a, um, adj. (tueor), *safe, secure:* tutum, subs., *a safe place:* hence

Tutor, āri, ātus, sum, dep. a., *to defend, protect.*

Tuus, a, um, poss. pron. (tu), *thy, your.*

Tyrannus, i, m., *a monarch, king; a tyrant.*

Tyrus, i, f., *Tyre, a city of Phœnicia.*

U.

Ubi, adv., *when.*

Ubique, adv., (ubi & que), *everywhere.*

Ubii, ōrum, m., *the Ubii, a people of Germany, on the banks of the Rhine.*

Ullus, a, um, adj., *any, any one.*

Ultrò, adv., (ulter, *that is beyond*), *of one's own accord, voluntarily.*

Umbra, æ, f., *a shade, shadow.*

Umquam (*or* Unquam), adv., unus & quam), *at any time, ever.*

Unda, æ, f., *a wave; water.*

Unde, adv., *whence.*

Undĕcim, num. adj. ind. (unus & decem), *eleven.*

Undetriginta, num. adj. ind. (unus, de & triginta), *twenty-nine.*

Undique, adv. (unde & que) *on all sides, on every side.*

Universus, a, um, adj. (unus & verto), *all, whole, universal.*

Unquam, *see* Umquam.

Unus, a, um, num. adj., *one; an or a; one only, alone.*

Urbs, is, f. (orbis, *a circle,*) *a walled town, a city.*

Ursus, i, m., *a bear.*

Usque, adv., *all the way; all the while, as long, as far as, until, even.*

Usus, a, ūm, part. (utor).

Usus, ûs, m., (utor), *use, advantage, profit, benefit; need, necessity.*

Ut *or* Uti, comp. & fin. conj. & adv., *as, like or just as, as if; that, so that; when, as soon as.*

Uterque, utrăque, utrumque, gen utriusque, adj. (uter, *which of the two* and que), *both, each.*

Uti, *see* Ut & Utor.

Utica, æ, f., *Utica, a maritime city of Africa, near Carthage.*

Utilis, e, adj. (utor), *useful.*

Utinam, adv. (uti & nam), *oh that! I wish that! would that!*

Utor, i, usus sum, dep., *to use, make use of, exercise, employ, exert; to enjoy, have.*

Utrum, adv. (uter, *which of the two*), in direct questions it is omitted in translation, in indirect questions, *whether:* utrum—an, *whether—or.*

Uxor, ōris, f., *a wife, spouse:* ducere uxorem, *to lead a wife home, i. e., to marry.*

V.

Vaco, āre, āvi, ātum, n., *to be empty, free from, destitute of*: hence

Vacuus, a, um, adj., *empty, void, free, free from, devoid of.*

Vae, interj., *ah! alas! woe!*

Valens, tis, part. & adj., *strong, powerful*: from

Valeo, ēre, ui, ĭtum, n., *to be strong; to be well* or *in health; to have weight* or *influence; to be powerful* or *strong, be able; to avail.*

Valerius, i, m., *Valerius, a Roman name.*

Vallum, i, n. (vallus, *a stake*), *a pallisaded rampart; a rampart, bulwark.*

Vanĭtas, ātis, f. (vanus, *empty*), *emptiness, vanity.*

Varius, a, um, adj., *diverse, changing, various; changeable, unsteady, fickle.*

Vectīgal, ālis, n. (vectus, *carried*), *a toll, tax; revenue.*

Vehementer, adv. (vehĕmens, *vehement*), *vehemently, ardently, eagerly, impetuously.*

Veii, ōr m, m, pl. (pronounced Veyi), *Veii, a very ancient city of Etruria.*

Vel, disj. conj. (imperative of volo), *or; even:* vel — vel, *either — or.*

Velox, ōcis, adj. (velum, *a sail*), *swift, rapid.*

Velut, adv. (vel & ut), *just as; as; as if.*

Vendo, ĕre, dĭdi, dĭtum. a. (venum, *sale*, & do), *to sell.*

Venĕror, āri, ātus, sum, dep. a., *to reverence, worship, adore, venerate; to beseech, implore.*

Venia, æ, f., *grace, indulgence, favor; leave, permission; pardon, forgiveness.*

Venio, īre, veni, ventum, n., *to come.*

Venor, āri, ātus, sum, dep. n. & a., *to hunt.*

Ventūrus, a, um, part. (venio), *about to come.*

Ventus, i, m., *the wind.*

Ver, veris, n., *spring*

Verbum, i, n., *a word:* verba facere, *to speak, discourse.*

Verè, adv. comp. verius, sup. verissĭmè, (verus), *truly.*

Vĕreor, ēri, ĭtus sum, dep. q. & n., *to revere, reverence; to fear, apprehend.*

Vergasillaunus, i, m, *Vergasillaunus, a chief of the Arverni, a people of Gaul.*

Verissĭmè, adv. (sup of vere), *most truly.*

Verĭtas, ātis, f. (verus), *truth.*

Verò, advers. conj. (verus), *in truth, truly, indeed: but in fact, but.*

Verres, is, m., *Verres,* (C. Cornelius), *a Roman praetor.*

Verso, āri, āvi, ātum, a. (verto), *to turn often; to turn, twist; to examine; to change, exercise.*

Versor, āri, ātus, sum, pass. (verso), *to frequent; to dwell, remain, stay, live, be; to be occupied, engaged, busied, employed, exercised.*

Verto, ĕre, ti, sum, a, & n., *to turn, turn round:* vertere terga, *to turn one's back, run away, betake one's self to flight.*

Verus, a, um, adj., *true, real.*

Vescor, vesci, dep. n., *to eat, feed; to subsist upon.*

Vesontio, ōnis, f., *Vesontio, the chief town of the Sequani, a people of Gaul.*

Vester, tra, trum, poss. pron. (vos), *your, yours.*

Vestigium, ii, n., *a footstep, track.*

Vestis, is, f., *a garment, robe, dress.*

Veto, āre, ui, ĭtum, a., *to forbid, hinder, prevent:* from

Vetus, ĕris, adj., *ancient, old.*

Vexo, āre, āvi, ātum, a. (veho, *to carry*), *to agitate; to trouble, vex, harass, disturb.*

Via, æ, f., *a way, road, path; a journey.*

Viātor, ōris, m. (vio, *to travel*), *a traveller.*

Vicesĭmus, a, um, num. adj. (viginti), *the twentieth.*

Vici, see Vinco.

Victor, ōris, m. (vinco), *a conqueror, victor:* hence

Victoria, æ, f., *victory.*

Victus, a, um. part. (vinco).

Vicus, i, m., *a street; a village.*

Video, ĕre, vidi, visum, a.; *to see; to perceive.*

Videor, ēri, visus, sum, pass. (video), *to be seen; to seem, appear:* impers., *to seem good, fit* or *proper.*

Vigilantia, æ, f. (vigilans, *watchful*), *vigilance, watchfulness, wakefulness.*

Vigilia, æ, f. (vigil, *awake*), *a watching, being awake; a watch; the watch, watchmen, sentinels.*

Viginti, num. adj. ind., *twenty.*

Vinco, ĕre, vici, victum, a., *to conquer, overcome.*

Vinculum, i, n, (vincio, *to bind*), *a band, bond, fetter . vincula chains, fetters; a prison.*

Vindico, āre, āvi, ātum, a. (vis & dico), *to claim, demand; to free, deliver, liberate, save, to avenge, revenge.*

Violo, āre, āvi, ātum, a. (vis), *to injure; to violate, dishonor.*

Vir, viri, m., *a man; a husband.*

Virgo, inis, f., (vireo, *to flourish*), *a ward, maiden, virgin.*

Virtus, ūtus, f. (vir), *manhood, manliness; strength, vigor; bravery, courage; virtue.*

Vis, vis, f., pl. vires, *strength, vigor, power, might, energy, virtue; force, violence.*

Vita, æ, f. (vivo), *life.*

Vitium, ii, n., *a fault, defect; a crime, vice.*

Vito, āre, āvi, ātum, a. & n., *to shun, avoid.*

Vivo, ĕre, vixi, victum, n., *to live; to live upon, eat or drink.*

Vix, adv., *hardly, scarcely.*

Vixi, *see* Vivo.

Voco, āre āvi, ātum, a. & n., (vox), *to call; to name; to cite, summon.*

Volo, āre, āvi, ātum, n., *to fly.*

Volo, velle, volui, irr. a., *to wish, be willing, will; to purpose, intend:* hence

Voluntas, ātis, f., *will, wish, desire.*

Voluptas, ātis, f. (volŭpe, *agreeably*), *enjoyment, pleasure, delight.*

Vos, pl. of tu *you.*

Vox, vocis, f., *a voice.*

Vulcānus, i, m., *Vulcan, the son of Jupiter and Juno.*

Vulgus, i, n. & m., *the multitude, the people, the public.*

Vulnĕro, āre, āvi, ātum, a, *to wound, hurt:* from

Vulnus, ĕris, n., *a wound; pain, grief, sorrow.*

Z.

Zeno, ōnis, m., *Zeno, a Grecian philosopher.*

23